Structured Query Language for all RDBMS and PL/SQL (SQL, PL/SQL)

Structured Query Language for all RDBMS and PL/SQL (SQL, PL/SQL)

Kriti Sinha

KALPAZ

ISBN: 978-93-5128-201-3

Price: ₹ 450

First Published, 2016

Published by

Kalpaz Publications
C-30, Satyawati Nagar,
Delhi – 110052
E-mail: kalpaz@hotmail.com
Ph.: 9212142040

Printed at: G. Print Process, Delhi

Cataloging in Publication Data—DK
Courtesy: D.K. Agencies (P) Ltd. <docinfo@dkagencies.com>

Sinha, Kriti, author.
Structured query language for all RDBMS and PL/SQL (SQL, PL/SQL) / Kriti Sinha.
pages cm
ISBN 9789351282013

1. SQL (Computer program language) 2. Relational databases. I. Title.

QA76.73.S67S56 2016 DDC 005.756 23

Contents

Acknowledgment and Dedications

First and foremost, I would like to thank my parents for standing beside me throughout my career and writing this book. Then I want to thank my spouse, he is my pillar. I also want to thank my wonderful children: Aradhya and Anvi from whom I got inspired for continuous learning, growing, for always making me smile and for understanding on those days when I was writing this book instead of playing games. I hope that one day my both daughter will read this book and can understand why I spent so much time in front of my computer. I dedicate this book to my daughters. I also acknowledge my entire family member who supported me and helped me to write this book.

Chapter - 1

Introduction of RDBMS

1.1 RDBMS stands for Relational Database Management System
A relational database management system is used to manage the integrity, security, storage and access of data. RDBMS is the basis for SQL, and for all modern database systems like Oracle, MS SQL Server and IBM DB2.

A RDBMS is a database management system (DBMS) that is based on the relational model. Relational Model first introduced by E. F. Codd (Edgar F. Codd). He normalized the data and created an "A Relational Model of Data for Large Shared Data Banks" in (1970).

A RDBMS lets you create, update and administer a Relational database.

RDBMS's use the Structured Query Language (SQL) to access the data from database.

1.2 Table

A Table is a database object and is a collection of related data entries and it consists of columns and rows. In RDBMS table represents relation with one or more tables there are some max limit for number of columns for a single table can have.

1.2.1 Max limit for number of columns for a single table can have – for different RDBMS

Oracle supports up to 1000 columns in a single table.

SQL. server supports up to 1024 columns per table.

Sybase supports 45000 columns in a single table.

IBM DB2 supports 1012 columns in a single table.

My SQL supports 4096 Columns in a single table.

So every RDBMS have its own capacity/limit for number of columns. Similarly each RDBMS having its own limit for each rows. Limits for rows depend on data types of related column. You will find depth knowledge about each data types for each RDBMS in chapter 4.

Note: Supporting Maximum column number may vary for different version/Release.

Example: 1.2.1

Table1.2.1:Employee

Employee ID	*First Name*	*Last Name*	*Email*	*Phone Number*	*Hire Date*
100	Steven	King	SKING	515.123.4567	6/17/1987
101	Neena	Kochhar	NKOCHHAR	515.123.4568	9/21/1989
102	Lex	De Haan	LDEHAAN	515.123.4569	1/13/1993
103	Alexander	Hunold	AHUNOLD	590.423.4567	1/3/1990
104	Bruce	Emst	BERMNST	590.423.4568	5/21/1991
107	Diana	Lorentz	DLORENTZ	590.423.5567	2/7/1999
124	Kevin	Mourgos	KMOURGOS	650.123.5234	11/16/1999
141	Trenna	Rajas	TRAJAS	650.121.8009	10/17/1995
142	Curtis	Davies	CDAVIES	650.121.2994	1/29/1997
143	Randall	Matos	RMATOS	650.121.2874	3/15/1998
144	Peter	Vargas	PVARGAS	650.121.2004	7/9/1998

1.2.2 Properties of the Relational Tables

Relational tables have the following six properties:

Values are atomic.

Column values are of the same kind.

Each row is unique.

The sequence of columns is insignificant.

The sequence of rows is insignificant.

Each column must have a unique name.

1.3 Field

Each entities of a table called as field. The fields in the Employee table consist of EMPLOYEE_ID, FIRST_NAME, LAST_NAME, EMAIL, PHONE_NUMBER and HIRE_DATE.

1.4 Row

Each individual entry that are horizontal in a table called as row or record. For example there are 11 records /row in the above Employee table. Following is a single row of data or record in the Employee table.

Example: 1.4.1

100	Steven	King	SKING	515.123.4567	6/17/1987

1.5 Column

Each individual Fields that exist Vertical in a table called as Column. For example, a column in the Employee table is FIRST_NAME which represents FIRST NAME description and would consist of the following:

Example : 1.5.1

FIRST_NAME
Steven
Neena
Lex
Alexander
Bruce
Diana
Kevin
Trenna

Exercise:

1. Draw a table to store data for 10 Students. Which will store ID, Student name, Address, Class and Section.

2. Draw a table to store data for 10 Employees. which will store Employee ID, Employee name, Address, Department, Salary, and hire_date.
3. Draw a table to store data for 10 order_items. Which will store item_ ID, order_ID, orderdate, order_details

Chapter - 2

Normalization

Normalization is the process of organizing the Data in the form of fields and tables of a relational database to minimize redundancy and dependency. Normalization usually involves dividing large tables into smaller (and less redundant) tables and defining relationships between them. The goal of normalization is to get isolated/relational data so that Insert/Update/Delete can be made easily and efficiently by using defined relation between one or more table or columns.

There are many benefits of normalizing data base. Few are as below:

Normalization makes free the database of modification anomalies.

Normalization Groups data logically, which avoids bias towards any pattern of query.

It reduces data Duplication, which reduces its size and prevents storing same data again and again in different table.

2.1 Types of Normalization

Edgar F. Codd, the inventor of the relational model, introduced the concept of normalization and what we now know as the First Normal Form (1NF) in 1970.

2.1.1 First Normal Form (1NF) sets the very basic rules for an organized database:

Rule 1: Define the data items required, because they become the columns in a table. Place related data items in a table.

Define the data items means organizing the data into columns, defining what type of data each column contains, and finally putting related columns into their own table.

Example: You put all the columns relating to locations of meetings in the Location table, those relating to members in the Member Details table, and so on.

Rule 2: Ensure that there are no repeating groups of data.

Consider we have following table student:

Name	*Age*	*Department*	*DCourse*	*Class Room*
Ramesh	10	IT	C++	C1
Jayesh	10	CS	Accounts	C2
Anita	12	MBA	BM	C4

So, if we populate this table for a single Student having multiple Courses then it would be something as follows:

Name	*Age*	*Department*	*DCourse*	*Class Room*
Ramesh	10	IT	C++	C1
Jayesh	10	CS	Accounts	C2
Ramesh	10	MCA	C	C3
Anita	12	MBA	BM	C4

As per 1NF, we need to ensure that there are no repeating groups of data. So let us break above table into two parts and join them using a key as follows:

Student

Student_ID	*Name*	*Age*
1.	Ramesh	10
2.	Jayesh	10
3.	Anita	12

Department

Department_Id	*Department*	*DCourse*	*ClassRoom*	*Student_ID*
d1	IT	C++	C1	1
d2	CS	Accounts	C2	2
d3	MCA	C	C3	1
d4	MBA	BM	C4	3

Rule 3: Ensure that there is a primary key.

The final rule of the first normal form is Create a primary key for each table which we have already created. Codd went on to define the Second Normal Form (2NF) and Third Normal Form (3NF) in 1971.

2.1.2 Second Normal Form (2NF)

A table is in Second normal form when the following conditions are met:

It is in First normal form.

There must be no partial dependencies of any of the columns on the primary key:

Consider a Student and Department relation and you want to store Student ID, Student name, Department ID and Department course detail:

Student

Student_ID	*Name*	*Age*
1	Ramesh	10
2	Jayesh	10
3	Ramesh	10
4	Anita	12

Department

Department_Id	*Department*	*DCourse*	*ClassRoom*	*Student_ID*
d1	IT	C++	C1	1
d2	CS	Accounts	C2	2
d3	MCA	C	C3	1
d4	MBA	BM	C4	4

This table is in first normal form, in that it obeys all the rules of first normal form. In this table, the primary key consists of Student_ID and Department_ID. Combined they are unique assuming same Student would hardly opt for same course.

However, the table is not in second normal form because there are partial dependencies of primary keys and columns. Student_NAME is dependent on Student_ID, and there's no real link between a student name and what course he enrolled. Department detail and department course are also dependent on Department_ID, but they are not dependent on Student_ID, because there's no link between a Student_ID and an Department_ID or their Course.

To make this table comply with second normal form, you need to separate the columns into three tables.

Student

Student_ID	*Name*	*Age*
1	Ramesh	10
2	Jayesh	10
3	Ramesh	10
4	Anita	12

Department

Department_Id	*Department*	*DCourse*	*ClassRoom*
d1	IT	C++	C1
d2	CS	Accounts	C2
d3	MCA	C	C3
d4	MBA	BM	C4

Student Department

Department_Id	*Student_ID*
d1	1
d2	2
d3	1
d4	4

2.1.3 Third Normal Form (3NF)

A table is in third normal form when the following conditions are met:

It is in second normal form. All non-primary fields are dependent on the primary key.

The dependency of non-primary fields is between the data.

Example: In the below table, Department Name , Course, and Class Room are unbreakably bound to the Department ID.

Department

Department_Id	*Department*	*DCourse*	*ClassRoom*
d1	IT	C++	C1
d2	CS	Accounts	C2
d3	MCA	C	C3
d4	MBA	BM	C4

The dependency between Department ID and Class Room is called a transitive dependency. To comply with third normal form, all you need to do is move the Department Id and Class Room fields into their own table, which you can call Department_ClassRoom table:

Department_ClassRoom

Department_Id	*ClassRoom*
d1	C1
d2	C2
d3	C3
d4	C4

Now your data base table will be like below:

Student

Student_ID	*Name*	*Age*
1	Ramesh	10
2	Jayesh	10
3	Ramesh	10
4	Anita	12

Department

Department_Id	*Department*	*DCourse*	*ClassRoom*
d1	IT	C++	CR1
d2	CS	Accounts	CR2
d3	MCA	C	CR3
d4	MBA	BM	CR4

Student_department

Department_Id	*Student_ID*
d1	1
d2	2
d3	1
d4	4

Department_ClassRoom

ClassRoom _ID	*ClassRoom*
CR1	C1
CR2	C2
CR3	C3
CR4	C4

The advantages of removing transitive dependencies are mainly twofold. First, the amount of data duplication is reduced and therefore your database becomes smaller.

The second advantage is data integrity. When duplicated data changes, there's a big risk of updating only some of the data, especially if it's spread out in a number of different places in the database.

Example: If Class Room and ClassRoom ID data were stored in different tables, then any changes in ClassRoom_Codes would need to ripple out to every record in those three or four tables.

Informally, a relational database table is often described as "normalized" if it is in the Third Normal Form. Most 3NF tables are free of insertion, update, and deletion anomalies.

Codd and Raymond F. Boyce defined the Boyce-Codd Normal Form (BCNF) in 1974.

2.1.4 Boyce-Codd Normal Form (BCNF)

Eliminates all redundancy that can be discovered by functional dependencies.

2.2. Benefit of Normalization

There are two benefit of the normalization

Eliminating redundant data

Ensuring data dependencies

2.3 Drawbacks of Normalization

There are some drawbacks of normalization:

By limiting redundancy, normalization helps maintain consistency and saves space.

But performance of querying can suffer because related information that was stored in a single relation is now distributed among several.

Example: 2.3.1 A join is required to get the Employee details along with Department and job details.

2.4 Relation Type- There are different types of Relation like ONE-To-ONE and MANY –TO-MANY. You can understand relation type with below example.

Table 1: Employee

Employee_id	*Last_name*	*Phone_number*	*Hire_date*	*Job_id*	*Salary*	*Depart-ment_id*
100	King	515.123.4567	6/17/1987	AD_PRES	24000	60
101	Kochhar	515.123.4568	9/21/1989	AD_VP	17000	60
102	De Haan	515.123.4569	1/13/1993	AD_VP	17000	60
103	Hunold	590.423.4567	1/3/1990	IT_PROG	9000	60
100	King	515.123.4567	6/17/1987	AD_PRES	24000	90
101	Kochhar	515.123.4568	9/21/1989	AD_VP	17000	90
102	De Haan	515.123.4569	1/13/1993	AD_VP	17000	90
103	Hunold	590.423.4567	1/3/1990	IT_PROG	9000	90
100	King	515.123.4567	6/17/1987	AD_PRES	24000	60
101	Kochhar	515.123.4568	9/21/1989	AD_VP	17000	60
102	De Haan	515.123.4569	1/13/1993	AD_VP	17000	60
103	Hunold	590.423.4567	1/3/1990	IT_PROG	9000	60
100	King	515.123.4567	6/17/1987	AD_PRES	24000	90
101	Kochhar	515.123.4568	9/21/1989	AD_VP	17000	90
102	De Haan	515.123.4569	1/13/1993	AD_VP	17000	90
103	Hunold	590.423.4567	1/3/1990	IT_PROG	9000	90

Table 2: Department

Department_id	*Department_name*	*Manager_id*
60	IT	103
90	Executive	100

Table 3: Job

Job_id (primary key)	*Job_title*	*Min_salary*	*Max_salary*
AD_PRES	President	20000	40000
AD_VP	Sales	15000	30000

Note: Employee table

Employee _Id is primary key and in Department table it is foreign key.

Department table: Department_ID is primary key and foreign key for Department_Id in employee table.

And Manager_ID is foreign key and primary key in Employee table.

Job table: Job_Id is primary key and foreign key for Job_Id column in employee table.

Relation type:

2.4.1 Many- to- Many: Two columns of Employee's table related to Department table. So relation is called many - to - many relations.

2.4.2 One-to-One-: One column of Employee table related to one column off of job table. So relation called as one - to- one.

First_Name	Last_Name	Phone_Number	Hire_Date	Job_Id	Salary	Manager_Name	Department_Name	Job_Title	Min_Salary	Max_Salary
Steven	King	515.123.4567	6/17/1987	AD_PRES	24000	Alexander	IT	President	20000	40000
Neena	Kochhar	515.123.4568	9/21/1989	AD_VP	17000	Alexander	IT	President	20000	40000
Lex	De Haan	515.123.4569	1/13/1993	AD_VP	17000	Alexander	IT	President	20000	40000
Alexander	Hunold	590.423.4567	1/3/1990	IT_PROG	9000	Alexander	IT	President	20000	40000
Steven	King	515.123.4567	6/17/1987	AD_PRES	24000	Steven	Executive	President	20000	40000
Neena	Kochhar	515.123.4568	9/21/1989	AD_VP	17000	Steven	Executive	President	20000	40000
Lex	De Haan	515.123.4569	1/13/1993	AD_VP	17000	Steven	Executive	President	20000	40000
Alexander	Hunold	590.423.4567	1/3/1990	IT_PROG	9000	Steven	Executive	President	20000	40000
Steven	King	515.123.4567	6/17/1987	AD_PRES	24000	Alexander	IT	Sales	15000	30000
Neena	Kochhar	515.123.4568	9/21/1989	AD_VP	17000	Alexander	IT	Sales	15000	30000
Lex	De Haan	515.123.4569	1/13/1993	AD_VP	17000	Alexander	IT	Sales	15000	30000
Alexander	Hunold	590.423.4567	1/3/1990	IT_PROG	9000	Alexander	IT	Sales	15000	30000
Steven	King	515.123.4567	6/17/1987	AD_PRES	24000	Steven	Executive	Sales	15000	30000
Neena	Kochhar	515.123.4568	9/21/1989	AD_VP	17000	Steven	Executive	Sales	15000	30000
Lex	De Haan	515.123.4569	1/13/1993	AD_VP	17000	Steven	Executive	Sales	15000	30000
Alexander	Hunold	590.423.4567	1/3/1990	IT_PROG	9000	Steven	Executive	Sales	15000	30000

Exercise: Consider below listed data for Normalization:

1. Make separate table for repeating Groups. – Need to separate repeating Groups.
2. Make relation between both tables.- Need to create primary key in each table.
3. Separate the column which required more time entries and relate it to primary key table. Create reference with dependent primary key column of other table.

Finally you will get result like below.

Table 1: Employee

Emplo-yee_id	*Last_name*	*Phone_number*	*Hire_date*	*Job_id*	*Salary*	*Depart-ment_id*
100	King	515.123.4567	6/17/1987	AD_PRES	24000	60
101	Kochhar	515.123.4568	9/21/1989	AD_VP	17000	60
102	De Haan	515.123.4569	1/13/1993	AD_VP	17000	60
103	Hunold	590.423.4567	1/3/1990	IT_PROG	9000	60
100	King	515.123.4567	6/17/1987	AD_PRES	24000	90
101	Kochhar	515.123.4568	9/21/1989	AD_VP	17000	90
102	De Haan	515.123.4569	1/13/1993	AD_VP	17000	90
103	Hunold	590.423.4567	1/3/1990	IT_PROG	9000	90
100	King	515.123.4567	6/17/1987	AD_PRES	24000	60
101	Kochhar	515.123.4568	9/21/1989	AD_VP	17000	60
102	De Haan	515.123.4569	1/13/1993	AD_VP	17000	60
103	Hunold	590.423.4567	1/3/1990	IT_PROG	9000	60
100	King	515.123.4567	6/17/1987	AD_PRES	24000	90
101	Kochhar	515.123.4568	9/21/1989	AD_VP	17000	90
102	De Haan	515.123.4569	1/13/1993	AD_VP	17000	90
103	Hunold	590.423.4567	1/3/1990	IT_PROG	9000	90

Table 2: Department

Department_id	*Department_name*	*Manager_id*
60	IT	103
90	Executive	100

Table3: Job

Job_id (primary key)	*Job_title*	*Min_salary*	*Max_salary*
AD_PRES	President	20000	40000
AD_VP	Sales	15000	30000

Chapter - 3

Introduction of Structured Query Language (SQL)

The original SQL standard declared that the official pronunciation for SQL is "es queue el". Reason behind it is its first version name 'Structured English Query Language' and the acronym was SEQUEL. Many English-speaking database professionals still use the original pronunciation like the word "sequel", including Donald Chamberlin himself. SQL stands for Structured Query Language, developed by IBM. SQL is non-procedural language that is designed specifically for data access operation on relational database structures. SQL is used to communicate with a database. According to ANSI (American National Standards Institute), it is the standard language for relational database management systems. SQL commands are interpreted by the DBMS engine.

SQL is a data manipulation language.

SQL is not a programming language.

SQL commands can be embedded within programming languages.

SQL statements also include the semicolon (";") statement terminator. Though not required on every platform, it is defined as a standard part of the SQL grammar, manly used in Oracle.

SQL commands can be used interactively as a query language within the RDBMS. Like MS SQL Server, Microsoft Access, Oracle, My SQL, DB2, Sybase, Postgre SQL and Informix. All are using different dialects, such as: MS SQL Server using T-SQL,

Oracle using PL/SQL and MS Access version of SQL is called JET SQL (native format).

3.1 SQL Revisions

Table: 3. 1

Year	*Name*	*Comments*
1986	SQL-86	Implemented by IBM. Became internationally accepted in 1987, when the ANSI adopted and documented.
1989	SQL-89	Minor revision also called as super set of SQL – 86. In which the major addition were integrity constraints and Binding for C and Ada, Unique and Not Null values, Primary key, check constraint and referential key –Introduced with this version and Adopted as FIPS 127-1.
1992	SQL-92	Major revision (ISO 9075), Entry Level SQL-92 adopted as FIPS 127. Date, Time, Time Stamp, Bit String, varchar string and national character string support introduced with this version, Union Join and natural join, check constraint and creating temporary table – introduced with this version.
1999	SQL:1999	Major Version. Added regular expression matching, recursive queries (e.g. transitive closure), triggers, support for procedural and control-of-flow statements, Boolean data type, non-scalar types, some object-oriented programming features (e.g. structured types). Support for embedding SQL in Java (SQL/OLB) and vice-versa (SQL/JRT), Role based access control, Order by and update through Union and joins- Introduced with this version.
2003	SQL:2003	XML-related Specification a brand new feature (SQL/XML), window functions, standardized sequences, and columns with auto-generated values (including identity-columns), Bigint, Multi set and combining insert and update into Merge - Introduced with this version.
2006	SQL:2006	ISO/IEC 9075-14:2006 defines ways in which SQL can be used in conjunction with XML. It defines ways of importing and storing XML data in an SQL database, manipulating it within the database and publishing both XML and conventional SQL-data in XML form. In addition, it enables applications to integrate into their SQL code the use of XQuery, the XML Query Language published by the World Wide Web Consortium (W3C), to concurrently access ordinary SQL-data and XML documents- Introduced with this version.
2008	SQL:2008	Legalizes ORDER BY outside cursor definitions. Adds INSTEAD OF database triggers. Adds the TRUNCATE statement, Merge comma separated When clause in a case expression – introduced with this version.

3.2 SQL Process

When a SQL command executes for any RDBMS, the system determines the best way to get the result of your request and SQL engine figures out how to interpret the task, which is called as a SQL Process.

These components of SQL process are SQL Statement, Parsing, optimization, Row Execution Plan Generation and execution etc. Classic query engine handles all non-SQL queries but SQL query engine won't handle logical files.

Following is a simple diagram showing SQL Architecture: Diagram 3.1

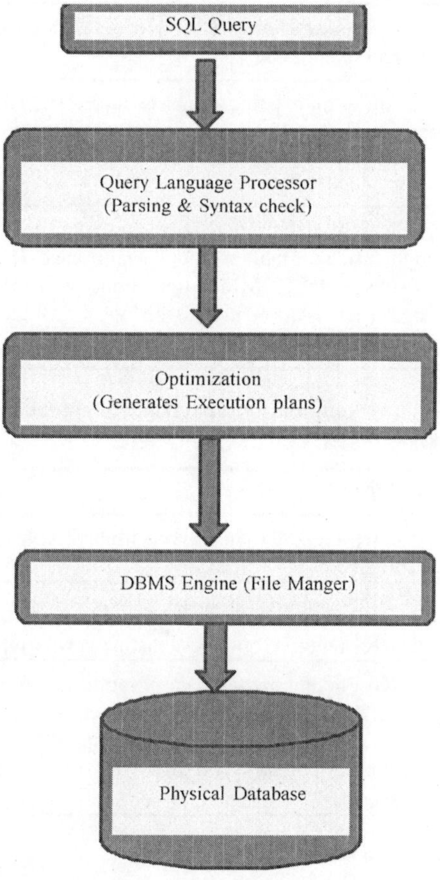

3.3 Types of SQL

There are different types of SQL:

1. DDL (Data Definition Language)
2. DML (Data Manipulation Language)
3. DCL (Data Control Language)
4. TCL/TCC (Transaction Control Language/Commands)
5. DQL (Data Query Language)

3.3.1. DDL - Data Definition Language: Commands that define a database - Create, Alter, Drop and Truncate

Command	***Description***
CREATE	Creates a new table, a view of a table, an Index or other object in database
ALTER	Modifies an existing database object, such as a table.
DROP	Deletes an entire table, a view of a table or other object in the database.it cannot be rolled back
TRUNCATE	Deletes all data from a table in a very fast way, deleting the data inside the table and not the table itself. It usually implies a subsequent COMMIT operation, i.e., it cannot be rolled back (data is not written to the logs for rollback later, unlike DELETE).

3.3.2 DML - Data Manipulation Language: Commands that maintain and query a database-Insert, update and Delete.

Command	***Description***
INSERT	Creates a record (adds rows (formally tuples) to an existing table).
UPDATE	Modifies records (modifies a set of existing table rows)
DELETE	Deletes records (removes existing rows from a table).
MERGE	Used to combine the data of multiple tables. It combines the **INSERT** and **UPDATE** elements. It is defined in the SQL: 2003 standard; prior to that, some databases provided similar functionality via different syntax, sometimes called "upsert".

3.3.3 DCL - Data Control Language: Commands that control a database, including administering privileges and committing data.

Command	***Description***
GRANT	Gives a privilege to user (authorizes one or more users to perform an operation or a set of operations on an object).
REVOKE	Takes back privileges granted from user (eliminates a grant, which may be the default grant).

3.3.4 TCL – Transaction Control Language: Transactions, if available, wrap DML operations: START TRANSACTION (or BEGIN WORK, or BEGIN TRANSACTION, depending on SQL dialect) marks the start of a database transaction, which either completes entirely or not at all. SAVE TRANSACTION (or SAVEPOINT) saves the state of the database at the current point in transaction.

Note: SQL Server does not require Commit and Rollback.

COMMIT	Allows all data changes in a transaction to be made permanent. Once the **COMMIT** statement completes, the transaction's changes cannot be rolled back
ROLLBACK	Allows all data changes since the last COMMIT or ROLLBACK to be discarded, leaving the state of the data as it was prior to those changes.
SAVEPOINT	Allows to temporarily save a transaction. Later on you can rollback to that point.

3.3.5. DQL - Data Query Language: Commands that access the database and returns the data.

Command	***Description***
SELECT	Retrieves certain records from one or more tables

Exercise: SQL Server doesn't required COMMIT and ROLLBACK why?

Chapter - 4

Data Types for Various RDBMS

4.1. Microsoft Access Data Types

Data type	*Description*	*Storage*
Text	Use for text or combinations of text and numbers (Alphanumeric value). 255 characters maximum. Mostly used for name field.	Up to 2.14 Gb
Memo	Memo is used for larger amounts of text. Note: You cannot sort a memo field. However, they are search-able. Mostly used for Brief description.	Stores up to 65,536 characters.
Byte	Allows whole numbers from 0 to 255	1 byte
Integer	Allows whole numbers between -32,768 and 32,767	2 bytes
Long	Allows whole numbers between -2,147,483,648 and 2,147,483,647	4 bytes
Single	Single precision floating-point. Will handle most decimals	4 bytes
Double	Double precision floating-point. Will handle most decimals	8 bytes
Currency	Use for currency (Monetary values). Holds up to 15 digits of whole dollars, plus 4 decimal places. Tip: You can choose which country's currency to use	8 bytes
AutoNumber	Auto Number fields automatically generates each record its own number, usually starting at 1	4 bytes
Date/Time	Use for dates and times value between the years 100 and 9999.	8 bytes
Yes/No	Boolean values.A logical field can be displayed as Yes/No, True/False, or On/Off. In code, use the constants True and False (equivalent to -1 and 0). Note: Null values are not allowed in Yes/No fields	1 bit
OLE Object	Can store pictures, audio, video, or other BLOBs (Binary Large objects) like Word Document.	up to 1GB

Hyperlink	Contain links to other files, including web pages mostly used for storing Email address/Link need to open on click.	
Lookup Wizard	Let you type a list of options, which can then be chosen from a drop-down list	bytes

4.2 MySQL Data Types

In MySQL there are three main types : Text, Number, and Date/ Time types.

Text types:

Data type	***Description***	***Storage***
CHAR (size)	Holds a fixed length string (can contain letters, numbers, and special characters). The fixed size is specified in parenthesis.	up to 255 characters
VARCHAR (size)	Holds a variable length string (can contain letters, numbers, and special characters). The maximum size is specified in parenthesis. Note: If you put a greater value than 255 it will be converted to a TEXT type	up to 65,535 characters
TINYTEXT	Holds a string. Note you can't specify a length of TINTEXT.	up to 255 characters
TEXT	Holds a string. not case sensitive.	up to 65,535 characters
BLOB	For BLOBs (Binary Large Objects) used to store large number of binary data.case sensitive.	up to 65,535 characters
MEDIUMTEXT	Holds a string. Note you can't specify a length of MIDIUMTEXT.	up to 16777215 characters
MEDIUMBLOB	For BLOBs (Binary Large Objects). Note you can't specify a length of MIDIUMBLOB.	up to 16777215 characters
LONGTEXT	Holds a string. Note you can't specify a length of LONGTEXT.	up to 4294967295 characters
LONGBLOB	For BLOBs (Binary Large OBjects).). Note you can't specify a length of LONGBLOB.	up to 4294967295 characters
ENUM (x,y,z,etc.)	Let you enter a list of possible values. If a value is inserted that is not in the list, a blank value will be inserted. Note: The values are sorted in the order you enter them.You enter the possible values in this format: ENUM('X','Y','Z'). Once defined the value for ENUM .you can only use those value along with NULL.	up to 65,535 characters
SET	Similar to ENUM except that SET may contain up to 64 list items and can store more than one choice	Up to 64 list items

4.2.1. Number types:

Data type	*Description*	*Storage*
TINYINT (size)	The maximum number of digits may be specified in parenthesis	-128 to 127 & . 0 to 255 UNSIGNED
SMALLINT (size)	The maximum number of digits may be specified in parenthesis	-32768 to 32767 normal. 0 to 65535 UNSIGNED
MEDIUMINT (size)	The maximum number of digits may be specified in parenthesis	-8388608 to 8388607 normal. 0 to 16777215 UNSIGNED
INT (size)	The maximum number of digits may be specified in parenthesis	-2147483648 to 2147483647 normal. 0 to 4294967295 UNSIGNED
BIGINT (size)	The maximum number of digits may be specified in parenthesis	-9223372036854775808 to 9223372036854775807 normal. 0 to 18446744073709551615 UNSIGNED*.
FLOAT (size,d)	A small number with a floating decimal point. The maximum number of digits may be specified in the size parameter. The maximum number of digits to the right of the decimal point is specified in the d parameter	Decimal precision can go to 24 places for a FLOAT.
DOUBLE(size,d)	A large number with a floating decimal point. The maximum number of digits may be specified in the size parameter. The maximum number of digits to the right of the decimal point is specified in the d parameter	Decimal precision can go to 53 places for a DOUBLE.
DECIMAL(size,d)	A DOUBLE stored as a string, allowing for a fixed decimal point. The maximum number of digits may be specified in the size parameter. The maximum number of digits to the right of the decimal point is specified in the d parameter	

*The integer types have an extra option called UNSIGNED. Normally, the integer goes from a negative to positive value. Adding the UNSIGNED attribute will move that range up so it starts at zero instead of a negative number.

4.2.2. Date types:

Data type	*Description*	*Storage*
DATE()	A date. Format: YYYY-MM-DD	from '1000-01-01' to '9999-12-31'
DATETIME()	*A date and time combination. Format: YYYY-MM-DD HH: MM:SS	is from '1000-01-01 00:00:00' to '9999-12-31 23:59:59'
TIMESTAMP()	*A timestamp. TIMESTAMP values are stored as the number of seconds since the Unix epoch ('1970-01-01 00:00:00' UTC). Format: YYYY-MM-DD HH: MM:SS	is from '1970-01-01 00:00:01' UTC to '2038-01-09 03:14:07' UTC
TIME()	A time. Format: HH:MM:SS	from '-838:59:59' to '838:59:59'
YEAR()	A year in two-digit or four-digit format. Note: Values allowed in four-digit format: 1901 to 2155. Values allowed in two-digit format: 70 to 69.	Year from 1901 to 2155

*Even if DATETIME and TIMESTAMP return the same format, they work very differently. In an INSERT or UPDATE query, the TIMESTAMP automatically set itself to the current date and time. TIMESTAMP also accepts various formats, like YYYYMMDDHHMMSS, YYMMDDHHMMSS, YYYYMMDD, or YYMMDD.

4.3. SQL Server Data Types

4.3.1 String types:

Data type	*Description*	*Storage*
char(n)	Fixed width, non-unicode character string	(n) bites n should be >=1 or <=8000
varchar(n)	Variable width, non-unicode character string	2 bytes + number of chars Maximum 8,000 characters
varchar(max)	Variable width, no-unicode	2 bytes + number of chars character string. Maximum 1,073,741,824 characters
text	Variable width character string. Not recommended in higher version instead their respective alternatives Varchar(Max) can be used.	4 bytes + number of chars Maximum 2GB of text data
nchar	Fixed width Unicode string.	Defined width x 2. Maximum 4,000 characters

nvarchar	Variable width Unicode string. The storage size is two times the actual length of the data entered + 2 bytes.	Maximum 8,000 bytes
nvarchar(max)	Variable width Unicode string. The actual length of the data entered + 2 bytes.	Maximum 2GB
ntext	Variable width Unicode string. Not recommended in higher version instead their respective alternatives NVarchar (Max) can be used.	Maximum 2GB of text data
bit	Allows 0, 1, or NULL	
binary(n)	Fixed width binary string. Maximum 8,000 bytes	(n) bytes
varbinary	Variable width binary string. the actual length of the data entered + 2 bytes.	Maximum 8,000 bytes
varbinary(max)	Variable width binary string. The actual length of the data entered + 2 bytes.	Maximum 2GB
image	Variable width binary string. It is not recommended instead it's alternative Varbinary (MAX) can be used.	Maximum 2GB

4.3.2 Number types:

Data type	***Description***	***Storage***
tinyint	Allows whole numbers from 0 to 255	1 byte
smallint	Allows whole numbers between -2^15 (-32,768) to 2^15-1 (32,767)	2 bytes
int	Allows whole numbers between -- 2^31 (-2,147,483,648) to 2^31-1 (2,147,483,647)	4 bytes
bigint	Allows whole numbers between - -2^63 (-9,223,372,036,854, 775,808) to 2^63-1 (9,223,372, 036,854,775,807)	8 bytes
decimal (p,s)	Fixed precision and scale numbers. Allows numbers from -10^38 +1 to 10^38 –1.	5-17 bytes – (10^38 +1 through 10^38 – 1)

	The p parameter indicates the maximum total number of digits that can be stored (both to the left and to the right of the decimal point). p must be a value from 1 to 38. Default is 18. The s parameter indicates the maximum number of digits stored to the right of the decimal point. s must be a value from 0 to p. Default value is 0	
numeric(p,s)	Fixed precision and scale numbers. Allows numbers from -10^38 +1 to 10^38 –1. The p parameter indicates the maximum total number of digits that can be stored (both to the left and to the right of the decimal point). p must be a value from 1 to 38. Default is 18. The s parameter indicates the maximum number of digits stored to the right of the decimal point. s must be a value from 0 to p. Default value is 0	5-17 bytes
smallmoney	Monetary data from -214,748.3648 to 214,748.3647	4 bytes
money	Monetary data from -922,337, 203,685,477.5808 to 922,337,203, 685,477.5807	8 bytes
float(n)	Floating precision number data from -1.79E + 308 to 1.79E + 308. The n parameter indicates whether the field should hold 4 or 8 bytes. float(24) holds a 4-byte field and float(53) holds an 8-byte field. Default value of n is 53.	4 or 8 bytes
real	Floating precision number data from -3.40E + 38 to 3.40E + 38	4 bytes

4.3.3 Date types:

Data type	*Description*	*Storage*
datetime	From January 1, 1753 to December 31, 9999 with an accuracy of 3.33 milliseconds. Format (YYYY-MM-DD hh:mm:ss[.nnn])	8 bytes
datetime2	From January 1, 0001 to December 31, 9999 with an accuracy of 100 nanoseconds	6-8 bytes
smalldatetime	From January 1, 1900 to June 6, 2079 with an accuracy of 1 minute. Format YYYY-MM-DD hh:mm:ss	4 bytes
date	Store a date only. From January 1, 0001 to December 31, 9999. Format YYYY-MM-DD	3 bytes
time	Store a time only to an accuracy of 100 nanoseconds. Format hh:mm:ss[.nnnnnnn]	3-5 bytes
datetimeoffset	The same as datetime2 with the addition of a time zone offset. Format YYYY-MM-DD hh:mm:ss [.nnnnnnn] [+/-]hh:mm	8-10 bytes
timestamp	Stores a unique number that gets updated every time a row gets created or modified. The timestamp value is based upon an internal clock and does not correspond to real time. Each table may have only one timestamp variable	

4.3.4 Other data types:

Data type	*Description*	*Storage*
sql_variant	Stores up to 8,000 bytes of data of various data types, except text, n text, and timestamp	up to 8,000 bytes
uniqueidentifier	Stores a globally unique identifier (GUID)	
xml	Stores XML formatted data. Maximum 2GB	Up to 2 GB
cursor	Stores a reference to a cursor used for database operations	
table	Stores a result-set for later processing	

4.4. Oracle Data Types:

Code	*Data Type*	*Description*	*Storage*
1	VARCHAR2 (*size* [BYTE | CHAR])	Variable-length character string having maximum length *size* bytes or characters. Maximum *size* is 4000 bytes(in 12c 32676 Note : Parameter MAX_STRING_SIZE should be set to EXTENDED) or characters, and minimum is 1 byte or 1 character. You must specify *size* for VARCHAR2. BYTE indicates that the column will have byte length semantics. CHAR indicates that the column will have character semantics.	32767 bytes or characters if MAX_STRING_SIZE = EXTENDED 4000 bytes or characters if MAX_STRING_SIZE = STANDARD
1	NVARCHAR2 (*size*)	Variable-length Unicode character string having maximum length *size* is 4000 bytes(in 12c 32676. Note : Parameter MAX_STRING_SIZE should be set to EXTENDED) or characters. The number of bytes can be up to two times *size* for AL16UTF16 encoding and three times *size* for UTF8 encoding. Maximum *size* is determined by the national character set definition, with an upper limit of 32,767 bytes. You must specify *size* for NVARCHAR2.	32767 bytes or characters if MAX_STRING_SIZE = EXTENDED 4000 bytes or characters if MAX_STRING_SIZE = STANDARD
2.	NUMBER [(*p* [, *s*])]	Number having precision *p* and scale *s*. The precision *p* can range from 1 to 38. The scale *s* can range from -84 to 127. Both precision and scale are in decimal digits. A NUMBER value requires from 1 to 22 bytes.	The precision *p* can range From 1 to 38. The scale scan range from -84 to127.
2.	FLOAT [(*p*)]	A subtype of the NUMBER data type having precision *p*. A FLOAT value is represented internally as NUMBER.	The precision *p* can range from 1 to 126 binary digits. A FLOAT value requires from 1 to 22 bytes.
8	LONG	Character data of variable length up to 2 gigabytes, or 2^{31} -1 bytes. Provided for backward compatibility.	2 Gigabytes -but now deprecated (provided for backward compatibility only)
12	DATE	Valid date range from January 1, 4712 BC, to December 31, 9999 AD. The default format is determined explicitly by the NLS_DATE_FORMAT parameter or implicitly by the NLS_TERRITORY parameter. The size is fixed at 7 bytes. This data type contains the datetime fields YEAR,	From January1, 4712 BC to December 31, 9999 AD.

		MONTH, DAY, HOUR, MINUTE, and SECOND. It does not have fractional seconds or a time zone.	
21	BINARY_FLOAT	32-bit floating point number. This data type requires 4 bytes.	32-bit floating point number.
22	BINARY_DOUBLE	64-bit floating point number. This data type requires 8 bytes.	64-bit floating point number.
180	TIMESTAMP [(fractional_seconds_precision)]	Year, month, and day values of date, as well as hour, minute, and second values of time, where *fractional_seconds_precision* is the number of digits in the fractional part of the SECOND datetime field. Accepted values of *fractional_seconds_precision* are 0 to 9. The default is 6. The default format is determined explicitly by the NLS_TIMESTAMP_FORMAT parameter or implicitly by the NLS_TERRITORY parameter. This data type contains the datetime fields YEAR, MONTH, DAY, HOUR, MINUTE, and SECOND. It contains fractional seconds but does not have a time zone.	Size 7 or 11 bytes, depending on the precision.
181	TIMESTAMP [(*fractional_seconds*)] WITH TIME ZONE	All values of TIMESTAMP as well as time zone displacement value, where *fractional_seconds_precision* is the number of digits in the fractional part of the SECOND datetime field. Accepted values are 0 to 9. The default is 6. The default format is determined explicitly by the NLS_TIMESTAMP_FORMAT parameter or implicitly by the NLS_TERRITORY parameter. This data type contains the datetime fields YEAR, MONTH, DAY, HOUR, MINUTE, SECOND, TIMEZONE_HOUR, and TIMEZONE_MINUTE. It has fractional seconds and an explicit time zone.	Size fixed at 13 bytes.
231	TIMESTAMP [(*fractional_seconds*)] WITH LOCAL TIME ZONE	All values of TIMESTAMP WITH TIME ZONE, with the following exceptions: Data is normalized to the database time zone when it is stored in the database. When the data is retrieved, users see the data in the session time zone.The default format is determined explicitly by the NLS_TIMESTAMP_FORMAT parameter or implicitly by the NLS_TERRITORY parameter. The size is 7 or 11 bytes, depending on the precision.	Size 7 or 11 bytes, depending on the precision.
182	INTERVAL YEAR [(*year_precision*)] TO MONTH	Stores a period of time in years and months, where *year_precision* is the number of digits in the YEAR datetime field. Accepted values are 0 to 9. The default is 2.	Size fixed at 5 bytes

183	INTERVAL DAY [(*day_precision*)] TO SECOND [(*fractional_seconds*)]	Stores a period of time in days, hours, minutes, and seconds, where *day_precision* is the maximum number of digits in the DAY datetime field. Accepted values are 0 to 9. The default is 2. *fractional_seconds_precision* is the number of digits in the fractional part of the SECOND field. Accepted values are 0 to 9. The default is 6.	Size fixed at 11 bytes.
23.	RAW(*size*)	Raw binary data of length *size* bytes. Maximum *size* is 4000 bytes (in 12c 32676 .Note : Parameter MAX_STRING_SIZE should be set to EXTENDED) or characters. You must specify *size* for a RAW value.	32767 bytes or characters if MAX_STRING_SIZE = EXTENDED 2000 bytes or characters if MAX_STRING_SIZE = STANDARD
24	LONG RAW	Raw binary data	Length up to 2 gigabytes.
69	ROWID	Base 64 string representing the unique address of a row in its table. This data type is primarily for values returned by the ROWID pseudocolumn.	
208	UROWID [(*size*)]	Base 64 string representing the logical address of a row of an index-organized table. The optional *size* is the size of a column of type UROWID. The maximum size and default is 4000 bytes.	
96	CHAR [(*size* [BYTE | CHAR])]	Fixed-length character data of length *size* bytes or characters. BYTE and CHAR have the same semantics as for VARCHAR2.	Maximum *size* is 2000 bytes or characters. Default and minimum *size* is 1 byte.
96	NCHAR[(*size*)]	Fixed-length character data of length *size* characters. The number of bytes can be up to two times *size* for AL16UTF16 encoding and three times *size* for UTF8 encoding.	1 to 2000 bytes.
112	CLOB	A character large object containing single-byte or multibyte characters. Both fixed-width and variable-width character sets are supported, both using the database character set.	Up to (4 gigabytes - 1) * (database block size).
112	NCLOB	A character large object containing Unicode characters. Both fixed-width and variable-width character sets are supported, both using the database national character set.	Up to (4 gigabytes - 1) * (database block size).
113	BLOB	A binary large object. Maximum size is (4 gigabytes - 1) * (database block size).	Up to (4 gigabytes - 1) * (database block size).

114	BFILE	Contains a locator to a large binary file stored outside the database. Enables byte stream I/O access to external LOBs residing on the database server. Maximum size is 4 gigabytes.	Up to 4 Giga bytes

Chapter - 5

Data Definition Language

DDL (Data Definition Language)–commands are used to create ,alter or drop a Schema object.) DDL command change the Schema of the data base with this command. Like Create a table will add a table in schema or Alter will change the structure of a schema object and Drop will reduce a schema object.

5.1 CREATE TABLE–The unique name or identifier for the table follows the CREATE TABLE statement. Each table structure must have a column. Each column must have name, data type and size of the data type.

A copy of an existing table can be created using a combination of the CREATE TABLE statement and the SELECT statement. You will cover this topic later in this chapter.

Example:

Following is an example which creates a CUSTOMERS table with ID as primary key and NOT NULL are the constraints showing that these fields cannot be NULL while creating records in this table:

Basic syntax of CREATE TABLE statement is as follows:

CREATE TABLE table_name (column1 datatype, column2 datatype, column3 datatype,

..... columnN datatype, PRIMARY KEY (one or more columns);

CREATE TABLE CUSTOMERS(

ID INT NOT NULL,

NAME VARCHAR (25) NOT NULL,

AGE INT NOT NULL,

ADDRESS CHAR (200),

SALARY DECIMAL (18,2),

PRIMARY KEY (ID));

Advanced Create table Command

CREATE TABLE [IF NOT EXISTS] [MEMORY] *table_name*

(*column_definition* [, ...]

index_definition [, ...]

) where *column_definition* is:

column_name data_type [*autoinc_options*] [*blob_settings*]

[NOT NULL | NULL]

[DEFAULT *default_value*]

[MINVALUE *min_value* | NOMINVALUE]

[MAXVALUE *max_value* | NOMAXVALUE]

and *index_definition* is:

[, PRIMARY [KEY] [*index_name*] (*column_name* [ASC | DESC] [CASE | NOCASE] [, ...])]

[, [UNIQUE] [INDEX] [*index_name*] (*column_name* [ASC | DESC] [CASE | NOCASE] [, ...])] [, ...]

IF NOT EXISTS

If this keyword is specified, the table will be created, only if there is no existing table with the same name. If this keyword is not specified then an exception will be raised in case any table exists with given name.

Table already exists

Data_type

The data type of the column. See the 'chapter 4' to know more about Data Types topic in more details about supported data types for each RDBMS.

NOT NULL: The column is not allowed to contain null values. (Default is NULL). One NULL value never equal to another NULL value.

My SQL differs from Oracle in the way it handles default value for a column that does not allow NULL value. In My SQL, for a column that does not allow NULL value and for which no data is provided for the column when data is inserted into the table, MySQL determines a default value for the column. This default value is the implicit default value for the column data type. However, if the strict mode is enabled, MySQL generates errors, and for transactional tables it rolls back the insert statement.

In Oracle, when data is inserted into a table, data must be provided for all columns that do not allow NULL value. Oracle does not generate a default value for columns that have the NOT NULL constraint.

UNIQUE: The UNIQUE constraint specifies that a column of a table may contain only unique values. For the purpose of a unique constraint, null values are considered equal.

PRIMARY KEY is merely a combination of UNIQUE and NOT NULL. Only one primary key can be specified for a table constraint.

Create table With Primary Key

```
CREATE TABLE ITEMS
(ItemID INT PRIMARY KEY AUTO_INCREMENT,
Item Name VARCHAR (50),
Item Price DECIMAL (8, 2),
Item Cat VARCHAR (50),
Item Desc TEXT);
```

Note: My SQL does not terminate a command until you give a semi colon (;) at the end of SQL command. SQL server does not need semicolon (;) to end command and Oracle needs it.

Auto increment

Auto-increment allows a unique number to be generated when a new record is inserted into a table.

AUTO INCREMENT a Field

Very often we would like the value of the primary key field to be created automatically every time a new record is inserted.

We would like to create an auto-increment field in a table.

5.1.1 Syntax for MySQL

The following SQL statement defines the "Customers_Id" column to be an auto-increment primary key field in the "Customers" table:

```
CREATE TABLE Customers
(Customer_Id int NOT NULL AUTO_INCREMENT,
Last Name varchar (255) NOT NULL,
First Name varchar (255),
```

```
Address varchar (255),
City varchar (255),
PRIMARY KEY (Customers_Id))
```

My SQL uses the AUTO_INCREMENT keyword to perform an auto-increment feature. By default, the starting value for AUTO_INCREMENT is 1, and it will increment by 1 for each new record. To let the AUTO_INCREMENT sequence start with another value, use the following SQL statement:

```
ALTER TABLE Customers AUTO_INCREMENT=100
```

To insert a new record into the "Customers" table, we will not have to specify a value for the "Customers_Id" column (a unique value will be added automatically):

```
INSERT INTO Customers (First Name, Last Name)
VALUES ('Lars','Monsen')
```

The SQL statement above would insert a new record into the "Customers" table. The "Customers_Id" column would be assigned a unique value. The "First Name" column would be set to "Lars" and the "Last Name" column would be set to "Monsen".

5.1.2 Syntax for SQL Server

The following SQL statement defines the "Customers_Id" column to be an auto-increment primary key field in the "Customers" table:

```
CREATE TABLE Customers
(Customers_Id int PRIMARY KEY IDENTITY,
Last Name varchar(255) NOT NULL,
First Name varchar(255),
Address varchar(255),
City varchar(255))
```

SQL Server uses the IDENTITY keyword to perform an auto-increment feature. By default, the starting value for IDENTITY is 1, and it will increment by 1 for each new record. To specify that the "Customers_Id" column should start at value 10 and increment by 5, change the identity to IDENTITY (10, 5).

To insert a new record into the "Customers" table, we will not have to specify a value for the "Customers_Id" column (a unique value will be added automatically):

INSERT INTO Customers (First Name, Last Name)VALUES ('Lars', 'Monsen').

The SQL statement above would insert a new record into the "Customers" table. The "Customers_Id" column would be assigned a unique value. The "First Name" column would be set to "Lars" and the "Last Name" column would be set to "Monsen".

5.1.3 Syntax for Access

The MS Access uses the Autoincrement keyword to perform an auto-increment feature.

The following SQL statement defines the "Customers_Id" column to be an auto-increment primary key field in the "Customers" table:

```
CREATE TABLE Customers
(Customers_Id PRIMARY KEY AUTOINCREMENT,
Last Name varchar (255) NOT NULL,
First Name varchar (255),
Address varchar (255),
City varchar (255))
```

By default, the starting value for AUTOINCREMENT is 1, and it will increment by 1 for each new record.

To specify that the "Customers _Id" column should start at value 10 and increment by 5, change the AUTOINCREMENT to AUTOINCREMENT (10, 5).

To insert a new record into the "Customers" table, we will not have to specify a value for the "Customers_Id" column (a unique value will be added automatically):

```
INSERT INTO Customers(First Name, Last Name)
VALUES ('Lars','Monsen')
```

The SQL statement above would insert a new record into the "Customers" table. The "Customers_Id" column would be assigned a unique value. The "First Name" column would be set to "Lars" and the "Last Name" column would be set to "Monsen".

5.1.4 Syntax for Oracle

In Oracle the code is a little bit different.You will have to create an auto-increment field with the sequence object (this object generates a number sequence).

Use the following CREATE SEQUENCE syntax:

```
CREATE SEQUENCE seq_Customers
MINVALUE 1
START WITH 1
INCREMENT BY 1
CACHE 10
```

The code above creates a sequence object called seq_Customers that starts with 1 and will increment by 1. It will also cache up to 10 values for performance. The cache option specifies how many sequence values will be stored in memory for faster access.

To insert a new record into the "Customers" table, we will have to use the nextval function (this function retrieves the next value from seq_person sequence):

```
INSERT INTO Customers (Customers_Id, First Name, Last Name)
VALUES (seq_Customers.nextval,'Lars','Monsen')
```

The SQL statement above would insert a new record into the "Customers" table. The "Customers_Id" column would be assigned the next number from the seq_Customers sequence. The "First Name" column would be set to "Lars" and the "Last Name" column would be set to "Monsen".

5.1.5 Creating a Table from an Existing Table

A table with copy of an existing table structure and data can be created using a combination of the CREATE TABLE statement and the SELECT statement.

The new table has the same column definitions. All columns or specific columns can be selected.

When you create a new table using existing table, new table would be populated using existing values in the old table.

Syntax:

The basic syntax for creating a table from another table is as follows:

```
CREATE TABLE NEW_TABLE_NAME AS
SELECT [ column1, column2...columnN ]
FROM EXISTING_TABLE_NAME
[ WHERE ]
```

Here column1, column 2...are the fields of existing table and same would be used to create fields of new table.

Example:

Following is an example which would create a table SALARY using CUSTOMERS table and having fields customer ID, and customer SALARY:

```
SQL> CREATE TABLE SALARY AS
SELECT ID, SALARY
FROM CUSTOMERS;
```

This would create new table SALARY which would have following records:

ID	*SALARY*
1	2000
2	3000
3	4000
4	5000
5	2000
6	3000
7	4000
8	3000

If you want to create a table with copy or existing table without and data(record) from existing table then you need to give a where clause with false condition like 1=2;

```
CREATE TABLE SALARY AS
SELECT ID, SALARY
FROM CUSTOMERS where 1=2;
```

With above command you can get an empty Customer table

ID	SALARY

Note: In SQL server you need to create an empty table with similar table structure as old table and you can insert all data from old table to new table. Or you can create new table similar as old table (Existing table) by using below syntax in SQL SERVER :

```
SELECT * INTO NewTableName
FROM OldTableName
select * from NewTableName
```

you will get New table created with all data similar to old table.

5.2 Alter

ALTER TABLE command is used to add, delete, or modify columns in an existing table. You can also use ALTER TABLE command to add and drop various constraints on existing table. The basic syntax of ALTER TABLE to add a new column in an existing table is as follows:

```
ALTER TABLE table_name ADD column_name datatype;
```

The basic syntax of ALTER TABLE to DROP COLUMN in an existing table is as follows:

```
ALTER TABLE table_name DROP COLUMN column_name;
```

5.2.1 Alter Table, Column, Data Type and constraints

My SQL alter to drop Column from table

```
ALTER TABLE table_name DROP column_name;
```

The basic syntax of ALTER TABLE to change the DATA TYPE of a column in a table is as follows:

```
ALTER TABLE table_name MODIFY COLUMN column_name
    datatype;
```

The basic syntax of ALTER TABLE to add a NOT NULL constraint to a column in a table is as follows:

```
ALTER TABLE table_name MODIFY column_name datatype NOT
    NULL;
```

The basic syntax of ALTER TABLE to ADD UNIQUE CONSTRAINT to a table is as follows:

```
ALTER TABLE table_name
ADD CONSTRAINT MyUniqueConstraint UNIQUE(column1,
    column 2...);
```

The basic syntax of ALTER TABLE to ADD CHECK CONSTRAINT to a table is as follows:

ALTER TABLE table_name

ADD CONSTRAINT MyUniqueConstraint CHECK (CONDITION);

The basic syntax of ALTER TABLE to ADD PRIMARY KEY constraint to a table is as follows:

ALTER TABLE table_name

ADD CONSTRAINT MyPrimaryKey PRIMARY KEY (column1, column 2...);

The basic syntax of ALTER TABLE to DROP CONSTRAINT from a table is as follows:

ALTER TABLE table_name

DROP CONSTRAINT MyUniqueConstraint;

If you're using MySQL, the code is as follows:

ALTER TABLE table_name

DROP INDEX MyUniqueConstraint;

The basic syntax of ALTER TABLE to DROP PRIMARY KEY constraint from a table is as follows:

ALTER TABLE table_name

DROP CONSTRAINT MyPrimaryKey;

MySQL:

ALTER TABLE table_name

DROP PRIMARY KEY;

Example:

Consider CUSTOMERS table is having following records:

ID	*Name*	*Age*	*Address*	*Salary*
1	Ramesh	32	Ahmedabad	2000
2	Khilan	25	Delhi	1500
3	Kaushik	23	Kota	2000
4	Chaitali	25	Mumbai	6500
5	Hardik	27	Bhopal	8500
6	Komal	22	MP	4500
7	Muffy	24	Indore	10000

Following is the example to ADD a new column in an existing table:

ALTER TABLE CUSTOMERS ADD SEX char(1);

Now CUSTOMERS table is changed and following would be output from SELECT statement:

ID	*Name*	*Age*	*Address*	*Salary*	*Sex*
1	Ramesh	32	Ahmedabad	2000	NULL
2	Khilan	25	Delhi	1500	NULL
3	kaushik	23	Kota	2000	NULL
4	Chaitali	25	Mumbai	6500	NULL
5	Hardik	27	Bhopal	8500	NULL
6	Komal	22	MP	4500	NULL
7	Muffy	24	Indore	10000	NULL

Following is the example to DROP sex column from existing table:

ALTER TABLE CUSTOMERS DROP SEX;

Now CUSTOMERS table is changed and following would be output from SELECT statement:

ID	*Name*	*Age*	*City*	*Salary*
1	Ramesh	32	Ahmedabad	2000
2	Khilan	25	Delhi	1500
3	kaushik	23	Kota	2000
4	Chaitali	25	Mumbai	6500
5	Hardik	27	Bhopal	8500
6	Komal	22	MP	4500
7	Muffy	24	Indore	10000

SQL DEFAULT Constraint on ALTER TABLE

To create a DEFAULT constraint on the "City" column when the table is already created, use the following SQL:

My SQL:

ALTER TABLE Customers
ALTER City SET DEFAULT 'PUNE'

SQL Server / MS Access:

ALTER TABLE Customers
ALTER COLUMN City SET DEFAULT 'PUNE'

Oracle:

ALTER TABLE Customers
MODIFY City DEFAULT 'PUNE'

5.3 Drop

The SQL DROP TABLE statement is used to remove a table definition and all data, indexes, triggers, constraints, and permission specifications for that table.

NOTE: You have to be careful while using this command because once a table is deleted then all the information available in the table would also be lost forever.

DROP TABLE Customers;

Example:

Let us first verify CUSTOMERS table, and then we would delete it from the database:

DESC CUSTOMERS;

Field	*Type*	*NULL*	*Key*	*Default*	*Extra*
ID	int(11)	No	Primary		
Name	varchar(20	NO			
Age	int(11)	NO			
City	char(20)	Yes		NULL	
Salary	int(18)	Yes		NULL	

This means CUSTOMERS table is available in the database, so Let us drop it as follows:

DROP TABLE CUSTOMERS;

Now if you would try DESC command then you would get the following error:

DESC CUSTOMERS;

ERROR 1146(42S02):Table'TEST.CUSTOMERS' doesn't exist

SQL SERVER: SQL server does not Support DESC to see the table structure. But you can see structure of table in sql server from INFORMATION_SCHEMA.Columns.

INFORMATION_SCHEMA.Columns is a system defined view. You can find it in System view tag on sql server.Suppose you want to see column name, Null, data type of a table CUSTOMERS than you will execute below query.

```
SELECT column_name AS [name],
DATA_TYPE AS [type],
IS_NULLABLE AS [null]
FROM INFORMATION_SCHEMA.Columns
WHERE table_name = 'CUSTOMERS'
```

Output you will get as below:

Field	*Type*	*NULL*
ID	int	No
Name	varchar	NO
Age	int	NO
City	char	Yes
Salary	int	Yes

To get Data type with width you need to use below query to execute.

```
SELECT column_name AS [name],
DATA_TYPE +
COALESCE('(' + CASE WHEN
CHARACTER_MAXIMUM_LENGTH = -1 THEN 'Max'
ELSE CAST(CHARACTER_MAXIMUM_LENGTH ASVRCHAR
(5))
END + ')', '') AS [type],
IS_NULLABLE AS [null?]
FROM INFORMATION_SCHEMA.Columns
WHERE table_name = 'CUSTOMERS'
```

Let's see another example

Note: if you will not give where table_name='CUSTOMERS' in above example and run the query, then you will get all table's structure (all columns, types and null from all tables from that data base.so, to get desired result you must execute above query with where clause.

My SQL code to describe the table structure

SHOW COLUMNS FROM CUSTOMERS;

5.3.2 DROP a DEFAULT Constraint

To drop a DEFAULT constraint, use the following SQL:

MySQL:

ALTER TABLE Customers

ALTER City DROP DEFAULT

SQL Server / Oracle / MS Access:

ALTER TABLE Customers

ALTER COLUMN City DROP DEFAULT

5.4 Truncate

TRUNCATE deletes all data from a table in a very fast way, deleting the data inside the table and not the table itself. It usually implies a subsequent COMMIT operation, i.e., it cannot be rolled back (data is not written to the logs for rollback later, unlike DELETE).You can't truncate parent table with child table. In oracle we get Error: unique/ primary keys in table referenced by enabled foreign keys.

TRUNCATE TABLE Table Name;

Note; In Oracle 12c you can use Truncate Table <Parent> cascade; if you have defined the FK as ON DELETE CASCADE.

Exercise:

1. Create a table to store data for 10 Students. Which will store ID, Student name, Address, Class and Section.
2. Create a table to store data for 10 Employees. Which will store Employee ID, Employee name, Address, Department and Salary, hire_date?
3. Create a table to store data for 10 order_items. Which will store item_ ID, order_ID,orderdate,order_details
4. What is Autoincrement? How it works in Oracle and sql server?
5. Differentiate truncate and Drop command.

Chapter - 6

Integrity Constraints

An integrity constraint is a schema object that is created and dropped using SQL. To enforce data integrity, use integrity constraints unless it is not possible. Advantages of integrity constraints over alternatives for enforcing data integrity include:

Declarative ease

Because you define integrity constraints using SQL statements, no additional programming is required when you define or alter a table.

Centralized rules

Integrity constraints are defined for tables and are stored in the data dictionary. Thus, data entered by all applications must adhere to the same integrity constraints. If the rules change at the table level, then applications need not change. Also, applications can use metadata in the data dictionary to immediately inform users of violations, even before the database checks the SQL statement.

Note: data Dictionary: A read-only collection of database tables and views containing reference information about the database, its structures, and its users.

Flexibility when loading data

You can disable integrity constraints temporarily to avoid performance overhead when loading large amounts of data. When the data load is complete, you can re-enable the integrity constraints.

6.1 Types of Integrity Constraints

Constraint Type	*Description*	*Notes*
NOT NULL	Allows or disallows inserts or updates of rows containing a **null** in a specified column.	You can only add a column with a NOT NULL constraint if the table does not contain any rows or if you specify a default value.
NULL	The SQL NULL is the term used to represent a missing value. A NULL value in a table is a value in a field that appears to be blank. The basic syntax of NULL while creating a table: CREATE TABLE CUSTOMERS ID INT NOT NULL, NAME VARCHAR (20) NOT NULL, AGE INT NOT NULL, ADDRESS CHAR (25), SALARY DECIMAL (18,2), PRIMARY KEY (ID);	A field with a NULL value is a field with no value. It is very important to understand that a NULL value is different than a zero value or a field that contains spaces. Here NOT NULL signifies that column should always accept an explicit value of the given data type. There are two columns where we did not use NOT NULL which means these column could be NULL. A field with a NULL value is one that has been left blank during record creation. You must use the IS NULL or IS NOT NULL operators in order to check for a NULL value.
Unique key	Prohibits multiple rows from having the same value in the same column or combination of columns but allows some values to be null. CREATE TABLE employees (..., email VARCHAR2(25) CONSTRAINT emp_email_nn NOT NULL..., CONSTRAINT emp_email_uk UNIQUE (email)...);	The term key refers only to the columns defined in the integrity constraint. Because the database enforces a unique constraint by implicitly creating or reusing an index on the key columns, the term unique key is sometimes incorrectly used as a synonym for unique key constraint or unique index Unless a NOT NULL constraint is also defined, a null always satisfies a unique key constraint. Thus, columns with both unique key constraints and NOT NULL constraints are typical. This combination forces the user to enter values in the unique key and eliminates the possibility that new row data conflicts with existing row data.

Primary key	Combines a **NOT NULL** constraint and a unique constraint. It prohibits multiple rows from having the same value in the same column or combination of columns and prohibits values from being null.	No two rows have duplicate values in the specified column or set of columns. The primary key columns do not allow nulls.
Foreign key	Designates a column as the foreign key and establishes a relationship between the foreign key and a primary or unique key, called the **referenced key**. The value of foreign keys can match either the referenced primary or unique key value, or be null. If any column of a composite foreign key is null, then the non-null portions of the key do not have to match any corresponding portion of a parent key. Foreign keys may be defined as multiple columns. However, a composite foreign key must reference a composite primary or unique key with the same number of columns and the same data types.	The unique key or primary key of the table referenced by a foreign key. For example, the department_id column in departments is the referenced key for the department_id column in employees. The table that is referenced by the foreign key of the child table. It is this table's referenced key that determines whether specific inserts or updates are allowed in the child table. For example, the departments table is a parent of employees.
Check	Requires a database value to obey a specified condition. A check constraint on a column or set of columns requires that a specified condition be true or unknown for every row. If DML results in the condition of the constraint evaluating to false, then the SQL statement is rolled back.	A single column can have multiple check constraints that reference the column in its definition. For example, the salary column could have one constraint that prevents values over 10000 and a separate constraint that prevents values less than 500. If multiple check constraints exist for a column, then they must be designed so their purposes do not conflict. No order of evaluation of the conditions can be assumed. The database does not verify that check conditions are not mutually exclusive.

REF	Dictates types of data manipulation allowed on values in a **REF** column and how these actions affect dependent values. In an object-relational database, a built-in data type called a **REF** encapsulates a reference to a row object of a specified object type. Referential integrity constraints on **REF** columns ensure that there is a row object for the **REF**.	Supports by ORACLE. A scoped REF is constrained to contain only references to a specified object table. You can specify a scoped REF when you declare a column type, collection element, or object type attribute to be a REF. Referential integrity constraints are scoped implicitly. For example, suppose the object type address_objtyp is used to create an object table named address_objtab: CREATE TABLE address_objtab OF address_objtyp;

6.2 DEFAULT Constraint

The DEFAULT constraint is used to insert a default value into a column.

The default value will be added to all new records, if no other value is specified.

SQL DEFAULT Constraint on CREATE TABLE

The following SQL creates a DEFAULT constraint on the "City" column when the "Customers" table is created:

My SQL / SQL Server / Oracle / MS Access:

```
CREATE TABLE Customers
(Customers_Id int NOT NULL,
LastName varchar(255) NOT NULL,
FirstName varchar(255),
City varchar(255) DEFAULT 'PUNE')
```

The DEFAULT constraint can also be used to insert system values, by using functions like GETDATE ():

```
CREATE TABLE Orders
(O_Id int NOT NULL,
OrderNo int NOT NULL,
Customers_Id int,
OrderDate date DEFAULT GETDATE())
```

Exercise:

Execute the script to create and populate the database which includes three tables Suppliers, quotation and inventory. Details are as below:

Supplier
Supplier_No (primary key)
SupplierName
Supplier_State

Quotation
Item_NO (Primary key)
Supplier_No (Foreign key)
Price
Delivery

Inventory
Inventory_No (Primary key)
Item_no (Foreign Key)
Quotation_Status
Component

1. Can a primary key contain more than one column?
2. What are the difference between primary key and unique key?
3. What are various constraints used in SQL?
4. How will you convert a date to char in Oracle give one example?
5. What are the differences between varchar, varchar2 and char data type.
6. What are Primary Keys and Foreign Keys?
7. When can you define a primary key for a column in a table?
   (i) Before creation of table
   (ii) After creation of table
   (iii) At the time of creating a table
   (iv) After inserting the rows in a table

Chapter - 7

Data Manipulation Language

7.1 Insert- Insert DML command is used to add one or more than one rows in an existing table. Only one row will get insert into Table with below example.

Example:

INSERT INTO My_table

(Column name 1,Column name 2,Column name 3) VALUES ('Test', 'N', NULL);

It is possible to write the INSERT INTO statement in two forms.

The first form does not specify the column names where the data will be inserted, only their values:

INSERT INTO table_nameVALUES (value1,value2,value3,...);

The second form specifies both the column names and the values to be inserted:

INSERT INTO table_name (column1,column2,column3,...) VALUES (value1,value2,value3,...);

Example Database

Below is a selection from the "Customers" table:

ID	Name	Age	City	Salary

7.1.1 INSERT INTO

Assume we wish to insert a new row in the "Customers" table.

We can use the following SQL statement (without specifying column names):

INSERT INTO CustomersVALUES (1, 'Muffy',24,' Indore',10000);

Or this SQL statement (including column names):

INSERT INTO Customers (ID, Name, Age, City, Salary)

VALUES (1, 'Muffy',24,' Indore',10000);

The selection from the "Customers" table will now look like this:

ID	*Name*	*Age*	*City*	*Salary*
1	Muffy	24	Indore	10000

AutoNumber is a type of data used in Microsoft Access tables to generate an automatically incremented numeric counter. The default AutoNumber type has a start value of 1 and an increment of 1.

The SQL INSERT INTO Statement is used to add new rows of data to a table in the database.

Syntax:To Delete all rows from Customers;

Delete from Customers;

Now your table is an empty table.

There are two basic syntax of INSERT INTO statement is as follows:

INSERT INTO TABLE_NAME (column1, column2, column 3,... columnN)]

VALUES (value1, value2, value3,...valueN);

Here column1, column2,...columnN are the names of the columns in the table into which you want to insert data.

You may not need to specify the column(s) name in the SQL query if you are adding values for all the columns of the table. But make sure the order of the values is in the same order as the columns in the table. The SQL INSERT INTO syntax would be as follows:

INSERT INTO TABLE_NAME VALUES (value1, value2, value3,... valueN);

Example:

Following statements would create six records in CUSTOMERS table:

INSERT INTO CUSTOMERS (ID, NAME, AGE, City, SALARY)
VALUES (1, 'Ramesh', 32, 'Ahmedabad', 2000.00);

INSERT INTO CUSTOMERS (ID, NAME, AGE, City, SALARY)
VALUES (2, 'Khilan', 25, 'Delhi', 1500.00);

INSERT INTO CUSTOMERS (ID, NAME, AGE, City, SALARY)
VALUES (3, 'kaushik', 23, 'Kota', 2000.00);

INSERT INTO CUSTOMERS (ID, NAME, AGE, City, SALARY)
VALUES (4, 'Chaitali', 25, 'Mumbai', 6500.00);

INSERT INTO CUSTOMERS (ID, NAME, AGE, City, SALARY)
VALUES (5, 'Hardik', 27, 'Bhopal', 8500.00);

INSERT INTO CUSTOMERS (ID, NAME, AGE, City, SALARY)
VALUES (6, 'Komal', 22, 'MP', 4500.00);

You can create a record in CUSTOMERS table using second syntax as follows:

INSERT INTO CUSTOMERS
VALUES (7, 'Muffy', 24, 'Indore', 10000.00);

All the above statement would product following records in CUSTOMERS table:

ID	*Name*	*Age*	*City*	*Salary*
1	Ramesh	32	Ahmedabad	2000
2	Khilan	25	Delhi	1500
3	kaushik	23	Kota	2000
4	Chaitali	25	Mumbai	6500
5	Hardik	27	Bhopal	8500
6	Komal	22	MP	4500
7	Muffy	24	Indore	10000

Populate one table using another table:

You can populate data into a table through select statement over another table provided another table has a set of fields which are required to populate first table. Here is the syntax:

```
INSERT INTO first_table_name [(column1, column 2,...columnN)]
SELECT column1, column 2,...columnN
FROM second_table_name
[WHERE condition];
```

7.1.2 Insert Data Only in Specified Columns

It is also possible to only insert data in specific columns.

The following SQL statement will insert a new row, but only insert data in the "CustomerName", "City", and "Country" columns (and the CustomerID field will of course also be updated automatically):

```
INSERT INTO Customers (Name, City)
VALUES ('Cardinal', 'Pune');
```

The selection from the "Customers" table will now look like this:

ID	*Name*	*Age*	*City*	*Salary*
1	Ramesh	32	Ahmedabad	2000
2	Khilan	25	Delhi	1500
3	kaushik	23	Kota	2000
4	Chaitali	25	Mumbai	6500
5	Hardik	27	Bhopal	8500
6	Komal	22	MP	4500
7	Muffy	24	Indore	10000
8	Cardinal		Pune	

We can also insert multiple rows with single insert statement

```
insert into tablename (column name)
select 'Column value' union all
select 'Column value' union all
select 'Column value'
insert into tablename (column1, column2, column3 ...)
select value1,value2,value3 union all
select value1,value2, value3
```

Note: few data base only supports multiline insertion like SQL server.

7.1.3 Inserting into a Remote Database:

Example The following statement inserts a row into the employees table owned by the user hr on the database accessible by the database link remote:

```
INSERT INTO employees@remote
VALUES (8002, 'Juan', 'Fernandez', 'juanf@example.com', NULL,
TO_DATE('04-OCT-1992', 'DD-MON-YYYY'), 'SH_CLERK',
    3000, NULL, 121, 20);
```

Note: few database only supports Inserting into a Remote Database. like Oracle .

Inserting Sequence Values: Example The following statement inserts a new row containing the next value of the departments_seq sequence into the departments table:

```
INSERT INTO departments
VALUES (departments_seq.nextval, 'Entertainment', 162, 1400);
```

Note: few data base only supports Inserting Sequence Values. like Oracle.

7.2 Update

The UPDATE statement is used to update records in an existing table.

SQL UPDATE Syntax

UPDATE ***table_name***

SET ***column1=value1,column2=value2,...***

WHERE ***some_column=some_value***;

Notice the WHERE clause in the SQL UPDATE statement!

The WHERE clause specifies which record or records that should be updated. If you omit the WHERE clause, all records will be updated!

Below is a selection from the "Customers" table:

ID	*Name*	*Age*	*City*	*Salary*
1	Ramesh	32	Ahmedabad	2000
2	Khilan	25	Delhi	1500
3	kaushik	23	Kota	2000
4	Chaitali	25	Mumbai	6500
5	Hardik	27	Bhopal	8500
6	Komal	22	MP	4500
7	Muffy	24	Indore	10000
8	Cardinal		Pune	

SQL UPDATE Example

Assume we wish to update the customer "Alfreds Futterkiste" with a new contact person and city.

We use the following SQL statement:

UPDATE Customers
SET Name='Rekha', City='Mumbai'
WHERE Name='Cardinal';

The selection from the "Customers" table will now look like this:

ID	*Name*	*Age*	*City*	*Salary*
1	Ramesh	32	Ahmedabad	2000
2	Khilan	25	Delhi	1500
3	kaushik	23	Kota	2000
4	Chaitali	25	Mumbai	6500
5	Hardik	27	Bhopal	8500
6	Komal	22	MP	4500
7	Muffy	24	Indore	10000
8	Rekha		Mumbai	

Update Warning!

Be careful when updating records. If we had omitted the WHERE clause in the example above, like this:

UPDATE Customers

SET Name='Rekha', City='Mumbai';

The "Customers" table would have looked like this:

ID	*Name*	*Age*	*City*	*Salary*
1	Rekha	32	Mumbai	2000
2	Rekha	25	Mumbai	1500
3	Rekha	23	Mumbai	2000
4	Rekha	25	Mumbai	6500
5	Rekha	27	Mumbai	8500
6	Rekha	22	Mumbai	4500
7	Rekha	24	Mumbai	10000
8	Rekha		Mumbai	

7.3 Delete

The SQL DELETE Statement

The DELETE statement is used to delete rows in a table.

SQL DELETE Syntax

DELETE FROM ***table_name***

WHERE ***some_column=some_value***;

Notice the WHERE clause in the SQL DELETE statement.

The WHERE clause specifies which record or records that should be deleted. If you omit the WHERE clause, all records will be deleted!

Below is a selection from the "Customers" table:

ID	*Name*	*Age*	*City*	*Salary*
1	Ramesh	32	Ahmedabad	2000
2	Khilan	25	Delhi	1500
3	kaushik	23	Kota	2000
4	Chaitali	25	Mumbai	6500
5	Hardik	27	Bhopal	8500
6	Komal	22	MP	4500
7	Muffy	24	Indore	10000

SQL DELETE Example

7.3.1 Delete specific Data

Assume we wish to delete the customer "Muffy" from the "Customers" table.

We use the following SQL statement:

DELETE FROM Customers

WHERE Name='Muffy' AND City='Indore';

The "Customers" table will now look like this:

ID	*Name*	*Age*	*City*	*Salary*
1	Ramesh	32	Ahmedabad	2000
2	Khilan	25	Delhi	1500
3	kaushik	23	Kota	2000
4	Chaitali	25	Mumbai	6500
5	Hardik	27	Bhopal	8500
6	Komal	22	MP	4500

7.3.2 Delete All Data

It is possible to delete all rows in a table without deleting the table. This means that the table structure, attributes, and indexes will be intact:

DELETE FROM ***table_name***;

If where Clause is given The WHERE clause specifies the conditions that identify which rows to delete. With no WHERE clause, all rows are deleted. If the ORDER BY clause is specified, the rows are deleted in the order that is specified. The LIMIT clause places a limit on the number of rows that can be deleted.

For the multiple-table syntax, DELETE deletes from each tbl_name the rows that satisfy the conditions. In this case, ORDER BY and LIMIT cannot be used.

7.3.3 Modifier for My SQL Delete statement

IN My SQL the DELETE statement supports the following modifiers:

- If you specify LOW_PRIORITY, the server delays execution of the DELETE until no other clients are reading from the table. This affects only storage engines that use only table-level locking (such as MyISAM, MEMORY, and MERGE).

- For MyISAM tables, if you use the QUICK keyword, the storage engine does not merge index leaves during delete, which may speed up some kinds of delete operations.
- The IGNORE keyword causes MySQL to ignore all errors during the process of deleting rows. Errors that are ignored due to the use of IGNORE are returned as warnings.

```
DELETE t1, t2 FROM t1 INNER JOIN t2 INNER JOIN t3
WHERE t1.id=t2.id AND t2.id=t3.id;
```

Or

```
DELETE FROM t1, t2 USING t1 INNER JOIN t2 INNER JOIN t3
WHERE t1.id=t2.id AND t2.id=t3.id;
```

7.4 MERGE–Merge (also known as UPSERT) is used to combine the data of multiple tables. It combines the INSERT and UPDATE elements. It is introduced in SQL: 2003 standard and expanded in the SQL: 2008; prior to that, some databases provided similar functionality via different syntax, sometimes called "upsert".

```
MERGE INTO targettable USING Sourcetable ON (condition)
WHEN MATCHED THEN
UPDATE SET column1 = value1 [, column2 = value2 ...]
WHEN NOT MATCHED THEN
INSERT (column1 [, column2 ...]) VALUES (value1 [, value2 ...
```

The Target table (table/view/sub-query) comes after the INTO and the Source table comes after USING (table/view/sub-query). That is: rows present in the Source but missing from the Target does run the action, specifically the NOT MATCHED action Rows missing from the Source and present in Target are ignored, no action is performed on the Target. If multiple Source rows match a given Target row, an error is mandated by SQL. You cannot update a Target row multiple times with MERGE statement Database management systems Oracle Database, DB2, Teradata and MS SQL support the standard syntax. Some also add non-standard SQL extensions. You can do similar through trigger. You can know more about Trigger in Trigger chapter.

Example:

```
CREATE TABLE TargetTable(EmployeeID int, EmployeeName
varchar(10),
```

```
CONSTRAINT Testtarget_PK PRIMARY KEY(EmployeeID));
CREATE TABLE SourceTable(EmployeeID int, EmployeeName
    varchar(10),
CONSTRAINT TestSource_PK PRIMARY KEY(EmployeeID));
INSERT into TargetTable(EmployeeID, EmployeeName) VALUES
    (100, 'Mary');
INSERT into TargetTable(EmployeeID, EmployeeName) VALUES
    (101, 'Sara');
INSERT into TargetTable(EmployeeID, EmployeeName) VALUES
    (102, 'Stefano');
INSERT into SourceTable(EmployeeID, EmployeeName) Values
    (103, 'Bob');
INSERT into SourceTable(EmployeeID, EmployeeName) Values
    (104, 'Steve');
select* from TargetTable
```

Table: TargetTable

Employee ID	*Employee Name*
100	Mary
101	Sara
102	Stefano

```
select* from SourceTable
```

Table: SourceTable

EmployeeID	*EmployeeName*
103	Bob
104	Steve

```
MERGE TargetTable AS T
USING SourceTable AS S
ON (T.EmployeeID = S.EmployeeID)
WHEN NOT MATCHED BY Target AND S.EmployeeName LIKE
'S%'
THEN INSERT (Employee ID, EmployeeName) VALUES
(S.Employee ID, S.EmployeeName);
```

You will get one addition row in Targettable as Employee name starts with S that is Steve.

Employee ID	***EmployeeName***
100	Mary
101	Sara
102	Stefano
104	Steve

Note: Semicolon (;) is mandatory at the end of Mearge statement.

Now if you want to update in case of match and Delete in case not matched, then execute below query:

```
MERGE TargetTable AS T
USING SourceTable AS S
ON (T.EmployeeID = S.EmployeeID)
WHEN NOT MATCHED BY Target AND S.EmployeeName LIKE
    'S%'
THEN INSERT(EmployeeID, EmployeeName) VALUES
    (S.Employee ID, S.EmployeeName)
WHEN MATCHED
THEN UPDATE SET T.EmployeeName = S.EmployeeName
WHEN NOT MATCHED BY SOURCE AND T.EmployeeName
    LIKE 'S%'
THEN DELETE;
```

You will get two rows in Targettable. Two rows which starts with 'S' and not matched with existing rows of source with given criteria will get deleted.

Select * from TargetTable

Employee ID	***Employee Name***
100	Mary
104	Steve

Exercise:

1. Differentiate DELETE command in Oracle/SQL server and DELETE command in MY SQL.
2. The____________clause specifies which record or records that should be deleted. If you omit the______________clause, all records will be deleted!

Chapter - 8

Synonym

A synonym is a database object that provides an alternative name for another database object, referred to as the base object that can exist on a local or remote server. You can create Synonyms for different objects of a database like: Table, View, Stored Procedure, Sequence, Functions, Package, Materialized View etc. Once created you can't Alter the Synonym. You can drop and recreate it again.

SQL Server syntax

CREATE SYNONYM [schema_name_1.] synonym_name FOR <object>

<object> :: =

{[server_name.[database_name] . [schema_name_2].| database_name . [schema_name_2].| schema_name_2.] object_name}

Arguments schema_name_1- Specifies the schema in which the synonym is created. If schema is not specified, SQL Server uses the default schema of the current user.

synonym_name -Is the name of the new synonym.

server_name -Is the name of the server on which base object is located.

database_name -Is the name of the database in which the base object is located.

If database_name is not specified, the name of the current database is used.

schema_name_2 -Is the name of the schema of the base object. If schema_name is not specified the default schema of the current user is used.

object_name -Is the name of the base object that the synonym references.

Note: To create a synonym in a given schema, a user must have CREATE SYNONYM permission and either owns the schema.

The CREATE SYNONYM permission is a grantable permission.

Example:

Creating a synonym for a local object

The following example first creates a synonym for the base object, Product in the database, and then queries the synonym.

select * from Departments

Department_id	*Department_name*	*Manager_id*	*Location_id*
10	Administration	200	1700
20	Marketing	201	1800
50	Shipping	124	1500
60	IT	103	1400
80	Sales	149	2500
90	Executive	100	1700
110	Accounting	205	1700
190	Contracting	NULL	1700

Create a table with above given data. And create a synonym with below given syntax:

create Synonym SynonymsDepartments for Departments

now you can use SynonymsDepartments same like Departments

select* from SynonymsDepartments

Department_id	*Department_name*	*Manager_id*	*Location_id*
10	Administration	200	1700
20	Marketing	201	1800
50	Shipping	124	1500
60	IT	103	1400
80	Sales	149	2500
90	Executive	100	1700
110	Accounting	205	1700
190	Contracting	NULL	1700

You can also use where and other conditions with this Synonym like Where

```
select * from SynonymsDepartments
where Department_Id <= 60
```

OutPut:

Department_id	*Department_name*	*Manager_id*	*Location_id*
10	Administration	200	1700
20	Marketing	201	1800
50	Shipping	124	1500
60	IT	103	1400

Note: My Sql, SQLite and Ms SQL server 2000 does not support synonym. Other higher version of MS SQL server supports to create synonyms or Alias.

8.1 Types of Synonyms: there are two types of Synonym Public Synonym and Private Synonym.

8.1.1 Public Synonym- Public Synonym is a synonym which is accessible to all database users. Creating a Public synonyms feature is supported by Oracle.

Syntax:

```
Create public Synonym SynonymsDepartments for Departments
```

8.1.2 Private Synonym- Private Synonym is a Synonym which visible to their owner only. BY default database creates Private Synonym only. There is no need of PRIVATE keyword to create a private Synonym.

Syntax:

```
create Synonym SynonymsDepartments for Departments
```

Exercise:

1. Create a Synonym for table Employees.
2. Create a Synonym for table Employees which gives output only for those employees who gets salary more than AVG salary..

Chapter - 9

Data Control Language

The Data Control Language (DCL) Gives or revoke Controls to users, to access and manipulate data.

9.1 Grant & Revoke – Grant and Revoke are DCL command mostly used to control (access/ permission) to the User.

GRANT authorizes one or more users to perform specific operation or a set of operations on an object. As a database administrator,

For example, application developers may want to take advantage of the Database Control interface to create or modify tables, indexes, views, and so on. You must grant access to Database Control to these users before they can log in.

Grant Type	*Privilege or Role Name*
System privileges	CREATEANYTABLE, CREATEANYVIEW
Object privileges	SELECT
Roles	APPDEV, SELECT_CATALOG_ROLE

GRANT SELECT, UPDATE

ON Employees

TO User1, User2;

REVOKE eliminates or denied a granted permission.You can also control default Granted permission also with this command.

Use the REVOKE statement to:

- Revoke system privileges from users and roles
- Revoke roles from users and roles
- Revoke object privileges for a particular object from users and roles

```
REVOKE SELECT, UPDATE
ON Employees
TO User1, User2;
```

To revoke a system privilege, you must have been granted the privilege with the ADMIN OPTION. You can revoke any privilege if you have the GRANT ANY PRIVILEGE system privilege.

To revoke a role, you must have been granted the role with the ADMIN OPTION. You can revoke any role if you have the GRANT ANY ROLE system privilege.

To revoke an object privilege, you must previously have granted the object privilege to the user and role or you must have the GRANT ANY OBJECT PRIVILEGE system privilege.

The REVOKE statement can revoke only privileges and roles that were previously granted directly with a GRANT statement. You can not use this statement to revoke:

- Privileges or roles not granted to the revokee
- Roles or object privileges granted through the operating system
- Privileges or roles granted to the revokee through roles

Granting and Revoking Object Privileges

You can grant DELETE, INSERT, SELECT and UPDATE privileges on the table orders to the user hr with the following statement:

```
GRANT ALL ON Employees TO User1;
```

To revoke the DELETE privilege on orders from User1, issue the following statement:

```
REVOKE DELETE ON Employees FROM User1;
```

To revoke the remaining privileges on orders that you granted to User1, issue the following statement:

```
REVOKE ALL ON Employees FROM User1;
```

Grant and Revoking an Object Privilege on a Sequence from a User

You can grant the user User2 the SELECT privilege on the Synonyms Departments sequence in the schema USER1 with the following statement:

GRANT SELECT ON User1. SynonymsDepartments TO User2;

To revoke the SELECT privilege on Synonyms Departments from User 2, with the following statement:

REVOKE SELECT ON User1. Synonyms Departments TO User2 ;

Exercise:

1. Grant updates permission to a user on Employees Table.
2. Revoke Update permission to a user on Employees table.

Chapter - 10

Transaction Control Language

Transactions Control Language Command used to Control or manage transactions in database.They are basically Commit, Savepoint and Rollback.

10.1 Commit: Commit command is used to save your transaction permanently of a transaction. A transaction is nothing but a sequence SQL of commands or Statements in a single unit. Commit Statement also erases all savepoints in the transaction and used to release locks also. Until you commit a transaction:

- You can see any changes you have made during the transaction by querying the modified tables, but other users cannot see the changes. After you commit the transaction, the changes are visible to other users' statements that execute after the commit.
- You can roll back (undo) any changes made during the transaction with the ROLLBACK statement.

Note: In SQL Server you no need to commit a transaction. By default sql server do commit.

In Oracle used syntax like below:

Commit;

10.2 Savepoint: Savepoint is used to save a transaction temporarily, so that you can rollback to that point.

Syntax:

Savepoint savepoint_name;

10.3 Rollback: ROLLBACK statement is used to undo the work done in the current transaction. This command get back the transaction till last commit.

Syntax:

Rollback;

You can also use it with savepoint command to jump back to a savepoint in a transaction.

Syntax:

Rollback savepoint_name;

Specify the savepoint to which you want to roll back the current transaction. If you omit this clause, then the ROLLBACK statement rolls back the entire transaction. Using ROLLBACK without the TOSAVE-POINT clause performs the following operations:

- Ends the transaction
- Undoes all changes in the current transaction
- Erases all savepoints in the transaction
- Releases any transaction locks

Transactions, if available, wrap DML operations:

START TRANSACTION (or BEGIN WORK, or BEGIN TRANS-ACTION, depending on SQL dialect) marks the start of a database transaction, which either completes entirely or not at all.

SAVE TRANSACTION (or SAVEPOINT) saves the state of the database at the current point in transaction

Example: targetable

Employee ID	***Employee Name***
100	Mary
104	Steve

INSERT into TargetTable(EmployeeID, EmployeeName) VALUES (101, 'Sara');

SavePoint A;

INSERT into TargetTable(EmployeeID, EmployeeName) VALUES (102, 'Stefano');

Select * from targetable

Employee ID	*Employee Name*
100	Mary
104	Steve
101	Sara
102	Stefano

Rollback to A;

Select * from targetable;

Employee ID	*Employee Name*
100	Mary
104	Steve
101	Sara

Exercise

1. TCL stands for……………………………………………………
2. Which Commands in SQL allows controlling access to data in current database.
3. Which command saves table insertion permanently?

Chapter - 11

Data Query Language

11.1 Select: The SELECT statement is used to fetch data from a database table or view.

SELECT - list of attributes and functions

* / list of columns-list of columns to get in result set or * for getting all column in result set

FROM - list of tables

WHERE - conditions / join conditions

GROUP BY - attributes not aggregated in select clause

HAVING - group condition

ORDER BY - list of attributes

The result is stored in a result table, called the result-set.

Below is a selection from the "Customers" table:

ID	*Name*	*Age*	*City*	*Salary*
1	Ramesh	32	Ahmedabad	2000
2	Khilan	25	Delhi	1500
3	kaushik	23	Kota	2000
4	Chaitali	25	Mumbai	6500
5	Hardik	27	Bhopal	8500
6	Komal	22	MP	4500
7	Muffy	24	Indore	10000

Where

WHERE clause is used to extract only those records that fulfill a specified criteria.

SELECT column_name, column_name

FROM table_name

WHERE column_name operator value;

Below is a selection from the "Customers" table:

ID	*Name*	*Age*	*City*	*Salary*
1	Ramesh	32	Ahmedabad	2000
2	Khilan	25	Delhi	1500
3	kaushik	23	Kota	2000
4	Chaitali	25	Mumbai	6500
5	Hardik	27	Bhopal	8500
6	Komal	22	MP	4500
7	Muffy	24	Indore	10000

The following SQL statement selects all the customers from the country "Mexico", in the "Customers" table:

Example

SELECT * FROM Customers

WHERE city='Indore';

ID	*Name*	*Age*	*Address*	*Salary*
7	Muffy	24	Indore	10000

11.2 ORDER BY

The ORDER BY keyword is used to sort the result-set by one or more columns.The ORDER BY keyword sorts the records in ascending order by default. You can't use it in Unions. To sort the records in a descending order, you can use the DESC keyword.

SELECT column_name,column_name

FROM table_name

ORDER BY column_name,column_name ASC|DESC;

ORDER BY Example

The following SQL statement selects all customers from the "Customers" table, sorted by the "Country" column:

SELECT * FROM Customers

ORDER BY City;

Id	*Name*	*Age*	*City*	*Salary*
1	Ramesh	32	Ahmedabad	2000
2	Khilan	25	Delhi	1500
3	Kaushik	23	Kota	2000
4	Chaitali	25	Mumbai	8500
5	Hardik	27	Bhopal	8500
6	Komal	22	MP	4500
7	Mufti	24	Indore	10000

Note: If an ORDER BY clause only references the primary key column or a prefix of it, then the optimizer avoids the sorting overhead, as the rows are returned sorted on the primary key columns.

The following queries avoid sorting overhead because the data is already sorted on the primary key (if Customer ID is primary key on table):

SELECT * FROM Customers ORDER BY Customer ID;

If, however, you have an ORDER BY clause on a non-primary-key columns, additional sorting is required (assuming no other secondary indexes are defined).

SELECT * FROM Customers

ORDER BY City;

Note:In MySQL You can sort returned result on any field provided that filed is being listed out.

ORDER BY DESC Example

The following SQL statement selects all customers from the "Customers" table, sorted DESCENDING by the "Country" column:

SELECT * FROM Customers

ORDER BY City DESC;

Id	*Name*	*Age*	*City*	*Salary*
1	Ramesh	32	Ahmedabad	2000
2	Khilan	25	Delhi	1500
3	Kaushik	23	Kota	2000
4	Chaitali	25	Mumbai	8500
5	Hardik	27	Bhopal	8500
6	Komal	22	MP	4500
7	Mufti	24	Indore	10000

ORDER BY Several Columns Example

The following SQL statement selects all customers from the "Customers" table, sorted by the "City" and the "Name" column:

The following SQL statement selects all customers from the "Customers" table, sorted by the "City" and the "Name" column:

```
SELECT * FROM Customers
ORDER BY city,Name;
```

Id	*Name*	*Age*	*City*	*Salary*
1	Ramesh	32	Ahmedabad	2000
2	Khilan	25	Delhi	1500
3	Kaushik	23	Kota	2000
4	Chaitali	25	Mumbai	8500
5	Hardik	27	Bhopal	8500
6	Komal	22	MP	4500
7	Mufti	24	Indore	10000

11.3 Group By

The SQL GROUP BY clause can be used in an SQL SELECT statement to collect data across multiple records and group the results by one or more columns.

The syntax for the SQL GROUP BY clause is:

```
SELECT column1, column2,...column_n, aggregate_function
(expression)
FROM tables
WHERE predicates
```

You need to create a table employees as below:

Employee id	**First_name**	**Last_name**	**Email**	**Phone_number**	**Hire_date**	**Job_id**	**Salary**	**Manager _id**	**Department _id**
100	Steven	King	SKING	515.123.4567	6/17/1987	AD_PRES	24000	NULL	90
101	Neena	Kochhar	NKOCHHAR	515.123.4568	9/21/1989	AD_VP	17000	100	90
102	Lex	De Haan	LDEHAAN	515.123.4569	1/13/1993	AD_VP	17000	100	90
103	Alexander	Hunold	AHUNOLD	590.423.4567	1/3/1990	IT_PROG	9000	102	60
104	Bruce	Emst	BERNST	590.423.4568	5/21/1991	IT_PROG	6000	103	60
107	Diana	Lorentz	DLORENTZ	590.423.5567	2/7/1999	IT_PROG	4200	103	60
124	Kevin	Mourgos	KMOURGOS	650.123.5234	11/16/1999	ST_MAN	5800	100	50
141	Trenna	Rajas	TRAJAS	650.121.8009	10/17/1995	ST_CLERK	3500	124	50
142	Curtis	Davies	CDAVIES	650.121.2994	1/29/1997	ST_CLERK	3100	124	50
143	Randall	Matos	RMATOS	650.121.2874	3/15/1998	ST_CLERK	2600	124	50
144	Peter	Vargas	PVARGAS	650.121.2004	7/9/1998	ST_CLERK	2500	124	50
149	Eleni	Zlotkey	EZLOTKEY	011-44-1344-429018	1/29/2000	SA_MAN	10500	100	80
174	Ellen	Abel	EABEL	011-44-1344-429267	5/11/1996	SA_REP,	1100	149	80
176	Jonathon	Taylor	JTAYLOR	011-44-1344-429265	3/24/1998	SA_REP	8600	149	80
178	Kimberely	Grant	KGRANT	011-44-1344-429263	5/24/1999	SA_REP	7000	149	NULL
200	Jennifer	Whalen	JWHALEN	515.123.4444	9/17/1987	AD_ASST	4400	101	10
201	Mitchael	Hartstein	MHARTSTE	515.123.5555	2/17/1996	MK_MAN	13000	100	20
202	Pat	Fay	PFAY	603.123.6666	8/17/1997	MK_REP	6000	201	20
205	Shelley	Higgins	SHIGGINS	515.123.8080	6/7/1994	AC_MGR	12000	101	110
206	William	Gietz	WGEITZ	515.123.8181	6/7/1994	AC_ACCOUNT	8300	205	110

GROUP BY column1, column2, ... column_n;

Aggregate_function can be a function such as SQL SUM, COUNT, MIN, MAX, AVG.

GROUP BY Clause - Using the SUM function example

You could also use the SQL SUM function to return the name of the department and the total salary (in the associated department).

SELECT department_id, SUM(Salary) as "Total sales"

FROM Employees

GROUP BY department_id;

Department_id	*Total sales*
NULL	7000
10	4400
20	19000
50	17500
60	19200
80	20200
90	58000
110	20300

Because you have listed one column in your SQL SELECT statement that is not encapsulated in the SQL SUM function, you must use the SQL GROUP BY clause. The department_ID field must be listed in the GROUP BY section.

GROUP BY Clause - Using the COUNT function example

You could use the SQL COUNT function to return the name of the department and the number of employees (in the associated department) that make over $25,000 / year.

SELECT DEPARTMENT_ID, COUNT(*) as "Number of employees"

FROM Employees

where SALARY>3000

GROUP BY department_id;

DEPARTMENT_ID	*Number of employees*
NULL	1
10	1
20	2
50	3
60	3
80	2
90	3
110	2

GROUP BY Clause - Using the MIN function example

You could also use the SQL MIN function to return the name of each department and the minimum salary in the department.

SELECT DEPARTMENT_ID, MIN(salary) as "Lowest salary"

FROM Employees

GROUP BY department_id;

DEPARTMENT_ID	*Lowest salary*
NULL	7000
10	4400
20	6000
50	2500
60	4200
80	1100
90	17000
110	8300

GROUP BY Clause - Using the MAX function example

You could also use the SQL MAX function to return the name of each department and the maximum salary in the department.

SELECT DEPARTMENT_ID, MAX(salary) as "Highest salary"

FROM Employees

GROUP BY department_id;

DEPARTMENT_ID	*Highest salary*
NULL	7000
10	4400
20	13000
50	5800
60	9000
80	10500
90	24000
110	12000

Now you need to create few table with below given details.

Table: Orders

Order ID	*Customer ID*	*Employee ID*	*Order Date*	*Shipper ID*
10248	90	5	7/4/1996	3
10249	81	6	7/5/1996	1
10250	34	4	7/8/1996	2

Table: Shippers

Shipper ID	*Shipper Name*	*Phone*
1.	Speedy Express	(503) 555-9831
2.	United Package	(503) 555-3199
3.	Federal Shipping	(503) 555-9931

Table. Employees

Emplo-yee ID	*Last Name*	*First Name*	*Birth Date*	*Notes*
1.	Davolio	Nancy	12/8/1968	Education includes a BA...
2.	Fuller	Andrew	2/19/1952	Andrew received his BTS...
3.	Leverling	Janet	8/30/1963	Janet has a BS degree...

SQL GROUP BY Example

Now if you want to find the number of orders sent by each shipper, then you need to use group by with two tables Orders and Shippers.

Example

```
SELECT Shippers.ShipperName, COUNT (Orders.OrderID) AS
    Number Of Orders
FROM Orders LEFT JOIN Shippers ON Orders.ShipperID=
    Shippers.ShipperID
GROUP BY Shipper Name;
```

GROUP BY More Than One Column

You can also use the GROUP BY statement on more than two tables, like below given example:

Example

```
SELECT Shippers.ShipperName, Employees.LastName,
COUNT(Orders.OrderID) AS NumberOfOrders
FROM ((Orders
INNER JOIN Shippers
ON Orders.ShipperID=Shippers.ShipperID)
INNER JOIN Employees
ON Orders.EmployeeID=Employees.EmployeeID)
GROUP BY ShipperName,LastName;
```

Note : In Oracle and sql server a query that includes a GROUP BY clause cannot refer to non-aggregated columns in the select list that are not named in the GROUP BY clause. For example, this query is illegal in standard SQL because the name column in the select list does not appear in the GROUP BY:

```
SELECT o.custid, c.name, MAX (o.payment)
FROM orders o, customers c
WHERE o.custid = c.custid
GROUP BY o.custid;
```

Above query will resulte Error as below:

"Column ' c.name' is invalid in the select list because it is not contained in either an aggregate function or the GROUP BY clause."

For the query to be legal, the name column must be omitted from the select list or named in the GROUP BY clause.

My SQL extends the use of GROUP BY so that the select list can refer to non-aggregated columns not named in the GROUP BY clause. Yes,This means that the above query is legal in MySQL.

Example: In below example we are listing both Shipper name and Last name columns after Select and after group by.

```
SELECT Shippers.ShipperName, Employees.LastName,
COUNT(Orders.OrderID) AS NumberOfOrders
FROM ((Orders
INNER JOIN Shippers
ON Orders.ShipperID=Shippers.ShipperID)
INNER JOIN Employees
ON Orders.EmployeeID=Employees.EmployeeID)
GROUP BY ShipperName,LastName;
```

In MySQL we do not required to list all columns after Group by.

```
SELECT Shippers.ShipperName, Employees.LastName,
COUNT(Orders.OrderID) AS NumberOfOrders
FROM ((Orders
INNER JOIN Shippers
ON Orders.ShipperID=Shippers.ShipperID)
INNER JOIN Employees
ON Orders.EmployeeID=Employees.EmployeeID)
GROUP BY ShipperName;
```

Here we can list only that column by which we want to group the data in result set.

Example:

```
SELECT MAX (id), col2, col3, col4 FROM mytable GROUP BY
col3
```

11.4 Having

The HAVING clause works with the GROUP BY clause to limit the results of groups according to the criteria you specify. Group by clause need to be use first to use having clause. When HAVING is used without GROUP BY, any expression or column name in the select list must appear within an aggregate function.The RID (of DB2) or ROWID (of oracle) built-in function and the ROW CHANGE (of DB2) expression cannot be specified in a HAVING clause unless they are within an aggregate function.

Note: The HAVING clause was added to SQL because the WHERE keyword could not be used with aggregate functions.

SQL HAVING Syntax

```
SELECT column_name, aggregate_function (column_name)
FROM table_name
WHERE column_name operator value
GROUP BY column_name
HAVING aggregate_function(column_name) operator value;
```

SQL HAVING Example

The following SQL statement finds if any of the employees has registered more than 10 orders:

Example

```
SELECT Employees.LastName, COUNT (Orders.OrderID) AS
    Number Of Orders FROM (Orders
INNER JOIN Employees
ON Orders.EmployeeID=Employees.EmployeeID)
GROUP BY LastName
HAVING COUNT(Orders.OrderID) > 10;
```

Having clause can have multiple operators also like below:

The following SQL statement finds if any of the employees has registered more than 10248 and less than 10250 orders:

Example

```
SELECT Employees.LastName, COUNT(Orders.OrderID) AS
    NumberOfOrders FROM Orders
INNER JOIN Employees
ON Orders.EmployeeID = Employees.EmployeeID)
GROUP BY LastName
HAVING (COUNT (Orders.OrderID)> 0) and
Orders.OrderID>10248) and (Orders.OrderID <10250);
```

Now you want to find, if the employees “Davolio” or “Fuller” have more than 25 orders

you add an ordinary WHERE clause to the SQL statement:

Example

```
SELECT Employees.LastName, COUNT(Orders.OrderID) AS
    NumberOfOrders FROM Orders
INNER JOIN Employees
```

```
ON Orders.EmployeeID = Employees.EmployeeID
WHERE LastName= 'Davolio' OR LastName= 'Fuller'
GROUP BY LastName
HAVING COUNT (Orders.OrderID) >2;
```

You can use order by after Having as below

```
SELECT Employees.LastName, COUNT (Orders.OrderID) AS
    NumberOfOrders FROM Orders
INNER JOIN Employees
ON Orders.EmployeeID = Employees.EmployeeID
WHERE LastName= 'Davolio' OR LastName= 'Fuller'
GROUP BY LastName
HAVING COUNT(Orders.OrderID) >2
Order by Employees.LastName;
```

11.5 Subquery

A query nested within another sql query and embedded with the WHERE clause is called as subquery. Sub queries can be used with the SELECT, INSERT, UPDATE, and DELETE statements along with the comparison operators like =, <, >, >=, <=, IN, BETWEEN, Exist etc.

There are a few rules that subqueries must follow:

Subqueries must be enclosed within parentheses.

A subquery can have only one column in the SELECT clause, unless multiple columns are in the main query for the subquery to compare its selected columns.

An ORDER BY cannot be used in a subquery, although the main query can use an ORDER BY.

The GROUP BY can be used to perform the same function as the ORDER BY in a subquery.

Subqueries that return more than one row can only be used with multiple value operators, such as the IN operator.

The SELECT list cannot include any references to values that evaluate to a BLOB, ARRAY, CLOB, or NCLOB.

A subquery cannot be immediately enclosed in a set function.

The BETWEEN operator cannot be used with a subquery; however, the BETWEEN can be used within the subquery.

Example: you want to see all the employees whose salary is above average salary.

Select * from emp where sal > (select avg(sal) from emp);

Similarly we want to see the name and empno of that employee whose salary is maximum salary.

Select max (SALARY) as Highestsalary from employees

Highest salary
24000

With subquery to get max salary you can use below query:

select salary from employees
where salary =(Select max(SALARY) as Highestsalary from employees)

To see second maximum salary

Select max(SALARY) as SecondHighestsalary from employees where

SALARY < (select max(SALARY) from employees);

secondHighestsalary
17000

Similarly to see the Third highest salary you can execute below query.

Select max(SALARY) as ThirdHighestsalary from employees where
SALARY < (select max(SALARY) from employees where
SALARY < (select max(SALARY) from employees));

ThirdHighestsalary
13000

You want to see how many employees are there whose salary is above average.

Select count(*) countofemp from employees where

SALARY > (select avg(SALARY) from employees);

countofemp
9

You want to see those employees who are working in DALLAS. Remember employees and Departments are joined on Department_ID column, is in the dept table. Assuming that wherever department is located the employee is working in that Loc.

```
Select * from emp where dept_no
    In (select dept_no from dept where Loc='DALLAS')
```

Emp_no	*E_name*	*Job*	*Mgr*	*Hire_date*	*Sal*	*Comm*	*Dept_no*
7369	SMITH	CLERK	7902	12/17/1980	800	NULL	20
7566	JONES	MANAGER	7839	4/2/1981	2975	NULL	20
7788	SCOTT	ANALYST	7566	12/9/1982	3000	NULL	20
7876	ADAMS	CLERK	7788	1/12/1983	1100	NULL	20
7902	FORD	ANALYST	7566	12/3/1981	3000	NULL	20

Let's create few more tables (in Oracle you can find below table as default table.)

In SQL SERVER you can run below script. And in Oracle you can replace int data type with Number data type in create statement rest all you can run as it is.

```
CREATE TABLE EMP
(EMP_NO int NOT NULL PRIMARY KEY,
E_NAME VARCHAR(10),
JOB VARCHAR(9),
MGR int,
HIRE_DATE DATE,
SAL DECIMAL(7, 2),
COMM DECIMAL(7, 2),
DEPT_NO int);
SELECT *
FROM EMP
INSERT INTO EMP
(EMP_NO, E_NAME, JOB, MGR, HIRE_DATE, SAL, COMM,
    DEPT_NO)
VALUES
(7369, 'SMITH', 'CLERK', 7902, '17-DEC-1980', 800, NULL, 20);
```

```
INSERT INTO EMP
(EMP_NO, E_NAME, JOB, MGR, HIRE_DATE, SAL, COMM,
    DEPT_NO)
VALUES
(7499, 'ALLEN', 'SALESMAN', 7698, '20-FEB-1981', 1600, 300,
    30);

INSERT INTO EMP
(EMP_NO, E_NAME, JOB, MGR, HIRE_DATE, SAL, COMM,
    DEPT_NO)
VALUES
(7521, 'WARD', 'SALESMAN', 7698, '22-FEB-1981', 1250, 500,
    30);

INSERT INTO EMP
(EMP_NO, E_NAME, JOB, MGR, HIRE_DATE, SAL, COMM,
    DEPT_NO)
VALUES
(7566, 'JONES', 'MANAGER', 7839, '02-APR-1981', 2975,
    NULL, 20);

INSERT INTO EMP
(EMP_NO, E_NAME, JOB, MGR, HIRE_DATE, SAL, COMM,
    DEPT_NO)
VALUES
(7654, 'MARTIN', 'SALESMAN', 7698, '28-SEP-1981', 1250,
    1400, 30);

INSERT INTO EMP
(EMP_NO, E_NAME, JOB, MGR, HIRE_DATE, SAL, COMM,
    DEPT_NO)
VALUES
(7698, 'BLAKE', 'MANAGER', 7839, '01-MAY-1981', 2850,
    NULL, 30);

INSERT INTO EMP
(EMP_NO, E_NAME, JOB, MGR, HIRE_DATE, SAL, COMM,
    DEPT_NO)
VALUES
(7782, 'CLARK', 'MANAGER', 7839, '09-JUN-1981', 2450,
    NULL, 10);
```

```
INSERT INTO EMP
(EMP_NO, E_NAME, JOB, MGR, HIRE_DATE, SAL, COMM,
    DEPT_NO)
VALUES
(7788, 'SCOTT', 'ANALYST', 7566, '09-DEC-1982', 3000, NULL,
    20);

INSERT INTO EMP
(EMP_NO, E_NAME, JOB, MGR, HIRE_DATE, SAL, COMM,
    DEPT_NO)
VALUES
(7839, 'KING', 'PRESIDENT', NULL, '17-NOV-1981', 5000,
    NULL, 10);

INSERT INTO EMP
(EMP_NO, E_NAME, JOB, MGR, HIRE_DATE, SAL, COMM,
    DEPT_NO)
VALUES
(7844, 'TURNER', 'SALESMAN', 7698, '08-SEP-1981', 1500, 0,
    30);

INSERT INTO EMP
(EMP_NO, E_NAME, JOB, MGR, HIRE_DATE, SAL, COMM,
    DEPT_NO)
VALUES
(7876, 'ADAMS', 'CLERK', 7788, '12-JAN-1983', 1100, NULL,
    20);

INSERT INTO EMP
(EMP_NO, E_NAME, JOB, MGR, HIRE_DATE, SAL, COMM,
    DEPT_NO)
VALUES
(7900, 'JAMES', 'CLERK', 7698, '03-DEC-1981', 950, NULL, 30);

INSERT INTO EMP
(EMP_NO, E_NAME, JOB, MGR, HIRE_DATE, SAL, COMM,
    DEPT_NO)
VALUES
(7902, 'FORD', 'ANALYST', 7566, '03-DEC-1981', 3000, NULL,
    20);
```

```
INSERT INTO EMP
(EMP_NO, E_NAME, JOB, MGR, HIRE_DATE, SAL, COMM,
    DEPT_NO)
VALUES
(7934, 'MILLER', 'CLERK', 7782, '23-JAN-1982', 1300, NULL,
    10);
```

Select * from emp;

EMP_NO	*E_NAME*	*JOB*	*MGR*	*HIRE_DATE*	*SAL*	*COMM*	*DEPT_NO*
7369	SMITH	CLERK	7902	12/17/1980	800	NULL	20
7499	ALLEN	SALESMAN	7698	2/20/1981	1600	300	30
7521	WARD	SALESMAN	7698	2/22/1981	1250	500	30
7566	JONES	MANAGER	7839	4/2/1981	2975	NULL	20
7654	MARTIN	SALESMAN	7698	9/28/1981	1250	1400	30
7698	BLAKE	MANAGER	7839	5/1/1981	2850	NULL	30
7782	CLARK	MANAGER	7839	6/9/1981	2450	NULL	10
7788	SCOTT	ANALYST	7566	12/9/1982	3000	NULL	20
7839	KING	PRESIDENT	NULL	11/17/1981	5000	NULL	10
7844	TURNER	SALESMAN	7698	9/8/1981	1500	0	30
7876	ADAMS	CLERK	7788	1/12/1983	1100	NULL	20
7900	JAMES	CLERK	7698	12/3/1981	950	NULL	30
7902	FORD	ANALYST	7566	12/3/1981	3000	NULL	20
7934	MILLER	CLERK	7782	1/23/1982	1300	NULL	10

```
CREATE TABLE DEPT
    (DEPT_NO int,
D_NAME VARCHAR(14),
    LOC VARCHAR(13) );
INSERT INTO DEPT
    (DEPT_NO, D_NAME, LOC)
VALUES
    (10, 'ACCOUNTING', 'NEW YORK');
INSERT INTO DEPT
    (DEPT_NO, D_NAME, LOC)
VALUES
    (20, 'RESEARCH', 'DALLAS');
INSERT INTO DEPT
    (DEPT_NO, D_NAME, LOC)
VALUES
    (30, 'SALES', 'CHICAGO');
```

```
INSERT INTO DEPT
    (DEPT_NO, D_NAME, LOC)
VALUES
    (40, 'OPERATIONS', 'BOSTON');
```

Select * from dept

DEPT_NO	*D_NAME*	*LOC*
10	ACCOUNTING	NEW YORK
20	RESEARCH	DALLAS
30	SALES	CHICAGO
40	OPERATIONS	BOSTON

```
CREATE TABLE SAL_GRADE
    (GRADE int,
LO_SAL NUMERIC,
    HI_SAL NUMERIC);

INSERT INTO SAL_GRADE
    (GRADE, LO_SAL, HI_SAL)
VALUES
    (1, 700, 1200);

INSERT INTO SAL_GRADE
    (GRADE, LO_SAL, HI_SAL)
VALUES
    (2, 1201, 1400);

INSERT INTO SAL_GRADE
    (GRADE, LO_SAL, HI_SAL)
VALUES
    (3, 1401, 2000);

INSERT INTO SAL_GRADE
    (GRADE, LO_SAL, HI_SAL)
VALUES
    (4, 2001, 3000);

INSERT INTO SAL_GRADE
    (GRADE, LO_SAL, HI_SAL)
VALUES
    (5, 3001, 9999);
```

Select * from SAL_GRADE

GRADE	*LO_SAL*	*HI_SAL*
1.	700	1200
2.	1201	1400
3.	1401	2000
4.	2001	3000
5.	3001	9999

To see the sum salary deptwise you can give the following query.

Select sum (sal) as sal from emp group by dept_no;

sal
8750
10875
9400

11.6 Subqueries with INSERT Statement

Subqueries also can be used with INSERT statements. The INSERT statement uses the data returned from the subquery to insert into another table. The selected data in the subquery can be modified with any of the character, date, or number functions.

Example:

```
CREATE TABLE EMP_new
(EMP_NO int NOT NULL PRIMARY KEY,
E_NAME VARCHAR(10),
JOB VARCHAR(9),
MGR int,
HIRE_DATE DATE,
SAL DECIMAL(7, 2),
COMM DECIMAL(7, 2),
DEPT_NO int);
```

SELECT * FROM EMP_new

EMP_NO	E_NAME	JOB	MGR	HIRE_DATE	SAL	COMM	DEPT_NO

```
INSERT INTO EMP_new
    SELECT * FROM emp
    WHERE emp_no IN (SELECT emp_no
            FROM emp where emp_no <= 7788 )
```

Select * from emp_new

EMP_NO	*E_NAME*	*JOB*	*MGR*	*HIRE_DATE*	*SAL*	*COMM*	*DEPT_NO*
7369	SMITH	CLERK	7902	12/17/1980	800	NULL	20
7499	ALLEN	SALESMAN	7698	2/20/1981	1600	300	30
7521	WARD	SALESMAN	7698	2/22/1981	1250	500	30
7566	JONES	MANAGER	7839	4/2/1981	2975	NULL	20
7654	MARTIN	SALESMAN	7698	9/28/1981	1250	1400	30
7698	BLAKE	MANAGER	7839	5/1/1981	2850	NULL	30
7782	CLARK	MANAGER	7839	6/9/1981	2450	NULL	10
7788	SCOTT	ANALYST	7566	12/9/1982	3000	NULL	20

You can also insert data from existing table to new table in few columns only.

Example:

```
INSERT INTO EMP_new (EMP_NO,E_name,DEPT_NO)
SELECT EMP_NO,E_name,DEPT_NO FROM emp
WHERE emp_no = 7839;
```

EMP_NO	*E_NAME*	*JOB*	*MGR*	*HIRE_DATE*	*SAL*	*COMM*	*DEPT_NO*
7369	SMITH	CLERK	7902	12/17/1980	800	NULL	20
7499	ALLEN	SALESMAN	7698	2/20/1981	1600	300	30
7521	WARD	SALESMAN	7698	2/22/1981	1250	500	30
7566	JONES	MANAGER	7839	4/2/1981	2975	NULL	20
7654	MARTIN	SALESMAN	7698	9/28/1981	1250	1400	30
7698	BLAKE	MANAGER	7839	5/1/1981	2850	NULL	30
7782	CLARK	MANAGER	7839	6/9/1981	2450	NULL	10
7788	SCOTT	ANALYST	7566	12/9/1982	3000	NULL	20
7839	KING	NULL	NULL	NULL	NULL	NULL	10

11.7 Subqueries with UPDATE Statement

The subquery can be used in conjunction with the UPDATE statement. Either single or multiple columns in a table can be updated when using a subquery with the UPDATE statement.

The basic syntax is as follows:

UPDATE table
SET column_name = new_value
[WHERE conditional column[operator]
(SELECT COLUMN_NAME
FROM TABLE_NAME)
[WHERE...)]

Example:

You have Emp_New_BKP table available which is backup of emp table.

Following example updates SALARY by 0.25 times in emp_new table for all the emp whose dep_no is greater than or equal to 20:

UPDATE EMP_new
SET sal = sal * 0.25
WHERE Dept_no IN (SELECT Dept_no FROM EMP_new
WHERE Dept_no >= 20);

This query will update all rows salary value except rows having dept_no=10, because you have dept_no 10, 20, and 30 and you are updating dept_no >=20 .

EMP_NO	*E_NAME*	*JOB*	*MGR*	*HIRE_DATE*	*SAL*	*COMM*	*DEPT_NO*
7369	SMITH	CLERK	7902	12/17/1980	200	NULL	20
7499	ALLEN	SALESMAN	7698	2/20/1981	400	300	30
7521	WARD	SALESMAN	7698	2/22/1981	312.5	500	30
7566	JONES	MANAGER	7839	4/2/1981	743.75	NULL	20
7654	MARTIN	SALESMAN	7698	9/28/1981	312.5	1400	30
7698	BLAKE	MANAGER	7839	5/1/1981	712.5	NULL	30
7782	CLARK	MANAGER	7839	6/9/1981	2450	NULL	10
7788	SCOTT	ANALYST	7566	12/9/1982	750	NULL	20
7839	KING	NULL	NULL	NULL	NULL	NULL	10

11.8 Subqueries with the DELETE Statement:

The subquery can be used in conjunction with the DELETE statement like with any other statements mentioned above.

The basic syntax is as follows:

DELETE FROM TABLE_NAME

[WHERE conditional column [operator]

(SELECT COLUMN_NAME
FROM TABLE_NAME)
[WHERE...)]

Example:

Following example deletes records from emp_new table for all the emp whose Job is NULL:

```
Delete from emp_new
WHERE Dept_no IN (SELECT Dept_no FROM EMP_new
    WHERE job is null);
```

This would impact those rows in emp_new table where job having Null value:

EMP_NO	*E_NAME*	*JOB*	*MGR*	*HIRE_DATE*	*SAL*	*COMM*	*DEPT_NO*
7369	SMITH	CLERK	7902	12/17/1980	200	NULL	20
7499	ALLEN	SALESMAN	7698	2/20/1981	400	300	30
7521	WARD	SALESMAN	7698	2/22/1981	312.5	500	30
7566	JONES	MANAGER	7839	4/2/1981	743.75	NULL	20
7654	MARTIN	SALESMAN	7698	9/28/1981	312.5	1400	30
7698	BLAKE	MANAGER	7839	5/1/1981	712.5	NULL	30
7788	SCOTT	ANALYST	7566	12/9/1982	750	NULL	20

11. 9 Subqueries with EXISTS or NOT EXISTS

If a subquery returns any rows at all, EXISTS *subquery* is TRUE, and NOT EXISTS *subquery* is FALSE. For example:

SELECT column1 FROM T1 WHERE EXISTS (SELECT * FROM T2);

Traditionally, an EXISTS subquery starts with SELECT *, but it could begin with SELECT 5 or SELECT column1 or anything per requirement. MySQL ignores the SELECT list in such a subquery, so it makes no difference.

For the preceding example, if T2 contains any rows, even rows with nothing but NULL values, the EXISTS condition is TRUE. This is actually an unlikely example because a NOT EXISTS subquery almost always contains correlations. Here are some more realistic examples:

What kind of store is present in one or more cities?

SELECT DISTINCT store_type FROM stores

```
WHERE EXISTS (SELECT * FROM cities_stores
WHERE cities_stores.store_type = stores.store_type);
```

What kind of store is present in no cities?

```
SELECT DISTINCT store_type FROM stores
WHERE NOT EXISTS (SELECT * FROM cities_stores
WHERE cities_stores.store_type = stores.store_type);
```

What kind of store is present in all cities?

```
SELECT DISTINCT store_type FROM stores s1
WHERE NOT EXISTS
SELECT * FROM cities WHERE NOT EXISTS
SELECT * FROM cities_stores
WHERE cities_stores.city = cities.city
AND cities_stores.store_type = stores.store_type);
```

The last example is a double-nested NOT EXISTS query. That is, it has a NOT EXISTS clause within a NOT EXISTS clause.

11.10 Correlated Subquery

A *correlated subquery* is a subquery that contains a reference to a table that also appears in the outer query.A correlated query can be easily identified if it contains any references to the parent subquery columns in its WHERE clause. For example:

```
SELECT * FROM t1
WHERE column1 = ANY (SELECT column1 FROM t2
WHERE t2.column2 = t1.column2);
```

While an ordinary subquery is evaluated for each table, a correlated subquery is evaluated for each row returned by the parent query. Example returns the name and salary of each employee whose salary exceeds the departmental average. For each row in the table, the correlated subquery computes the average salary for the corresponding department.

```
SELECT department_id, last_name, salary
FROM employees t
WHERE salary > ( SELECT AVG(salary)
    FROM employees
    WHERE t.department_id = department_id)
ORDER BY department_id, last_name;
```

Exercise:

1. What is subquery? Explain the Properties of a Subquery?
2. What is Difference between DELETE and TRUNCATE Commands?

Chapter - 12

Functions

12.1 Aggregate Functions

Aggregate function return a single value based upon a set of other values. If used among many other expressions in the item list of a **SELECT** statement, the **SELECT** must have a **GROUP BY** clause. No **GROUP BY** clause is required if the aggregate function is the only value retrieved by the **SELECT** statement. The supported aggregate functions:

Aggregate Functions:

Function	*Usage*	*Example*	*Out Put value*
AVG()	Computes the average value of a column Ignores NULL values supported by Microsoft SQL Server, MySQL, Oracle, and PostgreSQL.	SELECT AVG (SALARY) FROM Employees;	8280.000000
COUNT()	Counts the rows defined	SELECT Count (SALARY) FROM Employees;	20
COUNT(*)	Counts all rows in the specified table or view	SELECT Count (*) FROM Employees;	20
MIN()	Finds the minimum value in a column supported by Microsoft SQL Server, My SQL, Oracle, and Postgres SQL. My SQL also support for *LEAST*( ) to get min. value.	SELECT MIN (SALARY) FROM Employees;	1100.00
MAX()	Finds the maximum value in a column supported by Microsoft SQL Server, MySQL, Oracle, and Postgre SQL. MySQL also support for *GREATEST*( ) to get largest value.	SELECT MAX (SALARY) FROM Employees;	24000.00

SUM()	Computes the sum of column values Ignores NULL values supported by Microsoft SQL Server, MySQL, Oracle, and PostgreSQL.	SELECT SUM (SALARY) FROM Employees;	165600.00
STDDEV()	Calculate standard deviation	SELECT stdev (SALARY) FROM Employees;	5883.-30376216414
FIRST() / TOP 1() / LIMIT 1	returns the first value of the selected column Microsoft Access Supports First. SQL Server, MySQL and Oracle Supports TOP 1 And My SQL Supports LIMIT 1	MS Access SELECT FIRST (Employee_ID) FROM employees; SQL Server, MySQL and Oracle SELECT TOP 1 Employee_ID FROM employees ORDER BY Employee_ID ASC; My SQL SELECT Employee_ ID FROM employees ORDER BY Employee_ ID ASCLIMIT 1;	Employee_ ID100

ANY, EVERY, and SOME are considered aggregate functions. However, they have been discussed as range search criteria since they are most often used that way.

The number of values processed by an aggregate varies depending on the number of rows queried from the table. This behavior makes aggregate functions different from scalar functions, which require a fixed number and fixed type of parameters.

The general syntax of an aggregate function is:

aggregate_function_name ([ALL | DISTINCT] expression)

The DISTINCT clause uses only distinct values when evaluating the function.

The COUNT function has three variations. COUNT(*) counts all the rows in the target table whether they include nulls or not. COUNT (expression) computes the number of rows with non-NULL values in a specific column or expression. COUNT(DISTINCT expression) computes the number of distinct non-NULL values in a column or expression.

Examples

This query counts all rows in a table:

SELECT COUNT(*) FROM Employees;

The following query finds the number of different countries where publishers are located:

SELECT COUNT(DISTINCT country) "Count of Countries" FROM customers

MIN*(expression) and MAX(expression)* find the minimum and maximum value (string, datetime, or numeric) in a set of rows. *DISTINCT* or ALL may be used with these functions, but they do not affect the result.

Examples: The following query finds the best and worst sales for any title on record:

SELECT 'MIN' = MIN(Salary), 'MAX' = MAX(Salary) FROM Employees;

MIN	*MAX*
1100	24000

12.2 Built-in Scalar Functions

Function	*Usage*	*Supports by*
CURRENT_DATE	Identifies the current date.	Supports by Microsoft SQL Server, My SQL and PostgreSQL
CURRENT_TIME	Identifies the current time.	Supports by Microsoft SQL Server, My SQL and PostgreSQL.
CURRENT_TIMESTAMP	Identifies the current date and time.	Supports by Microsoft SQL Server, My SQL and PostgreSQL .Synonym for Oracle is SYSDATE MySQL also supports NOW( ) and UNIX_TIMESTAMP( )
CURRENT_USER	Identifies the currently active user within the database server.	Supports by Microsoft SQL Server, My SQL and Postgre SQL. Synonym for Oracle and PostgreSQL isUSER
SESSION_USER	Identifies the currently active Authorization ID, if it differs from the user.	Supports by Microsoft SQL Server and My SQL
SYSTEM_USER	Identifies the currently active user within the host operating system.	Supports by Microsoft SQL Server, My SQL and PostgreSQL

The following queries retrieve the values from built-in functions. Notice that the various vendors return dates in their own native formats:

SELECT CURRENT_TIMESTAMP;

Result set will be '2014-12-10 23:50:26'

Microsoft SQL

SELECT CURRENT_TIMESTAMP

GO

Result set will be 2014-12-10 23:50:03.667

12.3 Numeric Functions

Function	*Usage*
BIT_LENGTH(expression)	Returns an integer value representing the number of bits in an expression.
CHAR_LENGTH(expression)	Returns an integer value representing the number of characters in an expression.
EXTRACT(datetime_expression datepart FROM expression)	Allows the datepart to be extracted (YEAR, MONTH, DAY, HOUR, MINUTE, SECOND, TIMEZONE_HOUR, or TIMEZONE_MINUTE) from an expression.
OCTET_LENGTH (expression)	Returns an integer value representing the number of octets in an expression. This value is the same as BIT_LENGTH/8.
POSITION(starting_string IN search_string)	Returns an integer value representing the starting position of a string within the search string.

BIT_LENGTH, CHAR_LENGTH, and OCTET_LENGTH

The closest any of the vendors get to the BIT_LENGTH function is Oracle.

Oracle supports the LENGTHB function, which returns an integer value representing the number of bytes in an expression.

MySQL and PostgreSQL support CHAR_LENGTH and the SQL99 synonym CHARACTER_LENGTH( ).

PostgreSQL also supports EXTRACT( ), OCTET_LENGTH( ), and POSITION( ) as per the SQL99 standard. The other two vendors each have a similar function that provides identical functionality. SQL Server provides the LEN function and Oracle provides the LENGTH function.

MySQL and PostgreSQL also fully support the OCTET_LENGTH function.

Example

The following example determines the length of a string and a value retrieved from a column:

MySQL and PostgreSQL

```
SELECT CHAR_LENGTH('Hello World');
SELECT OCTET_LENGTH(First_Name) FROM Employees;
```

Microsoft SQL Server

```
SELECT DATALENGTH(Hire_date)
FROM Employees
WHERE EMPLOYEE_ID = 100
Or
SELECT Len(Hire_date)
FROM Employees
WHERE EMPLOYEE_ID = 100
```

Oracle

```
SELECT LENGTH('Hello World') "Length of characters"FROM dual;
```

Note: DUAL is a small table in the data dictionary that Oracle Database and user-written programs can reference to guarantee a known result. The dual table is useful when a value must be returned only once, for example, the current date and time. All database users have access to DUAL.

The DUAL table has one column called DUMMY and one row containing the value X. The following example queries DUAL to perform an arithmetical operation:

```
SELECT ((3*4)+5)/3 FROM DUAL;

((3*4)+5)/3
-----------
5.66666667
```

12.4 EXTRACT

The EXTRACT function is not supported by the database vendors, except for PostgreSQL and MySQL.

MySQL implementation is extended somewhat beyond the SQL99 standard. The SQL99 standard does not have a provision for returning multiple fields in the same call to EXTRACT( ) (e.g., “DAY_HOUR”). The MySQL extensions try to accomplish what the combination DATE_TRUNC( ) and DATE_PART( ) do in PostgreSQL. MySQL supports the dateparts.

12.5 MySQL Dateparts

Type value	*Meaning*	*Expected format*
SECOND	Seconds	SECONDS
MINUTE	Minutes	MINUTES
HOUR	Hours	HOURS
DAY	Days	DAYS
MONTH	Months	MONTHS
YEAR	Years	YEARS
MINUTE_SECOND	Minutes and seconds	“MINUTES:SECONDS”
HOUR_MINUTE	Hours and minutes	“HOURS:MINUTES”
DAY_HOUR	Days and hours	“DAYS HOURS”
YEAR_MONTH	Years and months	“YEARS-MONTHS”
HOUR_SECOND	Hours, minutes, seconds	“HOURS: MINUTES: SECONDS”
DAY_MINUTE	Days, hours, minutes	“DAYS HOURS: MINUTES”
DAY_SECOND	Days, hours, minutes, seconds	“DAYS HOURS: MINUTES: SECONDS”

Example

This example extracts dateparts from several datetime values:

MySQL

SELECT EXTRACT(YEAR FROM “2015-07-02”);

OutPut

2015

SELECT EXTRACT (YEAR_MONTH FROM "2015-07-02 02:23:03");

OutPut

2015 07

POSITION

The POSITION function returns an integer that indicates the starting position of a string within the search string. MySQL and PostgreSQL support the POSITION function with no variation from the SQL99 syntax. PostgreSQL has a synonymous function, TEXTPOS, while MySQL has the synonymous function, LOCATE.

Oracle's equivalent function is called INSTR. Microsoft SQL Server has both CHARINDEX and PATINDEX. The CHARINDEX and PATINDEX are very similar, except that PATINDEX allows the use of wildcard characters in the search criteria. For example:

MySQL
SELECT LOCATE('bar', 'foobar');
Result set will be 4

MySQL and PostgreSQL
SELECT POSITION ('chk' IN 'Hello');
Result set will be 0

Microsoft SQL Server
SELECT CHARINDEX ('de', 'abcdefg')
GO
Output
4
SELECT PATINDEX ('%fg', 'abcdefg')
GO
Output
6

12.6 String Functions

Basic string functions offer a number of capabilities and return a string value as a result set. Some string functions are dyadic, indicating that they operate on two strings at once. SQL99 supports the string functions listed in below table.

SQL String Functions

Function	*Usage*
CONCATENATE (expression ||	Appends two or more literal expressions, column values, or variables together into one string. expression)
CONVERT	Converts a string to a different representation within the same character set.
LOWER	Converts a string to all lowercase characters.
SUBSTRING	allows one character string to be extracted from another
TRANSLATE	Converts a string from one character set to another.
TRIM	Removes leading characters, trailing characters, or both from a character string. This function also removes other types of characters from a specified character string. The default function is to trim the specified character from both sides of the character string. If no removal string is specified, TRIM removes spaces by default.
UPPER	Converts a string to all uppercase characters.

TRIM

MySQL, PostgreSQL, and Oracle support the SQL99 syntax of *TRIM.*

Microsoft SQL Server (and the other vendors for that matter) provide the functions LTRIM and RTRIM to trim off leading spaces or trailing spaces, respectively. LTRIM and RTRIM cannot be used to trim other types of characters.

Examples

SELECT TRIM (‘ Hello World’);

Output

‘Hello World’

SELECT TRIM (LEADING ‘20’ FROM ‘2015 Hello World’);

Output

‘15 Hello World’

SELECT TRIM (BOTH 'x' FROM 'xxx Hello Worldxxx');
OutPut
'Hello World'

SELECT TRIM (TRAILING 'World' FROM '**Hello World'**);
Output
'Hello'

SUBSTRING
SQL99
SUBSTRING(extraction_string FROM starting_position [FOR length]
[COLLATE collation_name])

If any of the inputs are NULL, the SUBSTRING function returns a NULL. The extraction_string is where the character value is extracted from. It may be a literal string, a column in a table with a character data type, or a variable with a character data type. The starting_position is an integer value telling the function at which position to perform the extract. The optional length is an integer value that tells the function how many characters to extract, starting at the starting_position.

MySQL Syntax and Variations

SUBSTRING (extraction_string FROM starting_position)

MySQL's implementation assumes that the characters are to be extracted from the starting position continuing to the end of the character string.

Microsoft SQL Server Syntax and Variations

SUBSTRING (extraction_string [FROM starting_position] [FOR length])

Microsoft SQL Server largely supports the SQL99 standard, except that it does not allow the COLLATE clause. Microsoft allows this command to be applied to text, image, and binary datatypes; however, the starting_position and length represent the number of bytes rather than the number of characters to count.

Oracle Syntax and Variations

SUBSTR (extraction_string, starting_position [, length])

Oracle's implementation, SUBSTR, largely functions the same way as SQL99. It does not support the COLLATE clause. When a starting_ value is a negative number, Oracle counts from the end of the extraction_ string. If length is omitted, the remainder of the string (starting at starting_ position) is returned.

PostgreSQL Syntax and Variations

SUBSTRING(extraction_string [FROM starting_position] [FOR length])

PostgreSQL largely supports the SQL99 standard, except that it does not accept the *COLLATE* clause.

Examples

These examples generally work on any one of the four database vendors profiled in this book. Only the second Oracle example, with a negative starting position, fails on the others (assuming, of course, that Oracle's SUBSTR is translated into SUBSTRING):

Oracle, counting from the left

```
SELECT SUBSTR('ABCDEFG',3,4) FROM DUAL;
OUTPUT
CDEF
```

Oracle, counting from the right

```
SELECT SUBSTR('ABCDEFG',-5,4) FROM DUAL;
Output
CDEF
```

```
MySQL
SELECT SUBSTRING('Be vewy, vewy quiet',5);
Result set will be 'wy, vewy quiet"
```

PostgreSQL or SQL Server

```
SELECT FIRST_NAME, SUBSTRING(FIRST_NAME, 1, 1)
FROM Employees
WHERE FIRST_NAME = 'Steven'
```

```
Output
FIRST_NAME        (No column name)
Steven            S
```

12.7 Vacuum

SQLite and PostgreSQL supports VACUUM.

The VACUUM command rebuilds the entire database. SQLite or PostgreSQL is running in "auto_vacuum=FULL" mode, tuples that are deleted or obsoleted by an update are not physically removed from their table; they remain present until a VACUUM is done. This means the database file might be larger than strictly necessary. Running VACUUM to rebuild the database reclaims this space and reduces the size of the database file. Therefore it's necessary to do VACUUM periodically, especially on frequently-updated tables.VACUUM only works on the main database. It is not possible to VACUUM an attached database file.

In some cases, VACUUM may also reduce the number of partially filled pages in the database, reducing the size of the database file further. There is no VACUUM statement in the SQL standard

12.8 Rank

RANK orders the members of a dimension based on the values of an expression. The function returns the sequence numbers of the dimension members. Supports by Oracle and MS SQL server.

RANK assigns the same rank to identical values. For example, RANK may return 1, 2, 3, 3, 5 for a series of five dimension members.

Return Value

NUMBER

Syntax

RANK ( ) OVER (rank_clause)

rank_clause::={ DIMENSION dimension_id | HIERARCHY hierarchy_id }

ORDER BY order_by_clause [, order_by_clause]...

[WITHIN { PARENT | LEVEL | ANCESTOR AT { DIMENSION LEVEL dim_lvl_id | HIERARCHY LEVEL hier_level_id}}

[order_by_clause::=expression [ASC | DESC] [NULLS {FIRST | LAST}]

Arguments

dimension_id-The dimension over which the values are calculated using the default hierarchy.

hierarchy_id-The hierarchy over which the values are calculated. If *dimension_id* is used instead, the default hierarchy is used.

ORDER BY-Provides the basis for the ranking. You can provide additional ORDER BY clauses to break any ties in the order.

expression

Provides the values to use as the basis for the rankings.

ASC | DESC-Sorts the ranking from smallest to largest (ascending) or from largest to smallest (descending).

NULLS {FIRST | LAST}-Determines whether members with null values are listed first or last.

WITHIN-Selects a set of related dimension members to be ranked.

PARENT ranks members at the same level with the same parent.

LEVEL ranks all members at the same level.

ANCESTOR ranks all members at the same level and with the same ancestor at a specified level.

Example:

To return all employees who work in the IT and Sales department and then calculate a rank for each unique salary in the IT and Sales department. If two employees had the same salary, the RANK function would return the same rank for both employees. However, this will cause a gap in the ranks (ie: non-consecutive ranks). This is quite different from the DENSE_RANK function which generates consecutive rankings.

select FIRST_NAME, salary,

RANK() OVER (PARTITION BY department_id ORDER BY salary) Rankoutput

from employees

where department_id = 60 or department_id = 90;

FIRST_NAME	***salary***	***Rankoutput***
Diana	4200	1
Bruce	6000	2
Alexander	9000	3
Neena	17000	1
Lex	17000	1
Steven	24000	3

12. 9 Dense Rank

DENSE_RANK computes the rank of a row in an ordered group of rows and returns the rank as a NUMBER. The ranks are consecutive integers beginning with 1. The largest rank value is the number of unique values returned by the query. Rank values are not skipped in the event of ties. Rows with equal values for the ranking criteria receive the same rank. This function is useful for top-N and bottom-N reporting.Supports by Oracle and MS SQL server.

This function accepts as arguments any numeric data type and returns NUMBER.

Example

select FIRST_NAME, salary,Department_id,

DENSE_RANK() OVER (PARTITION BY department_id ORDER BY salary)DenseRankoutput

from employees

where department_id = 60 or department_id = 90;

FIRST_NAME	*salary*	*Department_id*	*DenseRankoutput*
Diana	4200	60	1
Bruce	6000	60	2
Alexander	9000	60	3
Neena	17000	90	1
Lex	17000	90	1
Steven	24000	90	2

12.10 ROW_Number

Row_Number Returns the serial number of the row order by specified column. Supports by Oracle and MS SQL server.

Example

select FIRST_NAME, salary,Department_id,
ROW_NUMBER() OVER (PARTITION BY department_id ORDER BY salary)Rownumberoutput
from employees
where department_id = 60 or department_id = 90;

FIRST_NAME	*salary*	*Department_id*	*Rownumberoutput*
Diana	4200	60	1
Bruce	6000	60	2
Alexander	9000	60	3
Neena	17000	90	1
Lex	17000	90	2
Steven	24000	90	3

12.11 NULL

SQL having ISNULL(), NVL(), IFNULL() and COALESCE() Functions

Microsoft's SQL Server ISNULL() function is used to specify how we want to treat NULL values.The NVL(), IFNULL(), and COALESCE() functions can also be used to achieve the same result.

In below case we want NULL values to be zero.

Below, if "Deaprtment_Id" is NULL then ISNULL() returns a zero.

SQL Server / MS Access

Select employee_id,department_id,ISNULL(department_id,0) from employees

employee_id	*department_id*	*(No column name)*
100	90	90
101	90	90
102	90	90
103	60	60
104	60	60
107	60	60
124	50	50
141	50	50
142	50	50
143	50	50
144	50	50
149	80	80
174	80	80
176	80	80

178	NULL	0
200	10	10
201	20	20
202	20	20
205	110	110
206	110	110

Oracle

we can use the NVL() function instead of ISNULL to achieve the same result:

Example:

Select employee_id,department_id,NVL(department_id,0) from employees

employee_id	*department_id*	*(No column name)*
100	90	90
101	90	90
102	90	90
103	60	60
104	60	60
107	60	60
124	50	50
141	50	50
142	50	50
143	50	50
144	50	50
149	80	80
174	80	80
176	80	80
178	NULL	0
200	10	10
201	20	20
202	20	20
205	110	110
206	110	110

MySQL

In MySQL we can use the IFNULL() function, like this:

Example

Select employee_id,department_id,IFNULL(department_id,0) from employees

employee_id	*department_id*	*(No column name)*
100	90	90
101	90	90
102	90	90
103	60	60
104	60	60
107	60	60
124	50	50
141	50	50
142	50	50
143	50	50
144	50	50
149	80	80
174	80	80
176	80	80
178	NULL	0
200	10	10
201	20	20
202	20	20
205	110	110
206	110	110

or we can use the COALESCE() function, like this:

Select employee_id,department_id, COALESCE (department_id,0) from employees

employee_id	*department_id*	*(No column name)*
100	90	90
101	90	90
102	90	90
103	60	60

104	60	60
107	60	60
124	50	50
141	50	50
142	50	50
143	50	50
144	50	50
149	80	80
174	80	80
176	80	80
178	NULL	0
200	10	10
201	20	20
202	20	20
205	110	110
206	110	110

12.12 Server Supported Functions

The following section provides a full listing and description of each SQL -supported function for different RDBMS server. These functions are Server-specific. Thus, a MySQL function, for example, is not guaranteed to be supported by any other RDBMS server. MySQL functions are provided to give an idea of the capabilities available within the RDBMS server products

12.12.1 Microsoft SQL Server Supported Functions:

Function	***Description***
abs(numeric_expression)	Returns absolute value.
acos(float_expression)	Returns angle (in radians) whose cosine is the specified argument.
app_name()	Returns application name for current session; set by application.
ascii(character_expression)	Converts character to a numeric ASCII code.
asin(float_expression)	Returns angle (in radians) whose sine is the specified argument.

atan(float_expression)	Returns angle (in radians) whose tangent is the specified argument.
atn2(float_expression, float_expressioin)	Returns angle (in radians) whose tangent is argument1/argument1.
avg([All| Distinct] Expression)	Computes average of a column.
binary_checksum(| expression [,...n])*	Returns binary checksum for list of expressions or row of a table.
cast(Expression as Data Type)	Converts a valid SQL Server expression to the specified datatype.
ceiling(numeric_expression)	Returns smallest integer greater than or equal to the argument.
char(integer_expression)	Converts a numeric ASCII code to a character.
charindex(expression1, expression2 [, start_location])	Returns position of the first occurrence of a substring in a string.
checksum(|* expression [,...n])	Returns checksum value (computed over row values or expressions provided).
checksum_agg([ALL | Distinct] expression)	Returns checksum of the values in group.
coalesce(expression [,...n])	Returns the first non-NULL argument from a list of arguments.
col_length('table', 'column')	Returns column length in bytes.
col_name(table_id, column_id)	Returns column name, given table ID and column ID.
contains({column | }, *'contains_search_condition'})*	Searches columns on exact or "fuzzy" matches of *contains_search_criteria*. It is an elaborate function used to perform full-text searches. Refer to the vendor documentation for more information.
containsable(table, column, contains_search_condition)	Returns a table with exact and "fuzzy" matches of *contains_search_condition*. It is an elaborate function used to perform full-text searches. Refer to the vendor documentation for more information.

convert(data_type [(length)], expression [, style])	Converts data from one datatype to another.
cos(float_expression)	Returns cosine.
cot(float_expression)	Returns cotangent.
count_big([All | Distinct] expression)	Same as *count* except returns big integer.
current_timestamp	Returns current date and time.
current_user	Returns username in the current database of the current session.
datalength(expression)	Returns number of bytes in a character or binary string.
databasepropertyex(database, property)	Returns database option or property.
dateadd(datepart, number, date)	Adds a number of dateparts (e.g., days) to a datetime value.
datediff(datepart, startdate, enddate)	Calculates difference between two datetime values expressed in certain dateparts.
db_id('[database_name]')	Returns database ID and given name.
db_name(database_id)	Returns the database name.
degrees(numeric_expression)	Converts radians to degrees.
difference(character_expression, character_expression)	Compares how two arguments sound and returns a number from 0 to 4. Higher result indicates better phonetic match.
exp(float_expression)	Returns exponential value.
floor(numeric_expression)	Returns largest integer less than or equal to the argument.
file_id('file_name')	Returns the file ID for the logical filename.
file_name(file_id)	Returns the logical filename for file ID.
filegroup_id ('filegroup_name')	Returns filegroup ID for the logical filegroup name.
filegroup_name (filegroup_id)	Returns the logical filegroup name for filegroup ID.

filegroupproperty (filegroup_name, property)	Returns filegroup property value for the specified property.
fileproperty (file, property)	Returns file property value for the specified property.
fulltextcatalog property(catalog_name, property)	Returns full-text catalog properties.
fulltextservice property(property)	Returns full-text service level properties.
formatmessage (msg_number, param_value [,... n])	Constructs a message from an existing message in SYSMESSAGES table (similar to RAISERROR).
freetexttable(table) { column |*}, 'freetext_string' [, top_n_by_rank])	Used for full-text search; returns a table with columns that match the meaning but don't exactly match value of *freetext_string*.
getdate( )	Returns current date and time.
getansinull(['database'])	Returns default nullability setting for new columns.
getutcdate( )	Returns Universal Time Coordinate (UTC) date.
grouping (column_name)	Returns 1 when the row is added by CUBE or ROLLUP; otherwise, returns 0.
host_id( )	Returns workstation ID of a given process.
host_name( )	Returns process hostname.
ident_incr ('table_or_view')	Returns identity-column increment value.
ident_seed ('table_or_view')	Returns identity seed value.
ident_current ('table_name')	Returns the last identity value generated for the specified table.

identity(data_type [, seed, increment]) As column_name	Used in SELECT INTO statement to insert an identity column into the destination table.
index_col('table', index_id, key_id)	Returns index column name, given table ID, index ID, and column sequential number in the index key.
indexproperty(table_id, index, property)	Returns index property (such as Fillfactor).
isdate(expression)	Validates if a character string can be converted to DATETIME.
is_member({'group' | 'role'})	Returns true or false (1 or 0) depending on whether user is a member of NT group or SQL Server role.
is_srvrolemember ('role' [,'login'])	Returns true or false (1 or 0) depending on whether user is a member of specified server role.
isnull(check_expression, replacement_value)	Returns the first argument if it is not NULL; otherwise, returns the second argument.
isnumeric(expression)	Validates if a character string can be converted to NUMERIC.
left(character_expression, integer_expression)	Returns a portion of a character expression, starting at *integer_expression* from left.
len(string_expression)	Returns the number of characters in the expression.
log(float_expression)	Returns natural logarithm.
log10(float_expression)	Returns base-10 logarithm.
month(date)	Returns month part of the date provided.
nchar(integer_expression)	Returns the unicode character with the given integer code.
newid( )	Creates a new unique identifier of type *uniqueidentifier*.
nullif(expression, expression)	Returns NULL if two specified expressions are equivalent.
object_id('object')	Returns object ID and given name.
object_name(object_id)	Returns object name and given ID.

objectproperty *(id, property)*	Returns properties of objects in the current database.

12.12.2 MySQL-Supported Functions

Function	*Description*
abs(X)	Returns the absolute value of *X*.
acos(X)	Returns the arc cosine of *X*, i.e., the value whose cosine is *X*; returns NULL if *X* is not in the range -1 to 1.
ascii(str)	Returns the ASCII code value of the leftmost character of the string *str*; returns 0 if *str* is the empty string; returns NULL if *str* is NULL.
asin(X)	Returns the arc sine of *X*, i.e., the value whose sine is *X*; returns NULL if *X* is not in the range -1 to 1.
atan(X)	Returns the arctangent of *X*, i.e., the value whose tangent is *X*.
atan2(X,Y)	Returns the arctangent of the two variables *X* and *Y*.
avg(expr)	Returns the average value of *expr*.
benchmark(count,expr)	Executes the expression *exprcount* times. It may be used to time how fast MySQL processes the expression. The result value is always 0.
binary	Casts the string following it to a binary string.
bin(N)	Returns a string representation of the binary value of *N*, where *N* is a long (*BIGINT*) number.
bit_count(N)	Returns the number of bits that are set in the argument *N*.
bit_and(expr)	Returns the bitwise *AND* of all bits in *expr*. The calculation is performed with 64-bit (*BIGINT*) precision.
bit_or(expr)	Returns the bitwise OR of all bits in *expr*. The calculation is performed with 64-bit (BIGINT) precision.

CASE value WHEN [compare-value] THEN result [WHEN [compare-value] THEN result ...] [ELSE result] END	The first version returns the result where *value=compare-value*. The second version returns the result for the first condition that is true.
CASE WHEN [condition] THEN result [WHEN [condition] THEN result ...] [ELSE result] END	If there is no matching result value, then the result after ELSE is returned. If there is no ELSE part, NULL is returned.
ceiling(X)	Returns the smallest integer value not less than *X*.
char(N,...)	Interprets the arguments as integers and returns a string consisting of the characters given by the ASCII code values of those integers. NULL values are skipped.
coalesce(list)	Returns first non-NULL element in the list.
concat(str1,str2,...)	Returns the string that results from concatenating the arguments.
concat_ws(separator, str1, str2,...)	Stands for CONCAT With Separator and is a special form of CONCAT( ). The first argument is the separator for the rest of the arguments. The separator and the rest of the arguments can be a string. If the separator is NULL, the result is NULL. The function skips any NULLs and empty strings after the separator argument. The separator is added between the strings to be concatenated.
connection_id( )	Returns the connection ID (*thread_id*) for the connection. Every connection has its own unique ID.
conv(N,from_base,to_base)	Converts numbers between different number bases; returns a string representation of the number *N*, converted from base *from_base* to base *to_base* ; returns NULL if any argument is NULL.
cos(X)	Returns the cosine of *X*, where *X* is given in radians.
cot(X)	Returns the cotangent of *X*.
count(DISTINCT expr,[expr...])	Returns a count of the number of different values.
count(expr)	Returns a count of the number of non-NULL values in the rows retrieved by a SELECT statement.

curdate() current_date	Returns today's date as a value in 'YYYY-MM-DD' or YYYYMMDD format, depending on whether the function is used in a string or numeric context.
curtime() current_time	Returns the current time as a value in 'HH:MM:SS' or HHMMSS format, depending on whether the function is used in a string or numeric context.
database()	Returns the current database name.
date_add(date,INTERVAL expr type)	These functions perform date arithmetic. *ADDDATE()* and *SUBDATE()* are synonyms for *DATE_ADD()* and *DATE_*
date_sub(date,INTERVAL expr type) *adddate(date,INTERVAL expr type)* *subdate(date,INTERVAL expr type)*	*SUB()*. *date* is a *DATETIME* or *DATE* value specifying the starting date. *expr* is an expression specifying the interval value to be added or subtracted from the starting date. *expr* may start with a - for negative intervals. *type* indicates how the expression should be interpreted.
date_ format (date, format)	Formats the date value according to the format string.
dayname(date)	Returns the name of the weekday for date.
dayofmonth(date)	Returns the day of the month for date, in the range 1 to 31.
dayofweek(date)	Returns the weekday index for date (1 = Sunday, 2 = Monday, . . . 7 = Saturday).
dayofyear(date)	Returns the day of the year for date, in the range 1 to 366.
decode(crypt_str, pass_str)	Decrypts the encrypted string *crypt_str* using *pass_str* as the password. *crypt_str* should be a string returned from *ENCODE()*.
degrees(X)	Returns the argument *X*, converted from radians to degrees.

elt(N,str1,str2,str3,...)	Returns *str1* if *N* = 1, *str2* if *N* = 2, and so on. Returns NULL if *N* is less than 1 or greater than the number of arguments. *ELT( )* is the complement of *FIELD( )*.
encode(str,pass_str)	Encrypts *str* using *pass_str* as the password. To decrypt the result, use *DECODE( )*. The result is a binary string the same length as the string.
encrypt(str[,salt])	Encrypts *str* using the Unix *crypt( )* system call. The *salt* argument should be a string with two characters.
exp(X)	Returns the value of *e* (the base of natural logarithms) raised to the power of *X*.
export_set (bits,on,off,[separator, [number_of_bits]])	Returns a string where every bit set in 'bit' gets an 'on' string and every reset bit gets an 'off ' string. Each string is separated with 'separator' (default ',') and only 'number_of_bits' (default 64) of 'bits' is used.
field(str,str1,str2,str3,...)	Returns the index of *str* in the *str1*, *str2*, *str3*, . . . list. Returns 0 if *str* is not found. *FIELD( )* is the complement of *ELT( )*.
find_in_set(str,strlist)	Returns a value 1 to *N* if the string *str* is in the list *strlist* consisting of *N* substrings. A string list is a string composed of substrings separated by ',' characters. Returns 0 if *str* is not in *strlist* or if *strlist* is the empty string. Returns NULL if either argument is NULL. This function does not work properly if the first argument contains a ','.
floor(X)	Returns the largest integer value not greater than *X*.
format(X,D)	Formats the number *X* to a format like '## ### ###', rounded to *D* decimals. If *D* is 0, the result has no decimal point or fractional part.
from_days(N)	Given a daynumber *N*, returns a *DATE* value. Not intended for use with values that precede the advent of the Gregorian calendar (1582), due to the days lost when the calendar was changed.

from_unixtime(unix_timestamp)	Returns a representation of the *unix_timestamp* argument as a value in 'YYYY-MM-DD HH:MM: SS' or YYYYMMDDHHMMSS format, depending on whether the function is used in a string or numeric context.
from_unixtime*(unix_timestamp, format)*	Returns a string representation of the *unix_ timestamp*, formatted according to the format string. Format may contain the same specifiers as those listed in the entry for the *DATE_FORMAT ( )* function.
get_lock(str,timeout)	Tries to obtain a lock with a name given by the string *str*, with a timeout of *timeout* seconds. Returns 1 if the lock is obtained successfully, 0 if the attempt times out, or NULL if an error occurs.
greatest(X,Y,...)	Returns the largest (maximum-valued) argument.
hex(N)	Returns a string representation of the hexadecimal value of *N*, where *N* is a long (*BIGINT*) number. This is equivalent to *CONV(N,10,16)*. Returns NULL if *N* is NULL.
interval(N,N1,N2,N3,...) <*Nn* for this function to work correctly.	Returns 0 if *N<N1*, 1 if *N<N2*, and so on. All arguments are treated as integers. It is required that *N1<N2<N3<...*
hour(time)	Returns the hour for time, in the range 0 to 23.
if(expr1,expr2,expr3)	If *expr1* is TRUE (*expr1*<> 0 and *expr1*<> NULL), then
	IF( ) returns *expr2*, else it returns *expr3*. *IF( )* returns a numeric or string value, depending on the context in which it is used.
ifnull(expr1,expr2)	If *expr1* is not NULL, *IFNULL( )* returns *expr1*; otherwise it returns *expr2*. *IFNULL( )* returns a numeric or string value, depending on the context in which it is used.
isnull(expr)	If *expr* is NULL, *ISNULL( )* returns 1; otherwise it returns 0.
insert(str,pos,len,newstr)	Returns the string *str*. The substring begins at position *pos* and is 10 characters long, replaced by the string *newstr*.

instr(str,substr)	Returns the position of the first occurrence of substring *substr* in string *str*.
last_insert_id([expr])	Returns the last automatically generated value that was inserted into an *AUTO_INCREMENT* column.
lcase(str) Lower(str)	Returns the string *str* with all characters changed to lowercase according to the current character-set mapping (default is ISO-8859-1 Latin1).
least(X,Y,...)	With two or more arguments, returns the smallest (minimum-valued) argument.
left(str,len)	Returns the leftmost *len* characters from the string *str*.
length(str) octet_length(str) char_length(str) character_length(str)	These functions return the length of the string *str*.
load_file(file_name)	Reads the file and returns the file contents as a string. The file must be on the server, and the user must specify the full pathname to the file and have the file privilege.
locate(substr,str) position(substr IN str)	Returns the position of the first occurrence of substring *substr* in string *str*. Returns 0 if *substr* is not in *str*.
locate(substr,str,pos)	Returns the position of the first occurrence of substring *substr* in string *str*, starting at position *pos*; returns 0 if *substr* is not in *str*.
log(X)	Returns the natural logarithm of *X*.
log10(X)	Returns the base-10 logarithm of *X*.
lpad(str,len,padstr)	Returns the string *str*, left-padded with the string *padstr* until *str* is 10 characters long.
ltrim(str)	Returns the string *str* with leading-space characters removed.
make_set(bits,str1,str2, . . .)	Returns a set (a string containing substrings separated by ',' characters) consisting of the strings

	that have the corresponding bits in bit set. *str1* corresponds to bit 0, *str2* to bit 1, etc. NULL strings in *str1, str2, . . .* are not appended to the result.
md5(string)	Calculates a MD5 *checksum* for the string. Value is returned as a 32-long hex number.
min(expr) max(expr)	Returns the minimum or maximum value of *expr*. *MIN()* and *MAX()* may take a string argument; in such cases they return the minimum or maximum string value.
minute(time)	Returns the minute for time, in the range 0 to 59.
mod(N,M)	% Modulo (like the % operator in C); returns the remainder of *N* divided by *M*.
month(date)	Returns the month for date, in the range 1 to 12.
monthname(date)	Returns the name of the month for date.
now() sysdate( ) current_timestamp	Returns the current date and time as a value in 'YYYY-MM-DD HH:MM:SS' or YYYYMMDDHHMMSS format, depending on whether the function is used in a string or numeric context.
nullif(expr1,expr2)	If *expr1* = *expr2* is true, returns NULL; otherwise returns *expr1*.
oct(N)	Returns a string representation of the octal value of *N*, where *N* is a long number. This is equivalent to *CONV(N,10,8)*. Returns NULL if *N* is NULL.
ord(str)	If the leftmost character of the string *str* is a multibyte character, returns the code of multibyte character by returning the ASCII code value of the character in the format of:
	((first byte ASCII code)*256+(second byte ASCII code))[*256+third byte ASCII code...]
	If the leftmost character is not a multibyte character, returns the same value as the *ASCII()* function does.

password(str)	Calculates a password string from the plain-text password *str*. This is the function that is used for encrypting MySQL passwords for storage in the Password column of the user grant table.
period_add(P,N)	Adds *N* months to period *P* (in the format YYMM or YYYYMM). Returns a value in the format YYYYMM. Note that the period argument *P* is not a date value.
period_diff(P1,P2)	Returns the number of months between periods *P1* and *P2*. *P1* and *P2* should be in the format YYMM or YYYYMM. Note that the period arguments *P1* and *P2* are not date values.
pi( )	Returns the value of π
pow(X,Y) power(X,Y)	Returns the value of *X* raised to the power of *Y*.
quarter(date)	Returns the quarter of the year for date, in the range 1 to 4.
radians(X)	Returns the argument *X*, converted from degrees to radians.
rand( )	Returns a random floating-point value in the range 0 to 1.0.
rand(N)	If an integer argument *N* is specified, it is used as the seed value.
release_lock(str)	Releases the lock named by the string *str* that was obtained with *GET_LOCK( )*. Returns 1 if the lock is released, 0 if the lock isn't locked by this thread (in which case the lock is not released), and NULL if the named lock doesn't exist.
repeat(str,count)	Returns a string consisting of the string *str* repeated *count* times. If *count*<= 0, returns an empty string. Returns NULL if *str* or *count* are NULL.
replace(str, from_str,to_str)	Returns the string *str* with all occurrences of the string *from_str* replaced by the string *to_str*.
reverse(str)	Returns the string *str* with the order of the characters reversed.

right(str,ten)	Returns the rightmost 10 characters from the string *str*.
round(X)	Returns the argument *X*, rounded to an integer.
round(X,D)	Returns the argument *X*, rounded to a number with *D* decimals. If *D* is 0, the result has no decimal point or fractional part.
rpad(str,len,padstr)	Returns the string *str*, right-padded with the string *padstr* until *str* is ten characters long.
rtrim(str)	Returns the string *str* with trailing space characters removed.
sec_to_time(seconds)	Returns the seconds argument, converted to hours, minutes, and seconds, as a value in 'HH:MM:SS' or HHMMSS format, depending on whether the function is used in a string or numeric context.
second(time)	Returns the second for time, in the range 0 to 59.
sign(X)	Returns the sign of the argument as -1, 0, or 1, depending on whether *X* is negative, zero, or positive.
sin(X)	Returns the sine of *X*, where *X* is given in radians.
soundex(str)	Returns a *soundex* string from *str*. Two strings that sound "about the same" should have identical *soundex* strings.
	A "standard" *soundex* string is four characters long, but the *SOUNDEX( )* function returns an arbitrarily long string. A *SUBSTRING( )* can be used on the result to get a "standard" *soundex* string. All non-alphanumeric characters are ignored in the given string. All international alphabetic characters outside the A-Z range are treated as vowels.
space(N)	Returns a string consisting of *N* space characters.
sqrt(X)	Returns the nonnegative square root of *X*.
std(expr) stddev(expr)	Returns the standard deviation of *expr*. The *STDDEV()* form of this function is provided for Oracle compatability.

strcmp(expr1,expr2)	*STRCMP()* returns 0 if the strings are the same, -1 if the first argument is smaller than the second according to the current sort order, and 1 otherwise.
substring(str,pos,len) substring(str FROM pos FOR len) mid(str,pos,len)	Returns a substring 10 characters long from string *str*, starting at position *pos*. The variant form that uses *FROM* is ANSI SQL92 syntax.
substring_index (str,delim,count)	Returns the substring from string *str* after *count* occurrences of the delimiter *delim*. If *count* is positive, everything to the left of the final delimiter (counting from the left) is returned. If *count* is negative, everything to the right of the final delimiter (counting from the right) is returned.
substring(str,pos) substring(str FROM pos)	Returns a substring from string *str* starting at position *pos*.
sum(expr)	Returns the sum of *expr*. Note that if the return set has no rows, it returns NULL.
tan(X).	Returns the tangent of *X*, where *X* is given in radians.
time_format (time, format)	This is used like *DATE_FORMAT(),* but the format string may contain only those format specifiers that handle hours, minutes, and seconds. Other specifiers produce a NULL value or 0.
time_to_sec(time)	Returns the time argument, converted to seconds.
to_days(date)	Given a date, returns a daynumber (the number of days since year 0).
trim([BOTH | LEADING | TRAILING] [remstr] FROM] str)	Returns the string *str* with all *remstr* prefixes and/or suffixes removed. If none of the specifiers *BOTH, LEADING,* or *TRAILING* are given, *BOTH* is assumed. If *remstr* is not specified, spaces are removed.

truncate(X,D)	Returns the number *X*, truncated to *D* decimals. If *D* is 0, the result has no decimal point or fractional part.
ucase(str)	Returns the string *str* with all characters changed to uppercase according to the current character set mapping (default is ISO-8859-1 Latin1).
upper(str)	
unix_timestamp() *unix_timestamp(date)*	If called with no argument, returns a Unix timestamp (seconds since '1970-01-01 00:00:00' GMT). If *UNIX_TIMESTAMP()* is called with a date argument, it returns. the value of the argument as seconds since '1970-01-01 00:00:00' GMT.
user() system_user( ) session_user( )	These functions return the current MySQL username.
version()	Returns a string indicating the MySQL server version.
week(date) week(date, first)	With a single argument, returns the week for date, in the range 0 to 53. (The beginning of a week 53 is possible during some years.) The two-argument form of WEEK( ) allows the user to specify whether the week starts on Sunday (0) or Monday (1).
weekday(date)	Returns the weekday index for date (0 = Monday, 1 = Tuesday,...6 = Sunday).
year(date)	Returns the year for date, in the range 1000 to 9999.
yearweek(date) *yearweek(date, first)*	Returns year and week for a date. The second argument works exactly like the second argument to*WEEK()*. Note that the year may be different from the year in the date argument for the first and the last week of the year.

12.12.3 Oracle SQL-Supported Functions

Function	***Description***
abs(number)	Returns the absolute value of *number.*
acos(number)	Returns the arc cosine of *number* ranging from -1 to 1. The result ranges from 0 to π and is expressed in radians.
add_months(date, int)	Returns the date *date* plus *int* months.
ascii(string)	Returns the decimal value in the database character set of the first character of *string*; returns an ASCII value when the database character set is 7-bit ASCII; returns EBCDIC values if the database character set is EBCDIC Code Page 500.
asin(number)	Returns the arc sine of *number* ranging from -1 to 1. The resulting value ranges from - π /2 to π /2 and is expressed in radians.
atan(number)	Returns the arctangent of any *number.* The resulting value ranges from - π /2 to p/2 and is expressed in radians.
atan2(number,nbr)	Returns the arctangent of *number* and *nbr.* The values for *number* and *nbr* are not restricted, but the results range from - π to π and are expressed in radians.
avg([DISTINCT] expression) over (analytics)	Returns the average value of *expr*. It can be used as an aggregate or analytic function (analytic functions are beyond the scope of this text).
bfilename('directory','filename')	Returns a *BFILE* locator associated with a physical LOB binary *filename* on the server's filesystem in *directory.*
ceil(number)	Returns smallest integer greater than or equal to *number.*
chartorowid(char)	Converts a value from a character datatype (*CHAR* or *VARCHAR2* datatype) to *ROWID* datatype.

chr(number [USING NCHAR_CS])	Returns the character having the binary equivalent to *number* in either the database character set (if *USING NCHAR_CS* is not included) or the national character set (if *USING NCHAR_CS* is included).
concat(string1, string2)	Returns *string1* concatenated with *string2*. It is equivalent to the concatenation operator (||).
convert(char_value, target_char_set, source_char_set)	Converts a character string from one character set to another; returns the *char_value* in the *target_ char_set* after converting *char_value* from the *source_char_set.*
corr(expression1, expression2) over (analytics)	Returns the correlation coefficient of a set of num bered pairs (*expressions* 1 and 2). It can be used as an aggregate or analytic function (analytic functions are beyond the scope of this text).
cos(number)	Returns the cosine of *number* as an angle expressed in radians.
cosh(number)	Returns the hyperbolic cosine of *number.*
count	Returns the number of rows in the query; refer to the earlier section on *COUNT* for more information.
covar_pop(expression1, over expression2) (analytics)	Returns the population covariance of a set of number pairs (*expressions* 1 and 2). It can be used as an aggregate or analytic function (analytic functions are beyond the scope of this text).
covar_samp(expression1, expression2) over(analytics)	Returns the sample covariance of a set of number pairs (*expressions* 1 and 2). It can be used as an aggregate or analytic function (analytic functions are beyond the scope of this text).
cume_dist( ) ([OVER (query)] ORDER BY...)	The cumulative distribution function computes the relative position of a specified value in a group of values.
decode(expr search , result [,. n] [,default])	Compares *expr* to the search value; if *expr* is equal to a search, returns the result. Without a match, *DECODE* returns default, or *NULL* if default is omitted. Refer to Oracle documentation for more details.

dense_rank( ) ([OVER (query)] ORDER BY...)	Computes the rank of each row returned from a query with respect to the other rows, based on the values of the *value_exprs* in the *ORDER_BY_ clause.*
deref (expression)	Returns the object reference of *expression*, where *expression* must return a *REF* to an object.
dump(expression [,return_ format [, starting_at [,length]]])	Returns a *VARCHAR2* value containing a datatype code, length in bytes, and internal representation of *expression*. The resulting value is returned in the format of *return_format*.
empth[B | C]lob( )	Returns an empty LOB locator that can be used to initialize a LOB variable. It can also be used to initialize a LOB column or attribute to empty in an *INSERT* or *UPDATE* statement.
exp(number)	Returns *E* raised to the *number* ed power, where E = 2.71828183.
first_value(expression) over (analytics)	Returns the first value in an ordered set of values.
floor(number)	Returns largest integer equal to or less than *number.*
greatest(expression [,...n])	Returns the greatest of the list of *expressions*. All *expressions* after the first are implicitly converted to the datatype of the first *expression* before the comparison.
grouping(expression)	Distinguishes null cause by a super-aggregation in *GROUP BY* extension from an actual null value.
hextoraw(string)	Converts *string* containing hexadecimal digits into a raw value.
initcap(string)	Returns *string*, with the first letter of each word in uppercase and all other letters in lowercase.
instr(string1, string2, start_at, occurrence)	Searches one character string for another character string. *INSRT* search *char1* with a starting position of *start_at* (an integer) looking for the numeric *occurrence* within *string2*. Returns the position of the character in *string1* that is the first character of this occurrence.
instrb(string1, string2, [start_ a[t, occurrence]])	The same as *INSTR*, except that *start_at* and the return value are expressed in bytes instead of characters.

lag(expression [,offset][,default]) over(analytics)	Provides access to more than one row of a table at the same time without a self join; refer to the vendor documentation for more information.
last_day(date)	Returns the date of the last day of the month that contains *date*.
last_value(expression) over (analytics)	Returns the last value in an ordered set of values; refer to the vendor documentation for more information.
lead(expression [,offset][,default]) over(analytics)	Provides access to more than one row of a table at the same time without a self join. Analytic functions are beyond the scope of this text.
least(expression [,...n])	Returns the least of the list of *expressions*.
length(string)	Returns the integer length of *string*, or null if *string* is null.
lengthb(string)	Returns the length of *char* in bytes; otherwise, the same as *LENGTH*.
ln(number)	Returns the natural logarithm of *number*, where the *number* is greater than 0.
log(base_number, number)	Returns the logarithm of any *base_number* of *number*.
lower(string)	Returns *string* in the same datatype as it was supplied with all characters lowercase.
lpad(string1, number [,string2])	Returns *string1*, left-padded to length *number* using characters in *string2*; *string2* defaults to a single blank.
ltrim(string[, set])	Removes all characters in *set* from the left of *string*. *Set* defaults to a single blank.
make_ref({table_name | view_name} , key [,...n])	Creates a reference (*REF*) to a row of an object view or a row in an object table whose object identifier is primary key-based.
max([DISTINCT] expression) over (analytics)	Returns maximum value of *expression*. It can be used as an aggregate or analytic function (analytic functions are beyond the scope of this text).
min([DISTINCT] expression) over (analytics)	Returns minimum value of *expression*. It can be used as an aggregate or analytic function (analytic functions are beyond the scope of this text).

mod(dividend, divider)	Returns remainder of *dividend* divided by *divider*; returns the *dividend* if *divider* is 0.
months_between (date1, date2)	Returns number of months between dates *date1* and *date2*. When *date1* is later than *date2*, the result is positive. If it is earlier, the result is negative.
new_time(date, time_zone1, time_zone2)	Returns the date and time in *time_zone2* when date and time in *time_zone1* are *date*. *Time_zones* 1 and 2 may be any of these text strings: AST, ADT: Atlantic Standard or Daylight Time BST, BDT: Bering Standard or Daylight Time CST, CDT: Central Standard or Daylight Time EST, EDT: Eastern Standard or Daylight Time GMT: Greenwich Mean Time HST, HDT: Alaska-Hawaii Standard Time or Daylight Time MST, MDT: Mountain Standard or Daylight Time NST: Newfoundland Standard Time PST, PDT: Pacific Standard or Daylight Time YST, YDT: Yukon Standard or Daylight Time
next_day(date, string)	Returns the date of the first weekday named by *string* that is later than *date*. The argument *string* must be either the full name or the abbreviation of a day of the week in the date language of the session.
nls_charset_decl_len(bytecnt, csid)	Returns the declaration width (*bytecnt*) of an *NCHAR* column using the character set ID (*csid*) of the column.
nls_charset_id(text)	Returns the NLS character set ID number corresponding to *text.*
nls_charset_name(number)	Returns the *VARCHAR2* name for the NLS character set corresponding to the ID *number.*
nls_initcap(string [,'nlsparameter'])	Returns *string* with the first letter of each word in uppercase and all other letters in lowercase. The *nlsparameter* offers special linguistic sorting features.
nls_lower(string, [,'nlsparameter'])	Returns *string* with all letters lowercase. The *nlsparameter* offers special linguistic sorting features.

nlssort(string [, 'nlsparameter'])	Returns the string of bytes used to sort *string*. The *nlsparameter* offers special linguistic sorting features.
nls_upper string [, 'nlsparameter'])	Returns *string* with all letters uppercase. The *nlsparameter* offers special linguistic sorting features.
ntile(expression) over (query_partition ORDER BY...)	Divides an ordered data set into a number of buckets numbered 1 to *expression* and assigns the appropriate bucket number to each row.
numtodsinterval (number, 'string')	Converts *number* to an *INTERVAL DAY TO SEC OND* literal, where *number* is a number or an expression resolving to a number, such as a numeric datatype column.
numtoyminterval (number, 'string')	Converts *number* to an *INTERVAL DAY TO MONTH* literal, where *number* is a number or an expression resolving to a number, such as a numeric datatype column.
nvl2(expression1, expression2, expression3)	Similar to *NLV*, except that if *expression1* is not null, *expression2* is returned. If *expression1* is null, *expression3* is returned. The expressions may be any datatype, except *LONG*.
percent_rank() over (query_partition ORDER BY...)	Similar to the *CUME_DIST* analytical function. Rather than return the cumulative distribution, it returns the percentage rank of a row compared to the others in its result set. Refer to the vendor documentation for more assistance.
power(number, power)	Returns *number* raised to the nth *power*. The base and the exponent can be any numbers, but if *number* is negative, *power* must be an integer.
ratio_to_report (value_exprs) over (query_partition)	Computes the ratio of a value to the sum of a set of values. If *values_expr* is null, the ratio-to-re port value also is null.
rawtohex(raw)	Converts a *raw* value to a string (character datatype) of its hexadecimal equivalent.
ref(table_alias)	*REF* takes a table alias associated with a row from a table or view. A special reference value is returned for the object instance that is bound to the variable or row.

reftohex(expression)	Converts argument *expression* to a character value containing its hexadecimal equivalent.
regr_ xxx(expression1, expression2) over (analytics)	Linear regression functions fit an ordinary-least-squares regression line to a set of number pairs where *expression1* is the dependent variable and *expression2* is the independent variable. The linear regression functions are:
	REGR_SLOPE: returns the slope of the line REGR_INTERCEPT: returns the y-intercept of the regression line REGR_COUNT: returns the number of non-null pairs fitting the regression line REGR_R2: returns the coefficient of determination for the regression REGR_AVGX: returns the average of the independent variable REGR_AVGY: returns the average of the dependent variable REGR_SXX: calculates *REGR_COUNT(exp1, exp2) ** VAR_POP(exp2) REGR_SYY: calculates *REGR_COUNT(exp1, exp2) ** VAR_POP(exp1) REGR_SXY: calculates *REGR_COUNT(exp1, exp2) * COVAR_POP(exp1, exp2)* These can be used as aggregate or analytic functions.
replace(string. search_string [,replacement_string])	Returns *string* with every occurrence of *search_string* replaced with *replacement_string.*
round (number, decimal)	Returns *number* rounded to *decimal* places right of the decimal point. When *decimal* is omitted, *number* is rounded to 0 places. Note that *decimal*, an integer, can be negative to round off digits left of the decimal point.
round (date[, format])	Returns the *date* rounded to the unit specified by the format model *format*. When *format* is omitted, *date* is rounded to the nearest day.
row_number ( ) over (query_partition ORDER BY...)	Assigns a unique number to each row where it is applied in the ordered sequence of rows specified by the *ORDER_BY_clause*, beginning with 1.

rowidtochar(rowid)	Converts a *rowid* value to *VARCHAR2* datatype, 18 characters long.
rpad(string1, number [, string2])	Returns *string1*, right-padded to length *number* with the value of *string2*, repeated as needed. *String2* defaults to a single blank.
rtrim(string[,set])	Returns *string*, with all the rightmost characters that appear in *set* removed; *set* defaults to a single blank.
sign(number)	When *number*< 0, returns -1. When *number* = 0, returns 0. When *number*> 0, returns 1.
sin(number)	Returns the sine of *number* as an angle expressed in radians.
sinh(number)	Returns the hyperbolic sine of *number.*
soundex(string)	Returns a character string containing the phonetic representation of *string*. This function allows words that are spelled differently but sound alike in English to be compared for equality.
sqrt(number)	Returns square root of *number*, a nonnegative number.
stddev([DISTINCT] expression) over (analytics)	Returns sample standard deviation of a set of numbers shown as *expression.*
stdev_pop(expression) over (analytics)	Computes the population standard deviation and returns the square root of the population variance.
seddev_samp(expression) over (analytics)	Computes the cumulative sample standard deviation and returns the square root of the sample variance.
substr(extraction_string [FROM starting_position] *[FOR length])*	Refer to the earlier section on *SUBSTR.*
substrb(extraction_string [FROM starting_position] [FOR length])	*SUBSTRB* is the same as *SUBSTR*, except that the arguments *m starting_position* and *length* are expressed in bytes, rather than in characters.
sum([DISTINCT] expression) over (analytics)	Returns sum of values of *expr* ; refer to vendor documentation for assistance with analytics and the *OVER* subclause.
sys_context ('namespace', 'attribute' [,length])	Returns the value of *attribute* associated with the context *namespace*, usable in both SQL and PL/SQL statements.

sys_guid( )	Generates and returns a globally unique identifier (*RAW* value) made up of 16 bytes.
tan(number)	Returns the tangent of *number* as an angle expressed in radians.
tanh(number)	Returns the hyperbolic tangent of *number*
to_char (date [, format [, 'nls_parameter']])	Converts *date* to a *VARCHAR2* in the format specified by the date format *format*. When *fmt* is omitted, *date* is converted to the default date format. The *nls_parameter* option offers additional control over formatting options.
to_char (number [, format [, 'nls_parameter']])	Converts *number* to a *VARCHAR2* in the format specified by the number format *format*. When *fmt* is omitted, *number* is converted to a string long enough to hold the *number*. The *nls_parameter* option offers additional control over formatting options.
to_date(string [, format [, 'nls_parameter']])	Converts *string* (in *CHAR* or *VARCHAR2)* to a *DATE* datatype. The *nls_parameter* option offers additional control over formatting options.
to_lob(long_column)	Usable only by *LONG* or *LONG RAW* expressions, it converts *LONG* or *LONG RAW* values in the column *long_column* to LOB values. It is usable only in the *SELECT* list of a subquery in an *INSERT* statement.
to_multi_byte(string)	Returns *string* with all of its single-byte characters converted to their corresponding multi-byte characters.
to_number(string [, format [,'nls_parameter']])	Converts a numeric *string* (of *CHAR* or *VARCHAR2* datatype) to a value of a NUMBER datatype in the format specified by the optional format model *format*. The *nls_parameter* option offers additional control over formatting options.
to_single_byte(string)	Returns *string* with all of its multi-byte characters converted to their corresponding single-byte characters.
translate('char_value', 'from_text', 'to_text')	Returns *char_value* with all occurrences of each character in *from_text* replaced by its corresponding character in *to_text*; refer to the section "CONVERT and TRANSLATE" earlier in this chapter for more information on *TRANSLATE*.

translate (text USING [CHAR_CS | NCHAR_CS])	Converts *text* into the character set specified for conversions between the database character set or the national character set.
trunc (base [, number])	Returns *base* truncated to *number* decimal places. When *number* is omitted, *base* is truncated to 0 places. *Number* can be negative to truncate (make zero) *number* digits left of the decimal point.
trunc (date [, format])	Returns *date* with any time data truncated to the unit specified by *format*. When *format* is omitted, *date* is truncated to the nearest whole day.
uid	Returns an integer that uniquely identifies the session user who logged on. No parameters are needed.
upper(string)	Returns *string* with all letters in uppercase.
user	Returns the name of the session user who logged on in *VARCHAR2*.
userenv(option)	Returns information about the current session in *VARCHAR2*.
value(table_alias)	Takes as a table alias associated with a row in an object table and returns object instances stored within the object table.
var_pop(expression) over (analytics)	Returns the population variance of a set of numbers after discarding the nulls in the *expression* numberset. Analytic functions are covered in the vendor documentation.
var_samp(expression) over (analytics)	Returns the sample variance of a set of numbers after discarding the nulls in the *expression* numberset. Analytic functions are covered in the vendor documentation.
variance([DISTINCT] expression) over (analytics)	Returns variance of *expression* calculated as follows: 0 if the number of rows in *expression* = 1 *VAR_SAMP* if the number of rows in *expression*> 1
vsize(expression)	Returns the number of bytes in the internal representation of *expression*. When *expression* is null, it returns null.

Exercise:

1. What are Ranking Functions?
2. What is ROW_NUMBER()?
3. What is Difference between GETDATE and SYSDATETIME in SQL Server?
4. What will be result set of the following;

Select to_number('1210.73', '9999.99')
Select to_number('546', '999')
Select to_number('1210.73');

Chapter - 13

Joins

The "JOIN" operation is an SQL keyword used to query data from itself or two or more related tables placed in, From clause and where clause, used to do query to combines rows from two or more tables, views, or materialized views

13.1 Join Conditions

A specific condition that makes a relationship between two or more table specified in from clause and where clause known as join condition. WHERE clause that contains a join conditions also contain other conditions that refer to columns of only one table. These conditions can further restrict the rows returned by the join query.

In most of the cases you will use primary key of first table and foreign key of secondary table to get data from tables by using this relationship you can reduce the duplication of data in every table. By using joins, you can also retrieve data from two or more tables based on logical relationships between the tables. Joins indicate how database should use data from one table to select the rows in another table.

SQL contains different types of Joins we will see each concept with example by using Employees and Departments tables.

Table Employees

Employee_Id	First_Name	Last_Name	E-mail	Phone_Number	Hire_Date	Job_Id	Salary	Commission_Pct	Manager_Id	Department_Id
100	Steven	King	SKING	515.123.4567	6/17/1987	AD_PRES	24000	NULL	NULL	90
101	Neena	Kochhar	NKOCHHAR	515.123.4568	9/21/1989	AD_VP	17000	NULL	100	90
102	Lex	De Haan	LDEHAAN	515.123.4569	1/13/1993	AD_VP	17000	NULL	100	90
103	Alexander	Hunold	AHUNOLD	590.423.4567	1/3/1990	IT_PROG	9000	NULL	102	60
104	Bruce	Emst	BERNST	590.423.4568	5/21/1991	IT_PROG	6000	NULL	103	60
107	Diana	Lorentz	DLORENTZ	590.423.5567	2/7/1999	IT_PROG	4200	NULL	103	60
124	Kevin	Mourgos	KMOURGOS	650.123.5234	11/16/1999	ST_MAN	5800	NULL	100	50
141	Trenna	Rajas	TRAJAS	650.121.8009	10/17/1995	ST_CLERK	3500	NULL	124	50
142	Curtis	Davies	CDAVIES	650.121.2994	1/29/1997	ST_CLERK	3100	NULL	124	50
143	Randall	Matos	RMATOS	650.121.2874	3/15/1998	ST_CLERK	2600	NULL	124	50
144	Peter	Vargas	PVARGAS	650.121.2004	7/9/1998	ST_CLERK	2500	NULL	124	50
149	Eleni	Zlotkey	EZLOTKEY	011-44-1344-42	1/29/2000	SA_MAN	10500	0.2	100	80
174	Ellen	Abel	EABEL	011-44-1344-42	5/11/1996	SA_REP,	1100	0.3	149	80
176	Jonathon	Taylor	JTAYLOR	011-44-1344-42	3/24/1998	SA_REP	8600	0.2	149	80
178	Kimberely	Grant	KGRANT	011-44-1344-42	5/24/1999	SA_REP	7000	0.15	149	NULL
200	Jennifer	Whalen	JWHALEN	515.123.4444	9/17/1987	AD_ASST	4400	NULL	101	10
201	Mitchael	Hartstein	MHARTSTE	515.123.5555	2/17/1996	MK_MAN	13000	NULL	100	20
202	Pat	Fay	PFAY	603.123.6666	8/17/1997	MK_REP	6000	NULL	201	20
205	Shelley	Higgins	SHIGGINS	515.123.8080	6/7/1994	AC_MGR	12000	NULL	101	110
206	William	Gietz	WGEITZ	515.123.8181	6/7/1994	AC_ACCOUNT	8300	NULL	205	110

Table Departments

Department_id	Department_name	Manager_id	Location_id
10	Administration	200	1700
20	Marketing	201	1800
50	Shipping	124	1500
60	IT	103	1400
80	Sales	149	2500
90	Executive	100	1700
110	Accounting	205	1700
190	Contracting	NULL	1700

JOINs allow us to query data from table/tables in a number of ways. Different Ways to query data from table or tables know as different types of join.

13.2 Types of Joins

(1) Inner Joins

(2) Outer Joins

(3) Self Join

13.2.1 Inner Join

The join that displays only the rows that have a match in both the joined tables is known as inner join. This is default join in the query and view designer.

Note: In My Sql keyword STRAIGHT_JOIN does an inner join but returns the table in exactly the order listed in the query.

INNER JOIN is the same as JOIN.

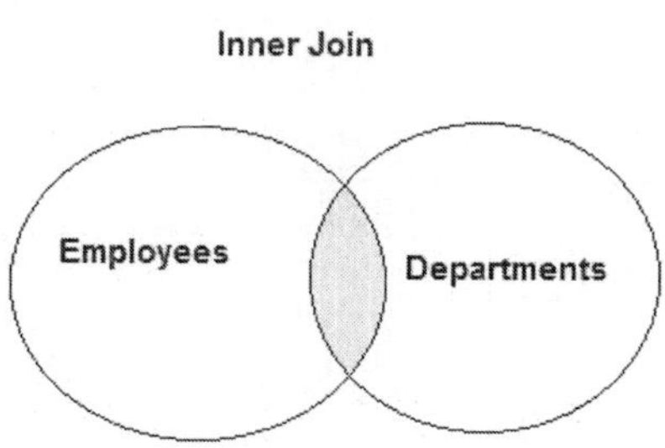

Syntax for Inner Join

```
SELECT t1.column_name,t2.column_name
FROM table_name1 t1
INNER JOIN table_name2 t2
ON t1.column_name=t2.column_name
Or
SELECT t1.column_name,t2.column_name
FROM table_name1 t1
JOIN table_name2 t2
ON t1.column_name=t2.column_name
```

INNER JOIN (or just JOIN)

Below Example will display all employee data who associated with department. So it will not display employee with department as NULL or empty.

Example

```
select EMPLOYEE_ID,e.FIRST_NAME,d.DEPARTMENT_ID,
d.DEPARTMENT_NAME,d.LOCATION_ID
from Employees e inner join Departments d on
e.DEPARTMENT_ID=d.department_id

select E. EMPLOYEE_ID,e.FIRST_NAME,d.DEPARTMENT_ID,
d.DEPARTMENT_NAME,d.LOCATION_ID
from Employees e , Departments d
where e.DEPARTMENT_ID=d.department_id
```

OutPut

Employee_id	First_name	Department_id	Department_name	Location_id
100	Steven	90	Executive	1700
101	Neena	90	Executive	1700
102	Lex	90	Executive	1700
103	Alexander	60	IT	1400
104	Bruce	60	IT	1400
107	Diana	60	IT	1400
124	Kevin	50	Shipping	1500
141	Trenna	50	Shipping	1500

(Contd...)

142	Curtis	50	Shipping	1500
143	Randall	50	Shipping	1500
144	Peter	50	Shipping	1500
149	Eleni	80	Sales	2500
174	Ellen	80	Sales	2500
176	Jonathon	80	Sales	2500
200	Jennifer	10	Administration	1700
201	Mitchael	20	Marketing	1800
202	Pat	20	Marketing	1800
205	Shelley	110	Accounting	1700
206	William	110	Accounting	1700

You can write inner join query like this also it will give same result.

Select E. EMPLOYEE_ID,e.FIRST_NAME,d.DEPARTMENT_ID, d. DEPARTMENT_NAME,d.LOCATION_ID

from Employees e join Departments d

on e.DEPARTMENT_ID=d.department_id

Based on above result we can say that INNER JOIN keyword return rows when there is at least one match in both tables. If there are rows in "Employees" that do not have matches in "Departments", those rows will NOT be listed.

In inner Join we are having different types of Joins those are–

(1) Equi Join
(2) Natural Join
(3) Cross Join

13.2.1.1 Equi Join

The Equi join is used to display all the matched records from the joined tables and also display redundant values. In this join we need to use = sign to join the table.

Syntax
SELECT * FROM table_name1 t1
INNER JOIN table_name2 t2
ON t1.column_name=t2.column_name

Now check the below query for Equi join

Once you run above query output will be like below

Employee	*First_Name*	*Last_Name*	*Email*	*Phone_Number*	*Hire_Date*	*Job_ID*	*Salary*	*Commission_PCT*	*Manager_ID*	*Department_ID*	*Department_ID*	*Department_ID*	*Department_ID*	*Location_ID*
100	Steven	King	Sking	515.123.4567	6-17-1987	AD_PRES	24000	NULL	NULL	90	90	Executive	100	1700
101	Neena	Kochhar	NKOCHHAR	515.123.4568	9-21-1989	AD_VP	17000	NULL	100	90	90	Executive	100	1700
102	Lex	De Haan	LDEHAAN	515.123.4569	1-13-1993	AD_VP	1700	NULL	100	90	90	Executive	100	1700
103	Alexander	Hunold	AHUNOLD	590.423.4567	1-3-1990	IT_PROG	9000	NULL	102	60	60	IT	103	1400
104	Bruce	Emst	BERNST	550.423.4568	5-21-1991	IT_PROG	6000	NULL	103	60	60	IT	103	1400
107	Diana	Lorentz	DLORENTZ	590.423.5567	2-7-1999	IT_PROG	4200	NULL	103	60	60	IT	103	1400
124	Keving	Mourgos	KMOURGOS	650.123.5234	11-16-1999	ST_MAN	5800	NULL	100	50	50	Shipping	124	1500
141	Trenna	Rajas	TRAJAS	650.121.8009	10-17-1995	ST_CLERK	3500	NULL	124	50	50	Spipping	124	1500
143	Randall	Matos	RMATOS	650.121.2874	3-15-1998	ST_CLERK	2600	NULL	124	50	50	Shipping	124	1500
144	Pater	Vargas	PVARGAS	650.121.2004	7-9-1998	ST_CLERK	2500	NULL	124	50	50	Shipping	124	1500
149	Eleni	Zlotkey	EZLOTKEY	011.44.1344.4290	1-29-2000	ST_MAN	10500	0.2	100	80	80	Sales	149	2500
174	Ellen	Abel	EABEL	011.44.1344.4290	1-29-200	SA_REP,	1100	0.3	149	80	80	Sales	149	2500
176	Jonathon	Taylor	JTAYLOR	011.44.1344.4292	5-11-1996	SA_REP	8600	0.2	149	80	80	Sales	149	2500
200	Jennifer	Whalen	JWHALEN	515.123.5555	2-17-1996	AD_ASST	4400	NULL	101	10	10	Administrat	200	1700
201	Mitchael	Hartstein	MHARTSTE	515.123.5555	2-17-1996	MK_MAN	13000	NULL	100	10	10	Administrat	200	1700
202	Pat	Fay	PFAY	603.123.666	8-17-1997	MK_REP	6000	NULL	201	20	20	Marketing	201	1800
205	Shelley	Higgins	SHIGGINS	515.123.8080	6-7-1994	AC_MGR	1200	NULL	101	110	110	Accounting	205	1700
206	William	Giets	WGEITZ	515.123.8181	6-7-1994	AC_ ACCOUNT	8300	NULL	205	.110	110	Accounting	205	1700

Example

```
select * from Employees e inner join Departments d on
e.DEPARTMENT_ID=d.department_id
```

or

```
select * from Employees e join Departments d
on e.DEPARTMENT_ID=d.department_id
```

In equi join you need to use only equality comparisons in the join relation.

If you use other operators such as (<,>) for our comparison condition then you Joins disqualifies for equi join.It will be a Non Equi Join.

13.2.1.2 Natural Joins

The Natural join is same as your Equi join but only the difference is it will restrict to display redundant values, because it compares all the common columns only.

Note: Natural join is not supported by SQL Server, it is supported by Oracle and MySQL.

Syntax for Natural Join

Example

```
SELECT * FROM table_name1 t1
NATURAL JOIN table_name2 t2
SELECT * FROM Employees
NATURAL JOIN Deapartments
```

These NATURAL Joins won't work in our SQL Server (only supports in Oracle and MySQL) it will throw syntax error"**Incorrect syntax near 'natural'.**". If you observe above code "NATURAL" is not highlighted, indicating that it is not recognized as a keyword.

13.2.1.3 Cross Join

A cross join produces Cartesian product of the tables that involved in the join. The size of a Cartesian product is the number of the rows in first table multiplied by the number of rows in the second table.

Syntax

```
SELECT * FROM table_name1
CROSS JOIN table_name2
```

Or you can write it as below

```
SELECT * FROM table_name1,table_name2
```

Example

```
select *
from Employees e cross join Departments d
```

OR

```
select * from Employees , Departments
```

Once you run above query output will display 160 rows (20 from employees * 8 from departments)

Emplo-Yee_Id	*First_ Name*	*Last_ Name*	*Email*	*Phone_Number*	*Hire_Date*	*Job_Id*	*Salary*	*Commi-Ssion_PCT*	*Mana-Ger_Id*	*Depart-Ment_Id*	*Depart-Ment_Id*	*Depart- Ment_ Name*	*Mana-Ger_Id*	*Loca-tion_id*
100	Steven	King	SKING	515.123.4567	6/17/1987	AD_PRES	24000	NULL	NULL	90	10	Administration	200	1700
101	Neena	Kochhar	NKOCHHAR	515.123.4568	9/21/1989	AD_VP	17000	NULL	100	90	10	Administration	200	1700
102	Lex	De Haan	LDEHAAN	515.123.4569	1/13/1993	AD_VP	17000	NULL	100	90	10	Administration	200	1700
103	Alexander	Hunold	AHUNOLD	590.423.4567	1/3/1990	IT_PROG	9000	NULL	102	60	10	Administration	200	1700
104	BruceNew	Emst	BERNST	590.423.4568	5/21/1991	IT_PROG	6000	NULL	103	60	10	Administration	200	1700
107	Diana	Lorentz	DLORENTZ	590.423.5567	2/7/1999	IT_PROG	4200	NULL	103	60	10	Administration	200	1700
124	Kevin	Mourgos	KMOURGOS	650.123.5234	11/16/1999	ST_MAN	5800	NULL	100	50	10	Administration	200	1700
141	Trenna	Rajas	TRAJAS	650.121.8009	10/17/1995	ST_CLERK	3500	NULL	124	50	10	Administration	200	1700
142	Curtis	Davies	CDAVIES	650.121.2994	1/29/1997	ST_CLERK	3100	NULL	124	50	10	Administration	200	1700
143	Randall	Matos	RMATOS	650.121.2874	3/15/1998	ST_CLERK	2600	NULL	124	50	10	Administration	200	1700
144	Peter	Vargas	PVARGAS	650.121.2004	7/9/1998	ST_CLERK	2500	NULL	124	50	10	Administration	200	1700
149	Eleni	Zlotkey	EZLOTKEY	011-44-1344-429018	1/29/2000	SA_MAN	10500	0.2	100	80	10	Administration	200	1700
174	Ellen	Abel	EABEL	011-44-1344-429267	5/11/1996	SA_REP,	1100	0.3	149	80	10	Administration	200	1700
176	Jonathon	Taylor	JTAYLOR	011-44-1344-429265	3/24/1998	SA_REP	8600	0.2	149	80	10	Administration	200	1700
178	Kimberely	Grant	KGRANT	011-44-1344-429263	5/24/1999	SA_REP	7000	0.15	149	NULL	10	Administration	200	1700
200	Jennifer	Whalen	JWHALEN	515.123.4444	9/17/1987	AD_ASST	4400	NULL	101	10	10	Administration	200	1700
201	Mitchael	Hartstein	MHARTSTE	515.123.5555	2/17/1996	MK_MAN	13000	NULL	100	20	10	Administration	200	1700
202	Pat	Fay	PFAY	603.123.6666	8/17/1997	MK_REP	6000	NULL	201	20	10	Administration	200	1700
205	Shelley	Higgins	SHIGGINS	515.123.8080	6/7/1994	AC_MGR	12000	NULL	101	110	10	Administration	200	1700
206	William	Gietz	WGEITZ	515.123.8181	6/7/1994	AC_ACCOUNT	8300	NULL	205	110	10	Administration	200	1700
100	Steven	King	SKING	515.123.4567	6/17/1987	AD_PRES	24000	NULL	NULL	90	20	Marketing	201	1800
101	Neena	Kochhar	NKOCHHAR	515.123.4568	9/21/1989	AD_VP	17000	NULL	100	90	20	Marketing	201	1800

(Contd...)

102	Lex	De Haan	LDEHAAN	515.123.4569	1/13/1993	AD_VP	17000	NULL	100	90	20	Marketing	201	1800
103	Alexander	Hunold	AHUNOLD	590.423.4567	1/3/1990	IT_PROG	9000	NULL	102	60	20	Marketing	201	1800
104	BruceNew	Ernst	BERNST	590.423.4568	5/21/1991	IT_PROG	6000	NULL	103	60	20	Marketing	201	1800
107	Diana	Lorentz	DLORENTZ	590.423.5567	2/7/1999	IT_PROG	4200	NULL	103	60	20	Marketing	201	1800
124	Kevin	Mourgos	KMOURGOS	650.123.5234	11/16/1999	ST_MAN	5800	NULL	100	50	20	Marketing	201	1800
141	Trenna	Rajas	TRAJAS	650.121.8009	10/17/1995	ST_CLERK	3500	NULL	124	50	20	Marketing	201	1800
142	Curtis	Davies	CDAVIES	650.121.2994	1/29/1997	ST_CLERK	3100	NULL	124	50	20	Marketing	201	1800
143	Randall	Matos	RMATOS	650.121.2874	3/15/1998	ST_CLERK	2600	NULL	124	50	20	Marketing	201	1800
144	Peter	Vargas	PVARGAS	650.121.2004	7/9/1998	ST_CLERK	2500	NULL	124	50	20	Marketing	201	1800
149	Eleni	Zlotkey	EZLOTKEY	011-44-1344-429018	1/29/2000	SA_MAN	10500	0.2	100	80	20	Marketing	201	1800
174	Ellen	Abel	EABEL	011-44-1344-429267	5/11/1996	SA_REP,	1100	0.3	149	80	20	Marketing	201	1800
176	Jonathon	Taylor	JTAYLOR	011-44-1344-429265	3/24/1998	SA_REP	8600	0.2	149	80	20	Marketing	201	1800
178	Kimberely	Grant	KGRANT	011-44-1344-429263	5/24/1999	SA_REP	7000	0.15	149	NULL	20	Marketing	201	1800
200	Jennifer	Whalen	JWHALEN	515.123.4444	9/17/1987	AD_ASST	4400	NULL	101	10	20	Marketing	201	1800
201	Mitchael	Hartstein	MHARTSTE	515.123.5555	2/17/1996	MK_MAN	13000	NULL	100	20	20	Marketing	201	1800
202	Pat	Fay	PFAY	603.123.6666	8/17/1997	MK_REP	6000	NULL	201	20	20	Marketing	201	1800
205	Shelley	Higgins	SHIGGINS	515.123.8080	6/7/1994	AC_MGR	12000	NULL	101	110	20	Marketing	201	1800
206	William	Gietz	WGEITZ	515.123.8181	6/7/1994	AC_ACCOUNT	8300	NULL	205	110	20	Marketing	201	1800
100	Steven	King	SKING	515.123.4567	6/17/1987	AD_PRES	24000	NULL	NULL	90	50	Shipping	124	1500
101	Neena	Kochhar	NKOCHHAR	515.123.4568	9/21/1989	AD_VP	17000	NULL	100	90	50	Shipping	124	1500
102	Lex	De Haan	LDEHAAN	515.123.4569	1/13/1993	AD_VP	17000	NULL	100	90	50	Shipping	124	1500
103	Alexander	Hunold	AHUNOLD	590.423.4567	1/3/1990	IT_PROG	9000	NULL	102	60	50	Shipping	124	1500
104	BruceNew	Ernst	BERNST	590.423.4568	5/21/1991	IT_PROG	6000	NULL	103	60	50	Shipping	124	1500
107	Diana	Lorentz	DLORENTZ	590.423.5567	2/7/1999	IT_PROG	4200	NULL	103	60	50	Shipping	124	1500
124	Kevin	Mourgos	KMOURGOS	650.123.5234	11/16/1999	ST_MAN	5800	NULL	100	50	50	Shipping	124	1500

(Contd...)

141	Trenna	Rajas	TRAJAS	650.121.8009	10/17/1995	ST_CLERK	3500	NULL	124	50	50	Shipping	124	1500
142	Curtis	Davies	CDAVIES	650.121.2994	1/29/1997	ST_CLERK	3100	NULL	124	50	50	Shipping	124	1500
143	Randall	Matos	RMATOS	650.121.2874	3/15/1998	ST_CLERK	2600	NULL	124	50	50	Shipping	124	1500
144	Peter	Vargas	PVARGAS	650.121.2004	7/9/1998	ST_CLERK	2500	NULL	124	50	50	Shipping	124	1500
149	Eleni	Zlotkey	EZLOTKEY	011-44-1344-429018	1/29/2000	SA_MAN	10500	0.2	100	80	50	Shipping	124	1500
174	Ellen	Abel	EABEL	011-44-1344-429267	5/11/1996	SA_REP.	1100	0.3	149	80	50	Shipping	124	1500
176	Jonathon	Taylor	JTAYLOR	011-44-1344-429265	3/24/1998	SA_REP	8600	0.2	149	80	50	Shipping	124	1500
178	Kimberely	Grant	KGRANT	011-44-1344-429263	5/24/1999	SA_REP	7000	0.15	149	NULL	50	Shipping	124	1500
200	Jennifer	Whalen	JWHALEN	515.123.4444	9/17/1987	AD_ASST	4400	NULL	101	10	50	Shipping	124	1500
201	Mitchael	Hartstein	MHARTSTE	515.123.5555	2/17/1996	MK_MAN	13000	NULL	100	20	50	Shipping	124	1500
202	Pat	Fay	PFAY	603.123.6666	8/17/1997	MK_REP	6000	NULL	201	20	50	Shipping	124	1500
205	Shelley	Higgins	SHIGGINS	515.123.8080	6/7/1994	AC_MGR	12000	NULL	101	110	50	Shipping	124	1500
206	William	Gietz	WGEITZ	515.123.8181	6/7/1994	AC_ACCOUNT	8300	NULL	205	110	50	Shipping	124	1500
100	Steven	King	SKING	515.123.4567	6/17/1987	AD_PRES	24000	NULL	NULL	90	60	Inforamtion Technology	103	1400
101	Neena	Kochhar	NKOCHHAR	515.123.4568	9/21/1989	AD_VP	17000	NULL	100	90	60	Inforamtion Technology	103	1400
102	Lex	De Haan	LDEHAAN	515.123.4569	1/13/1993	AD_VP	17000	NULL	100	90	60	Inforamtion Technology	103	1400
103	Alexander	Hunold	AHUNOLD	590.423.4567	1/3/1990	IT_PROG	9000	NULL	102	60	60	Inforamtion Technology	103	1400
104	BruceNew	Ernst	BERNST	590.423.4568	5/21/1991	IT_PROG	6000	NULL	103	60	60	Inforamtion Technology	103	1400
107	Diana	Lorentz	DLORENTZ	590.423.5567	2/7/1999	IT_PROG	4200	NULL	103	60	60	Inforamtion Technology	103	1400
124	Kevin	Mourgos	KMOURGOS	650.123.5234	11/16/1999	ST_MAN	5800	NULL	100	50	60	Inforamtion Technology	103	1400

(Contd...)

141	Trenna	Rajas	TRAJAS	650.121.8009	10/17/1995	ST_CLERK	3500	NULL	124	50	60	Inforamtion Technology	103	1400
142	Curtis	Davies	CDAVIES	650.121.2994	1/29/1997	ST_CLERK	3100	NULL	124	50	60	Inforamtion Technology	103	1400
143	Randall	Matos	RMATOS	650.121.2874	3/15/1998	ST_CLERK	2600	NULL	124	50	60	Inforamtion Technology	103	1400
144	Peter	Vargas	PVARGAS	650.121.2004	7/9/1998	ST_CLERK	2500	NULL	124	50	60	Inforamtion Technology	103	1400
149	Eleni	Zlotkey	EZLOTKEY	011-44-1344-429018	1/29/2000	SA_MAN	10500	0.2	100	80	60	Inforamtion Technology	103	1400
174	Ellen	Abel	EABEL	011-44-1344-429267	5/11/1996	SA_REP,	1100	0.3	149	80	60	Inforamtion Technology	103	1400
176	Jonathon	Taylor	JTAYLOR	011-44-1344-429265	3/24/1998	SA_REP	8600	0.2	149	80	60	Inforamtion Technology	103	1400
178	Kimberely	Grant	KGRANT	011-44-1344-429263	5/24/1999	SA_REP	7000	0.15	149	NULL	60	Inforamtion Technology	103	1400
200	Jennifer	Whalen	JWHALEN	515.123.4444	9/17/1987	AD_ASST	4400	NULL	101	10	60	Inforamtion Technology	103	1400
201	Mitchael	Hartstein	MHARTSTE	515.123.5555	2/17/1996	MK_MAN	13000	NULL	100	20	60	Inforamtion Technology	103	1400
202	Pat	Fay	PFAY	603.123.6666	8/17/1997	MK_REP	6000	NULL	201	20	60	Inforamtion Technology	103	1400
205	Shelley	Higgins	SHIGGINS	515.123.8080	6/7/1994	AC_MGR	12000	NULL	101	110	60	Inforamtion Technology	103	1400
206	William	Gietz	WGEITZ	515.123.8181	6/7/1994	AC_ACCOUNT	8300	NULL	205	110	60	Inforamtion Technology	103	1400
100	Steven	King	SKING	515.123.4567	6/17/1987	AD_PRES	24000	NULL	NULL	90	80	Product Sales	149	2500
101	Neena	Kochhar	NKOCHHAR	515.123.4568	9/21/1989	AD_VP	17000	NULL	100	90	80	Product Sales	149	2500
102	Lex	De Haan	LDEHAAN	515.123.4569	1/13/1993	AD_VP	17000	NULL	100	90	80	Product Sales	149	2500
103	Alexander	Hunold	AHUNOLD	590.423.4567	1/3/1990	IT_PROG	9000	NULL	102	60	80	Product Sales	149	2500
104	BruceNew	Emst	BERNST	590.423.4568	5/21/1991	IT_PROG	6000	NULL	103	60	80	Product Sales	149	2500

(Contd...)

107	Diana	Lorentz	DLORENTZ	590.423.5567	2/7/1999	IT_PROG	4200	NULL	103	60	80	Product Sales	149	2500
124	Kevin	Mourgos	KMOURGOS	650.123.5234	11/16/1999	ST_MAN	5800	NULL	100	50	80	Product Sales	149	2500
141	Trenna	Rajas	TRAJAS	650.121.8009	10/17/1995	ST_CLERK	3500	NULL	124	50	80	Product Sales	149	2500
142	Curtis	Davies	CDAVIES	650.121.2994	1/29/1997	ST_CLERK	3100	NULL	124	50	80	Product Sales	149	2500
143	Randall	Matos	RMATOS	650.121.2874	3/15/1998	ST_CLERK	2600	NULL	124	50	80	Product Sales	149	2500
144	Peter	Vargas	PVARGAS	650.121.2004	7/9/1998	ST_CLERK	2500	NULL	124	50	80	Product Sales	149	2500
149	Eleni	Zlotkey	EZLOTKEY	011-44-1344-429018	1/29/2000	SA_MAN	10500	0.2	100	80	80	Product Sales	149	2500
174	Ellen	Abel	EABEL	011-44-1344-429267	5/11/1996	SA_REP,	1100	0.3	149	80	80	Product Sales	149	2500
176	Jonathon	Taylor	JTAYLOR	011-44-1344-429265	3/24/1998	SA_REP	8600	0.2	149	80	80	Product Sales	149	2500
178	Kimberely	Grant	KGRANT	011-44-1344-429263	5/24/1999	SA_REP	7000	0.15	149	NULL	80	Product Sales	149	2500
200	Jennifer	Whalen	JWHALEN	515.123.4444	9/17/1987	AD_ASST	4400	NULL	101	10	80	Product Sales	149	2500
201	Mitchael	Hartstein	MHARTSTE	515.123.5555	2/17/1996	MK_MAN	13000	NULL	100	20	80	Product Sales	149	2500
202	Pat	Fay	PFAY	603.123.6666	8/17/1997	MK_REP	6000	NULL	201	20	80	Product Sales	149	2500
205	Shelley	Higgins	SHIGGINS	515.123.8080	6/7/1994	AC_MGR	12000	NULL	101	110	80	Product Sales	149	2500
206	William	Gietz	WGEITZ	515.123.8181	6/7/1994	AC_ACCOUNT	8300	NULL	205	110	80	Product Sales	149	2500
100	Steven	King	SKING	515.123.4567	6/17/1987	AD_PRES	24000	NULL	NULL	90	90	Executive	100	1700
101	Neena	Kochhar	NKOCHHAR	515.123.4568	9/21/1989	AD_VP	17000	NULL	100	90	90	Executive	100	1700
102	Lex	De Haan	LDEHAAN	515.123.4569	1/13/1993	AD_VP	17000	NULL	100	90	90	Executive	100	1700
103	Alexander	Hunold	AHUNOLD	590.423.4567	1/3/1990	IT_PROG	9000	NULL	102	60	90	Executive	100	1700
104	BruceNew	Ernst	BERNST	590.423.4568	5/21/1991	IT_PROG	6000	NULL	103	60	90	Executive	100	1700
107	Diana	Lorentz	DLORENTZ	590.423.5567	2/7/1999	IT_PROG	4200	NULL	103	60	90	Executive	100	1700
124	Kevin	Mourgos	KMOURGOS	650.123.5234	11/16/1999	ST_MAN	5800	NULL	100	50	90	Executive	100	1700
141	Trenna	Rajas	TRAJAS	650.121.8009	10/17/1995	ST_CLERK	3500	NULL	124	50	90	Executive	100	1700
142	Curtis	Davies	CDAVIES	650.121.2994	1/29/1997	ST_CLERK	3100	NULL	124	50	90	Executive	100	1700

(Contd...)

143	Randall	Matos	RMATOS	650.121.2874	3/15/1998	ST_CLERK	2600	NULL	124	50	90	Executive	100	1700
144	Peter	Vargas	PVARGAS	650.121.2004	7/9/1998	ST_CLERK	2500	NULL	124	50	90	Executive	100	1700
149	Eleni	Zlotkey	EZLOTKEY	011-44-1344-429018	1/29/2000	SA_MAN	10500	0.2	100	80	90	Executive	100	1700
174	Ellen	Abel	EABEL	011-44-1344-429267	5/11/1996	SA_REP,	1100	0.3	149	80	90	Executive	100	1700
176	Jonathon	Taylor	JTAYLOR	011-44-1344-429265	3/24/1998	SA_REP	8600	0.2	149	80	90	Executive	100	1700
178	Kimberely	Grant	KGRANT	011-44-1344-429263	5/24/1999	SA_REP	7000	0.15	149	NULL	90	Executive	100	1700
200	Jennifer	Whalen	JWHALEN	515.123.4444	9/17/1987	AD_ASST	4400	NULL	101	10	90	Executive	100	1700
201	Mitchael	Hartstein	MHARTSTE	515.123.5555	2/17/1996	MK_MAN	13000	NULL	100	20	90	Executive	100	1700
202	Pat	Fay	PFAY	603.123.6666	8/17/1997	MK_REP	6000	NULL	201	20	90	Executive	100	1700
205	Shelley	Higgins	SHIGGINS	515.123.8080	6/7/1994	AC_MGR	12000	NULL	101	110	90	Executive	100	1700
206	William	Gietz	WGEITZ	515.123.8181	6/7/1994	AC_ACCOUNT	8300	NULL	205	110	90	Executive	100	1700
100	Steven	King	SKING	515.123.4567	6/17/1987	AD_PRES	24000	NULL	NULL	90	110	Accounting	205	1700
101	Neena	Kochhar	NKOCHHAR	515.123.4568	9/21/1989	AD_VP	17000	NULL	100	90	110	Accounting	205	1700
102	Lex	De Haan	LDEHAAN	515.123.4569	1/13/1993	AD_VP	17000	NULL	100	90	110	Accounting	205	1700
103	Alexander	Hunold	AHUNOLD	590.423.4567	1/3/1990	IT_PROG	9000	NULL	102	60	110	Accounting	205	1700
104	BruceNew	Emst	BERNST	590.423.4568	5/21/1991	IT_PROG	6000	NULL	103	60	110	Accounting	205	1700
107	Diana	Lorentz	DLORENTZ	590.423.5567	2/7/1999	IT_PROG	4200	NULL	103	60	110	Accounting	205	1700
124	Kevin	Mourgos	KMOURGOS	650.123.5234	11/16/1999	ST_MAN	5800	NULL	100	50	110	Accounting	205	1700
141	Trenna	Rajas	TRAJAS	650.121.8009	10/17/1995	ST_CLERK	3500	NULL	124	50	110	Accounting	205	1700
142	Curtis	Davies	CDAVIES	650.121.2994	1/29/1997	ST_CLERK	3100	NULL	124	50	110	Accounting	205	1700
143	Randall	Matos	RMATOS	650.121.2874	3/15/1998	ST_CLERK	2600	NULL	124	50	110	Accounting	205	1700
144	Peter	Vargas	PVARGAS	650.121.2004	7/9/1998	ST_CLERK	2500	NULL	124	50	110	Accounting	205	1700
149	Eleni	Zlotkey	EZLOTKEY	011-44-1344-429018	1/29/2000	SA_MAN	10500	0.2	100	80	110	Accounting	205	1700
174	Ellen	Abel	EABEL	011-44-1344-429267	5/11/1996	SA_REP,	1100	0.3	149	80	110	Accounting	205	1700
176	Jonathon	Taylor	JTAYLOR	011-44-1344-429265	3/24/1998	SA_REP	8600	0.2	149	80	110	Accounting	205	1700

(Contd...)

178	Kimberely	Grant	KGRANT	011-44-1344-429263	5/24/1999	SA_REP	7000	0.15	149	NULL	110	Accounting	205	1700
200	Jennifer	Whalen	JWHALEN	515.123.4444	9/17/1987	AD_ASST	4400	NULL	101	10	110	Accounting	205	1700
201	Mitchael	Hartstein	MHARTSTE	515.123.5555	2/17/1996	MK_MAN	13000	NULL	100	20	110	Accounting	205	1700
202	Pat	Fay	PFAY	603.123.6666	8/17/1997	MK_REP	6000	NULL	201	20	110	Accounting	205	1700
205	Shelley	Higgins	SHIGGINS	515.123.8080	6/7/1994	AC_MGR	12000	NULL	101	110	110	Accounting	205	1700
206	William	Gietz	WGEITZ	515.123.8181	6/7/1994	AC_ACCOUNT	8300	NULL	205	110	110	Accounting	205	1700
100	Steven	King	SKING	515.123.4567	6/17/1987	AD_PRES	24000	NULL	NULL	90	190	Contracting	NULL	1700
101	Neena	Kochhar	NKOCHHAR	515.123.4568	9/21/1989	AD_VP	17000	NULL	100	90	190	Contracting	NULL	1700
102	Lex	De Haan	LDEHAAN	515.123.4569	1/13/1993	AD_VP	17000	NULL	100	90	190	Contracting	NULL	1700
103	Alexander	Hunold	AHUNOLD	590.423.4567	1/3/1990	IT_PROG	9000	NULL	102	60	190	Contracting	NULL	1700
104	BruceNew	Ernst	BERNST	590.423.4568	5/21/1991	IT_PROG	6000	NULL	103	60	190	Contracting	NULL	1700
107	Diana	Lorentz	DLORENTZ	590.423.5567	2/7/1999	IT_PROG	4200	NULL	103	60	190	Contracting	NULL	1700
124	Kevin	Mourgos	KMOURGOS	650.123.5234	11/16/1999	ST_MAN	5800	NULL	100	50	190	Contracting	NULL	1700
141	Trenna	Rajas	TRAJAS	650.121.8009	10/17/1995	ST_CLERK	3500	NULL	124	50	190	Contracting	NULL	1700
142	Curtis	Davies	CDAVIES	650.121.2994	1/29/1997	ST_CLERK	3100	NULL	124	50	190	Contracting	NULL	1700
143	Randall	Matos	RMATOS	650.121.2874	3/15/1998	ST_CLERK	2600	NULL	124	50	190	Contracting	NULL	1700
144	Peter	Vargas	PVARGAS	650.121.2004	7/9/1998	ST_CLERK	2500	NULL	124	50	190	Contracting	NULL	1700
149	Eleni	Zlotkey	EZLOTKEY	011-44-1344-429018	1/29/2000	SA_MAN	10500	0.2	100	80	190	Contracting	NULL	1700
174	Ellen	Abel	EABEL	011-44-1344-429267	5/11/1996	SA_REP,	1100	0.3	149	80	190	Contracting	NULL	1700
176	Jonathon	Taylor	JTAYLOR	011-44-1344-429265	3/24/1998	SA_REP	8600	0.2	149	80	190	Contracting	NULL	1700
178	Kimberely	Grant	KGRANT	011-44-1344-429263	5/24/1999	SA_REP	7000	0.15	149	NULL	190	Contracting	NULL	1700
200	Jennifer	Whalen	JWHALEN	515.123.4444	9/17/1987	AD_ASST	4400	NULL	101	10	190	Contracting	NULL	1700
201	Mitchael	Hartstein	MHARTSTE	515.123.5555	2/17/1996	MK_MAN	13000	NULL	100	20	190	Contracting	NULL	1700
202	Pat	Fay	PFAY	603.123.6666	8/17/1997	MK_REP	6000	NULL	201	20	190	Contracting	NULL	1700

13.2.2 Outer Joins

A join that return all rows that satisfy the condition and unmatched rows in the joined table is an Outer Join. You have three types of Outer join left, right and full join. For using different join types you need to apply keyword like Left outer join, Right outer join or Full Outer join. In oracle you can also use outer join operator (+) instead of using keywords. You have some limitation and Rules with (+) operator in oracle.

1. You cannot specify the (+) operator in a query block that also contains FROM clause join syntax.
2. You can Use the (+) operator only in the WHERE clause or, in the context of left-correlation in the FROM clause, and can be applied only to a column of a table or view.
3. The (+) operator can't produce an outer join if you specify one table in the outer query and the other table in an inner query.
4. You cannot use the (+) operator to outer-join a table to itself, although self joins are valid.
5. The (+) operator can be applied only to a column, not to an arbitrary expression. However, an arbitrary expression can contain one or more columns marked with the (+) operator.
6. A WHERE condition containing the (+) operator cannot be combined with another condition using the OR logical operator.
7. A WHERE condition cannot use the IN comparison condition to compare a column marked with the (+) operator with an expression.
8. A WHERE condition cannot compare any column marked with the (+) operator with a subquery.
9. You cannot use the (+) operator to outer-join a table to itself, although self joins are valid. For example, the following statement is not valid:

Example: Invalid statement

```
SELECT e.employee_id, e.manager_id
FROM employees e
WHERE e.manager_id (+) = e.employee_id;
```

Valid Statement

```
SELECT e1.employee_id, e1.manager_id, e2.employee_id
```

FROM employees e1, employees e2

WHERE e1.manager_id (+) = e2.employee_id;

You are having three types of Outer Joins

1. Left Outer Join
2. Right Outer Join
3. Full Outer Join

You will learn each type of outer join in more brief now.

13.2.2.1 Left Outer Join: The left outer join displays all the rows from the first table and matched rows from the second table.

In some databases LEFT OUTER JOIN is called LEFT JOIN(In My SQL).

Left Outer Join

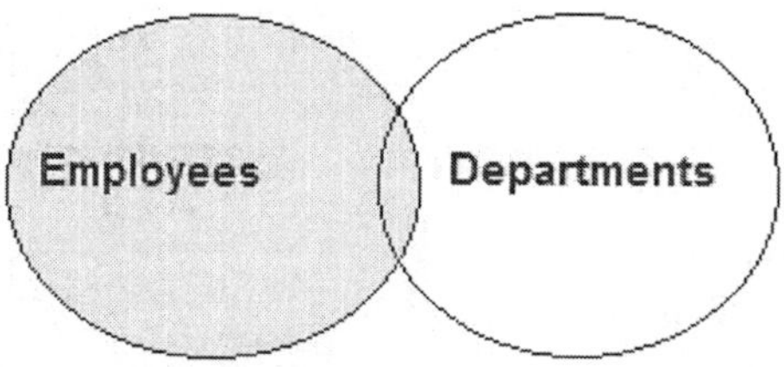

Syntax

```
SELECT Column_List FROM table_name1 t1
LEFT OUTER JOIN table_name2 t2
ON t1.column_name=t2.column_name
```

Example

```
select e.employee_ID, e.First_name,d.DEPARTMENT_ID, d.DEPARTMENT_NAME
from Employees e left outer join Departments d
on e.DEPARTMENT_ID=d.department_id
```

output will be

Employee_Id	*First_name*	*DEPARTMENT_ID*	*DEPARTMENT_ NAME*
100	Steven	90	Executive
101	Neena	90	Executive
102	Lex	90	Executive
103	Alexander	60	IT
104	Bruce	60	IT
107	Diana	60	IT
124	Kevin	50	Shipping
141	Trenna	50	Shipping
142	Curtis	50	Shipping
143	Randall	50	Shipping
144	Peter	50	Shipping
149	Eleni	80	Sales
174	Ellen	80	Sales
176	Jonathon	80	Sales
178	Kimberely	NULL	NULL
200	Jennifer	10	Administration
201	Mitchael	20	Marketing
202	Pat	20	Marketing
205	Shelley	110	Accounting
206	William	110	Accounting

13.2.2.2 Right Outer Join :The right outer join displays all the rows from the second table and matched rows from the first table.

In some databases RIGHT OUTER JOIN is called RIGHT JOIN(in mysql).

Right Outer Join

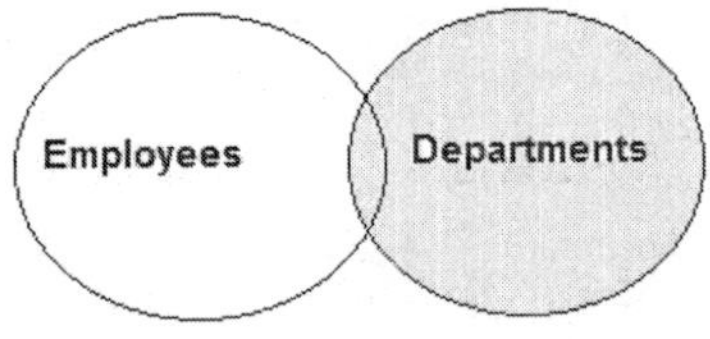

Syntax

```
SELECT Column_List FROM table_name1 t1
RIGHT OUTER JOIN table_name2 t2
ON t1.column_name=t2.column_name
```

Example

Select e.Employee_Id, e. First_name,

d.DEPARTMENT_ID, d.DEPARTMENT_NAME

From Employees e Right outer join Departments d

On e.DEPARTMENT_ID=d.department_id

output

Employee_Id	*First_name*	*DEPARTMENT_ID*	*DEPARTMENT_NAME*
200	Jennifer	10	Administration
201	Mitchael	20	Marketing
202	Pat	20	Marketing
124	Kevin	50	Shipping
141	Trenna	50	Shipping
142	Curtis	50	Shipping
143	Randall	50	Shipping
144	Peter	50	Shipping
103	Alexander	60	IT
104	Bruce	60	IT
107	Diana	60	IT
149	Eleni	80	Sales
174	Ellen	80	Sales
176	Jonathon	80	Sales
100	Steven	90	Executive
101	Neena	90	Executive
102	Lex	90	Executive
205	Shelley	110	Accounting
206	William	110	Accounting
NULL	NULL	190	Contracting

13.2.2.3 Full Outer Join: Full Outer Join displays all the matching and non-matching rows from both the tables.

The FULL OUTER JOIN keyword combines the result of both LEFT and RIGHT joins.

Note: My SQL does not SUPPORT FULL JOIN

Full Outer Join

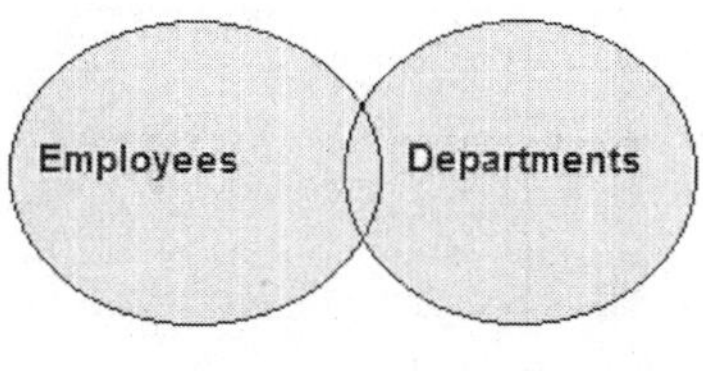

Syntax

SELECT Column_List FROM table_name1 t1

FULL OUTER JOIN table_name2 t2

ON t1.column_name=t2.column_name

Example

select e. Employee_Id, e. First_name,

d.DEPARTMENT_ID,d.DEPARTMENT_NAME

From Employees e Full Outer join Departments d on

e.DEPARTMENT_ID=d.department_id

output

Employee_Id	*First_name*	*DEPARTMENT_ID*	*DEPARTMENT_ NAME*
100	Steven	90	Executive
101	Neena	90	Executive
102	Lex	90	Executive
103	Alexander	60	IT
104	Bruce	60	IT
107	Diana	60	IT
124	Kevin	50	Shipping
141	Trenna	50	Shipping
142	Curtis	50	Shipping
143	Randall	50	Shipping
144	Peter	50	Shipping
149	Eleni	80	Sales
174	Ellen	80	Sales
176	Jonathon	80	Sales
178	Kimberely	NULL	NULL
200	Jennifer	10	Administration
201	Mitchael	20	Marketing
202	Pat	20	Marketing
205	Shelley	110	Accounting
206	William	110	Accounting
NULL	NULL	190	Contracting

13.2.3 Self Join

Joining the table itself called self join. Self join is used to retrieve the records having some relation or similarity with other records in the same table. Here we need to use aliases for the same table to set a self join between single table and retrieve records satisfying the condition in where clause.You can know more about alias name in a dedicated chapter for Aliases in this book.

To implement self join first design table and give a name as "EmployeeDetails"

```
create view EmpDetails as
select     e.Employee_Id,e.First_name,d.department_ID,
    d.MANAGER_ID
from Employees e left Outer join Departments d
on e.DEPARTMENT_ID=d.department_id
```

You will get a view which will work for you like a table for join exercise.

You will know more about view in dedicated chapter of view in this book.

Now see the table/View with all data.

```
select * from EmpDetails
```

Employee_Id	*First_name*	*DEPARTMENT_ID*	*MANAGER_ID*
100	Steven	90	100
101	Neena	90	100
102	Lex	90	100
103	Alexander	60	103
104	Bruce	60	103
107	Diana	60	103
124	Kevin	50	124
141	Trenna	50	124
142	Curtis	50	124
143	Randall	50	124
144	Peter	50	124
149	Eleni	80	149
174	Ellen	80	149
176	Jonathon	80	149
178	Kimberely	NULL	NULL
200	Jennifer	10	200
201	Mitchael	20	201
202	Pat	20	201
205	Shelley	110	205
206	William	110	205

Now if you want to get manager names of particular employee for that we need to write query like this with Inner Join

select e2.First_name,e1.First_name as 'Manager'

from EmpDetails e1

INNER JOIN EmpDetails e2

on e1.Employee_Id=e2.MANAGER_ID

Here if you observe above query EmpDetails table joined itself using table aliases e1 and e2.

output will be like this

First_name	***Manager***
Steven	Steven
Neena	Steven
Lex	Steven
Alexander	Alexander
Bruce	Alexander
Diana	Alexander
Kevin	Kevin
Trenna	Kevin
Curtis	Kevin
Randall	Kevin
Peter	Kevin
Eleni	Eleni
Ellen	Eleni
Jonathon	Eleni
Jennifer	Jennifer
Mitchael	Mitchael
Pat	Mitchael
Shelley	Shelley
William	Shelley

13.2.4 Antijoins

An antijoin returns rows from the left side of the predicate for which there are no corresponding rows on the right side of the predicate. It returns rows that fail to match (**NOT IN**) the subquery on the right side.

Now remember the data and structure of Employees and departments table

Here you can see data and structure of departments table:

Department_Id	*Department_Name*	*Manager_Id*	*Location_Id*
10	Administration	200	1700
20	Marketing	201	1800
50	Shipping	124	1500
60	IT	103	1400
80	Sales	149	2500
90	Executive	100	1700
110	Accounting	205	1700
190	Contracting	NULL	1700

You have Location_Id =1700 only for Department_Id 10,90,110 and 190.

```
SELECT * FROM employees
WHERE department_id NOT IN
(SELECT department_id FROM departments
WHERE location_id = 1700)
ORDER BY last_name;
```

Output

Employee_ID	*First_Name*	*Last_Name*	*E-mail*	*Phone_Number*	*Hire_Date*	*Job_ID*	*Commis-sion_pct*	*Mana-ger_ID*	*Depart-ment_ID*
174	Ellen	Abel	EABEL	011-44-1344-429267	5/11/1996	SA_REP,	0.3	149	80
142	Curtis	Davies	CDAVIES	650.121.2994	1/29/1997	ST_CLERK	NULL	124	50
104	Bruce	Emst	BERNST	590.423.4568	5/21/1991	IT_PROG	NULL	103	60
202	Pat	Fay	PFAY	603.123.6666	8/17/1997	MK_REP	NULL	201	20
201	Mitchael	Hartstein	MHARTSTE	515.123.5555	2/17/1996	MK_MAN	NULL	100	20
103	Alexander	Hunold	AHUNOLD	590.423.4567	1/3/1990	IT_PROG	NULL	102	60
107	Diana	Lorentz	DLORENTZ	590.423.5567	2/7/1999	IT_PROG	NULL	103	60
143	Randall	Matos	RMATOS	650.121.2874	3/15/1998	ST_CLERK	NULL	124	50
124	Kevin	Mourgos	KMOURGOS	650.123.5234	11/16/1999	ST_MAN	NULL	100	50
141	Trenna	Rajas	TRAJAS	650.121.8009	10/17/1995	ST_CLERK	NULL	124	50
176	Jonathon	Taylor	JTAYLOR	011-44-1344-429265	3/24/1998	SA_REP	0.2	149	80
144	Peter	Vargas	PVARGAS	650.121.2004	7/9/1998	ST_CLERK	NULL	124	50
149	Eleni	Zlotkey	EZLOTKEY	011-44-1344-429018	1/29/2000	SA_MAN	0.2	100	80

So, you get data except those Employee data which belongs to department_id 10, 90,110 and 190.

13.2.5 Semijoins

A semijoin returns rows that match an EXISTS subquery without duplicating rows from the left side of the predicate when multiple rows on the right side satisfy the criteria of the subquery.

Semijoin and antijoin transformation cannot be done if the subquery is on an OR branch of the WHERE clause. It can be used if no index has been defined on the conditional column in table to improve query performance.

Example

```
SELECT * FROM departments
WHERE EXISTS
(SELECT * FROM employees
WHERE departments.department_id = employees.department_id
AND employees.salary > 2500)
ORDER BY department_name;
```

Output

Department_ID	*Department_Name*	*Manager_ID*	*Location_ID*
110	Accounting	205	1700
10	Administration	200	1700
90	Executive	100	1700
60	IT	103	1400
20	Marketing	201	1800
80	Sales	149	2500
50	Shipping	124	1500

Exercise:

1. What is the difference between inner and outer join?
2. What is Self Join and why is it required?
3. What are different Types of Join?

Chapter - 14

Wild Cards Character

Wild card character are character used with Like operator along with single quote ‘ ’with % (percent) or _ (underscore). used to select data from a table with matching word with given pattern with wildcard character in where clause.

Let’s see how the per cent wildcard works in the SQL LIKE condition.

Select EMPLOYEE_ID,FIRST_NAME

from Employees where FIRST_NAME like ‘%t%’

Will return all rows where Employees First_name contains as t.

EMPLOYEE_ID	*FIRST_NAME*
100	Steven
141	Trenna
142	Curtis
144	Peter
176	Jonathon
201	Mitchael
202	Pat

Now you will see use of not like in below example.

Select EMPLOYEE_ID,FIRST_NAME

from Employees where FIRST_NAME not like‘%t%’

Will return all rows where Employees First_name not contains as t.

EMPLOYEE_ID	*FIRST_NAME*
101	Neena
102	Lex
103	Alexander
104	Bruce
107	Diana
124	Kevin
143	Randall
149	Eleni
174	Ellen
178	Kimberely
200	Jennifer
205	Shelley
206	William

With LIKE operator "you can also implements a pattern match comparison" that attempts to match "a string value against a pattern string containing wild-card characters."

Example:

Select EMPLOYEE_ID,FIRST_NAME

from Employees where FIRST_NAME like'El %'

Output

EMPLOYEE_ID	*FIRST_NAME*
149	Eleni
174	Ellen

LIKE is generally used only with strings and equals. Equal is faster in case of searching full string. The equal's operator treats wildcard characters as literal characters. The difference in results returned is as follows:

Select EMPLOYEE_ID,FIRST_NAME

from Employees where FIRST_NAME ='Ellen'

And

Select EMPLOYEE_ID,FIRST_NAME

from Employees where FIRST_NAME like'Ellen'

Both query will return the same result as below

EMPLOYEE_ID	*FIRST_NAME*
174	Ellen

Using LIKE will generally take longer as its a pattern match. However,

Select EMPLOYEE_ID,FIRST_NAME

from Employees where FIRST_NAME ='Ellen'

And

Select EMPLOYEE_ID,FIRST_NAME

from Employees where FIRST_NAME like'Ellen%'

Would return different results, where using "=" results in only results **like'Ellen%'** being returned and the LIKE operator will return anything starting with **'Ellen'**.

14.1 SQL supports following wildcard operators in conjunction with the LIKE operator:

Wild cards	*Description*
The percent sign (%)	Matches one or more characters. Note that MS Access uses the asterisk (*) wildcard character instead of the percent sign (%) wildcard character.
The underscore (_)	Matches one character. Note that MS Access uses a question mark (?) instead of the underscore (_) to match any one character.

The percent sign represents zero, one, or multiple characters. The underscore represents a single number or character. The symbols can be used in combinations.

Here are number of examples showing WHERE part having different LIKE clause with '%' and '_' operators:

Statement	*Description*
WHERE SALARY LIKE '2000 %'	Finds any values that start with 2000
WHERE SALARY LIKE '%2000%'	Finds any values that have 2000 in any position
WHERE SALARY LIKE '_00%'	Finds any values that have 00 in the second and third positions
WHERE SALARY LIKE '2_%_%'	Finds any values that start with 2 and are at least 3 characters in length
WHERE SALARY LIKE '%2'	Finds any values that end with 2
WHERE SALARY LIKE '_2%3'	Finds any values that have a 2 in the second position and end with a 3
WHERE SALARY LIKE '2___3'	Finds any values in a five-digit number that start with 2 and end with 3

Let us take a real example, consider Employees table:

To display all the records from Employees table where Hire_Date starts with 2000:

```
SELECT * FROM Employees
WHERE hire_Date LIKE '2000%';
```

output

Exercise:

1. Write 3 queries to fetch data from employees table where
   I. First name starts with S
   II. Department Id not contains two 0 (00).
   III. second character of Last name is a.

Chapter - 15

Operators

An operator manipulates data items and gives a result. Syntactically, an operator appears before or after an operand or between two operands.

15.1 Unary: An unary operator operates on only one operand. An unary operator typically appears with its operand as below:

Operator operand

Operator	*Description*
+	Unary plus operator; indicates positive value (numbers are positive without this, however)
-	Unary minus operator; negates an expression
++	Increment operator; increments a value by 1
—	Decrement operator; decrements a value by 1
!	Logical complement operator; inverts the value of a boolean

SQL Comparison Operators:

Assume variable a holds 10 and variable b holds 20 then:

Show Examples

Operator	*Description*	*Example*
=	Checks if the value of two operands is equal or not, if yes then condition becomes true.	(a = b) is not true.

!=	Checks if the value of two operands is equal or not, if values are not equal then condition becomes true.	(a != b) is true.
<>	Checks if the value of two operands is equal or not, if values are not equal then condition becomes true.	(a <> b) is true.
>	Checks if the value of left operand is greater than the value of right operand, if yes then condition becomes true.	(a > b) is not true.
<	Checks if the value of left operand is less than the value of right operand, if yes then condition becomes true.	(a < b) is true.
>=	Checks if the value of left operand is greater than or equal to the value of right operand, if yes then condition becomes true.	(a >= b) is not true.
<=	Checks if the value of left operand is less than or equal to the value of right operand, if yes then condition becomes true.	(a <= b) is true.
!<	Checks if the value of left operand is not less than the value of right operand, if yes then condition becomes true.	(a !< b) is false.
!>	Checks if the value of left operand is not greater than the value of right operand, if yes then condition becomes true.	(a !> b) is true.

15.2 Arithmetic Operators

Operator	*Purpose*	*Example*
+ -	When these denote a positive or negative expression, they are unary operators.	SELECT * FROM order_items WHERE quantity = -1 ORDER BY order_id, line_item_id, product_id;SELECT * FROM employees WHERE -salary < 0 OR DER BY employee_id;

+ -	When they add or subtract, they are binary operators.	SELECT hire_date FROM employees WHERE SYS-DATE - hire_date > 365 ORDER BY hire_date;
* /	Multiply, divide. These are binary operators.	UPDATE employees SET salary = salary * 1.1;

Precedence Example in the following expression, multiplication has a higher precedence than addition, so Oracle first multiplies 2 by 3 and then adds the result to 1.

If you check for 1+2*3 result will 7

Select 1+2*3 in sql Server and SQLlite

Select 1+2*3 from dual; in Oracle

You can use parentheses in an expression to override operator precedence. Oracle evaluates expressions inside parentheses before evaluating those outside.

If you check for (1+2)*3 result will 9

15.3 Concatenation Operator

<table>
<tr><th>Operator</th><th>Purpose</th><th>Example</th></tr>
<tr><td>||</td><td>Concatenates character strings and CLOB data.</td><td>SELECT 'Name is' || last_name FROM employees ORDER BY last_name;</td></tr>
</table>

NOTE:

On most platforms, the concatenation operator is two solid vertical bar.

Oracle provides the CONCAT character function as an alternative to the vertical bar operator.

SQL server supports + marks to concatenate the two or more than two column values.

Example:

In MS Sql server you can use + as a concatenation operator and in Oracle you can use ||

Example:

To get full name from employees table you need to concatenate first name and last name o employee.

SELECT FIRST_NAME + LAST_NAME as FullName FROM Employees

Output
FullName
StevenKing
NeenaKochhar
LexDe Haan
AlexanderHunold
BruceEmst
DianaLorentz
KevinMourgos
TrennaRajas
CurtisDavies
RandallMatos
PeterVargas
EleniZlotkey
EllenAbel
JonathonTaylor
KimberelyGrant
JenniferWhalen
MitchaelHartstein
PatFay
ShelleyHiggins
WilliamGietz

Now you need to add a single space between First name and last name. For this you need to add a single space between two columns.

Example:

SELECT FIRST_NAME + ' ' + LAST_NAME as FullName FROM Employees

Output
FullName
Steven King
Neena Kochhar
Lex De Haan
Alexander Hunold
Bruce Emst
Diana Lorentz
Kevin Mourgos
Trenna Rajas
Curtis Davies
Randall Matos
Peter Vargas
Eleni Zlotkey
Ellen Abel
Jonathon Taylor
Kimberely Grant
Jennifer Whalen
Mitchael Hartstein
Pat Fay
Shelley Higgins
William Gietz
AND and OR

The AND operator displays a record if both the first condition AND the second condition are true.

Example:

The following SQL statement selects all from Employees where Department_ID=90 AND the First_Name='Peter'

SELECT Employee_id,FIRST_NAME,DEPARTMENT_ID FROM Employees

WHERE DEPARTMENT_ID=90

AND FIRST_NAME='Lex';

Employee_id	*FIRST_NAME*	*DEPARTMENT_ID*
102	Lex	90

The OR operator displays a record if either the first condition OR the second condition is true.

Example

The following SQL statement selects all from Employees where Department_ID=90OR the First_Name='Kevin

SELECT Employee_id,FIRST_NAME,DEPARTMENT_ID FROM Employees

WHERE DEPARTMENT_ID=90

OR FIRST_NAME='Kevin';

Employee_id	*FIRST_NAME*	*DEPARTMENT_ID*
100	Steven	90
101	Neena	90
102	Lex	90
124	Kevin	50

15.4 Combining AND & OR

You can also combine AND and OR (use parenthesis to form complex expressions).

The following SQL statement selects all from Employees where Department_ID=90And the First_Name='Steven' or First_Name='Lex'

SELECT Employee_id,FIRST_NAME,DEPARTMENT_ID FROM Employees.

WHERE DEPARTMENT_ID=90

AND (FIRST_NAME='Steven' or FIRST_NAME='Lex');

Employee_id	*FIRST_NAME*	*DEPARTMENT_ID*
100 102	Steven Lex	90 90

In below table you can see more Operators with description.

Operator	*Description*
ALL	The ALL operator is used to compare a value to all values in another value set.
AND	The AND operator allows the existence of multiple conditions in an SQL statement's WHERE clause.
ANY	The ANY operator is used to compare a value to any applicable value in the list according to the condition.
BETWEEN	The BETWEEN operator is used to search for values that are within a set of values, given the minimum value and the maximum value.
EXISTS	The EXISTS operator is used to search for the presence of a row in a specified table that meets certain criteria.
IN	The IN operator is used to compare a value to a list of literal values that have been specified.
LIKE	The LIKE operator is used to compare a value to similar values using wild card operators.
NOT	The NOT operator reverses the meaning of the logical operator with which it is used. Eg. NOT EXISTS, NOT BETWEEN, NOT IN etc. This is negate operator.
OR	The OR operator is used to combine multiple conditions in an SQL statement's WHERE clause.
IS NULL	The NULL operator is used to compare a value with a NULL value.
UNIQUE	The UNIQUE operator searches every row of a specified table for uniqueness (no duplicates).

15.5 DISTINCT

The DISTINCT keyword eliminates duplicate rows from the results of a SELECT statement. If DISTINCT is not specified, all rows are returned, including duplicates.

SELECT DEPARTMENT_ID from Employees

DEPARTMENT_ID
90
90
90
60
60
60
50
50

50
50
50
80
80
80
NULL
10
20
20
110
110

SELECT Distinct DEPARTMENT_ID from Employees

DEPARTMENT_ID
NULL
10
20
50
60
80
90
110

Exercise:

1. How to get Full name from Employees table in Oracle with single space in between?
2. How to get employee detail where First name starts with s and department id is 90?

Chapter - 16

Aliases & Dot Notation

Aliases for table names can be created after the FROM keyword of the SELECT statement. You can use the alias in place of the full table name when referring to columns in that table to save yourself considerable typing.

Note: Alias name should be relevant to table name, So that you can easily identify the correspondence table name with alias name in query.

select e.Employee_Id, e.First_name,d.DEPARTMENT_ID, d.MANAGER_ID

from Employees e left outer join Departments d

on e.DEPARTMENT_ID=d.department_id

You can understand it with blow example. Consider two table Employees and departments as you have already.

Note: It require double quotation marks or square brackets if the column name contains spaces. For better practice you can use some special character like Underscore instead of spaces in column name while creating table or alias name for table or column.

Example:

SELECT CustomerName AS Customer, ContactName AS [Contact Person]

FROM Customers;

In the following SQL statement we combine two columns (First_Name and Last_name)and create an alias name as "Full_Name":

Example:

SELECT FIRST_NAME + ' ' + LAST_NAME as Full_Name FROM Employees

Full_Name
Steven King
Neena Kochhar
Lex De Haan
Alexander Hunold
Bruce Emst
Diana Lorentz
Kevin Mourgos
Trenna Rajas
Curtis Davies
Randall Matos
Peter Vargas
Eleni Zlotkey
Ellen Abel
Jonathon Taylor
Kimberely Grant
Jennifer Whalen
Mitchael Hartstein
Pat Fay
Shelley Higgins
William Gietz

Example the following SQL query of left outer join. In this querye is used as an Alias name for table employees and d is as alias name for table departments.

Example

select e. Employee_Id, e. First_name,d.DEPARTMENT_ID, d.MANAGER_ID from Employees e left outer join Departments d on

e.DEPARTMENT_ID=d.department_id

The same SQL statement without aliases:

Example

select Employees. Employee_Id, Employees. First_name,

Departments.DEPARTMENT_ID,Departments.MANAGER_ID

from Employees left outer join Departments

on Employees.DEPARTMENT_ID=Departments.department_id

Aliases can be useful when:

There is more than one table involved in a query

Functions are used in the query

Column names are big or not very readable

Two or more columns are combined together

Exercise

1. Select Employee Id, First_name, and manager_name as alias name 'Employee_Manager' from employees and Departments table.

Chapter - 17

Conditional (CASE) expressions

SQL supports a case expression. Whenever you require fetching or modifying the records based on some conditions. In this situation Case expression is best alternative for Cursor/looping and also provides better performance. To know more about Cursor and looping you can refer Cursor and Introduction of PL/SQL chapter in this book.

You can use CASE expressions anywhere in the SQL Query like CASE expressions can be used with in SELECT statement, In WHERE clauses, In Order by clause, In HAVING clauses, In (Insert, UPDATE and DELETE statements).

In its most general form, which is called a "searched case" in the SQL standard, it works like 'else if' in other programming languages like PL/SQL

Note: Case supports in SQL server /Oracle/DB2

```
CASE expression
WHEN expression1 THEN Result1
WHEN expression2 THEN Result2
ELSE ResultN
END
```

The WHEN conditions are tested in the order in which they appear in the source. If no ELSE expression is specified, it defaults to ELSE NULL.

```
CASE n
WHEN 1 THEN'one'
WHEN 2 THEN'two'
ELSE'i cannot count more'
END
```

17.1 Searched CASE expressions

This expression evaluates a set of Boolean expressions to find the result. This expression allows comparison operators, and logical operators AND/OR with in each Boolean expression.

Syntax for SQL SERVER/ Oracle / DB2

```
CASE
WHEN Boolean_expression1 THEN Result1
WHEN Boolean_expression2 THEN Result2
ELSE Else_value
END
```

17.2 SELECT statement with CASE expressions

```
SELECT * FROM departments
```

OutPut

Department_ID	*Department_Name*	*Manager_ID*	*Location_ID*
10	Administration	200	1700
20	Marketing	201	1800
50	Shipping	124	1500
60	IT	103	1400
80	Sales	149	2500
90	Executive	100	1700
110	Accounting	205	1700
190	Contracting	NULL	1700

```
select DEPARTMENT_ID,DEPARTMENT_NAME=
(CASE Department_Name
when 'IT' then 'Inforamtion Technology'
when 'Sales' then 'Product Sales'
```

```
else DEPARTMENT_NAME
End), Manager_ID, LOCATION_ID
From Departments
```

OutPut

Department_ID	*Department_Name*	*Manager_ID*	*Location_ID*
10	Administration	200	1700
20	Marketing	201	1800
50	Shipping	124	1500
60	Information Technology	103	1400
80	Product Sales	149	2500
90	Executive	100	1700
110	Accounting	205	1700
190	Contracting	NULL	1700

17.3 Update statement with CASE expression

```
SELECT * FROM departments
```

OutPut

Department_ID	*Department_Name*	*Manager_ID*	*Location_ID*
10	Administration	200	1700
20	Marketing	201	1800
50	Shipping	124	1500
60	IT	103	1400
80	Sales	149	2500
90	Executive	100	1700
110	Accounting	205	1700
190	Contracting	NULL	1700

```
Update Departments set DEPARTMENT_NAME=
(CASE Department_Name
when ‘IT’ then ‘Information Technology’
when ‘Sales’ then ‘Product Sales’
else DEPARTMENT_NAME
End)
From Departments
```

SELECT * FROM departments

OutPut

Department_ID	*Department_Name*	*Manager_ID*	*Location_ID*
10	Administration	200	1700
20	Marketing	201	1800
50	Shipping	124	1500
60	Information Technology	103	1400
80	Product Sales	149	2500
90	Executive	100	1700
110	Accounting	205	1700
190	Contracting	NULL	1700

17.4 ORDER BY clause with CASE expressions

select EMPLOYEE_ID, FIRST_NAME, LAST_NAME, DEPARTMENT_ID from Employees

where DEPARTMENT_ID in (90,60)

OutPut

Employee_ID	*First_Name*	*Last Name*	*Department_ID*
100	Steven	King	90
101	Neena	Kochhar	90
102	Lex	De Haan	90
103	Alexander	Hunold	60
104	Bruce	Emst	60
107	Diana	Lorentz	60

select EMPLOYEE_ID,FIRST_NAME,LAST_NAME, DEPARTMENT_ID from Employees

where DEPARTMENT_ID in (90,60)

ORDER BY CASE DEPARTMENT_ID WHEN 60 THEN FIRST_NAME END DESC, CASE WHEN DEPARTMENT_ID = 90 THEN FIRST_NAME END;

OutPut

Employee_ID	*First_Name*	*Last Name*	*Department_ID*
107	Diana	Lorentz	60
104	Bruce	Emst	60
103	Alexander	Hunold	60
102	Lex	De Haan	90
101	Neena	Kochhar	90
100	Steven	King	90

17.5 Having Clause with CASE expression

Without case statement

select EMPLOYEE_ID, FIRST_NAME, LAST_NAME, DEPARTMENT_ID, SUM (Salary) as Total_salary
from Employees
group by EMPLOYEE_ID, FIRST_NAME, LAST_NAME, DEPARTMENT_ID
Having max (SALARY)>=6000 and department_id =60 or
max (SALARY)>=17000 and department_id =90
order by Total_salary desc

OutPut

Employee_ID	*First_Name*	*Last Name*	*Department_ID*	*Total_salary*
100	Steven	King	90	24000
101	Neena	Kochhar	90	17000
102	Lex	De Haan	90	17000
103	Alexander	Hunold	60	9000
104	Bruce	Emst	60	6000

With case statement

select EMPLOYEE_ID, FIRST_NAME, LAST_NAME, DEPARTMENT_ID, SUM (Salary) as Total_salary from Employees
group by EMPLOYEE_ID, FIRST_NAME, LAST_NAME, DEPARTMENT_ID Having max(
CASE DEPARTMENT_ID WHEN 60 THEN Salary else Null End)>=6000 or max(CASE WHEN DEPARTMENT_ID = 90 THEN Salary else Null End)>=17000 order by Total_salary desc

OutPut

Employee_ID	*First_Name*	*Last Name*	*Department_ID*	*Total_salary*
100	Steven	King	90	24000
101	Neena	Kochhar	90	17000
102	Lex	De Haan	90	17000
103	Alexander	Hunold	60	9000
104	Bruce	Emst	60	6000

17.6 DECODE

In Oracle you have an equivalent **DECODE** construct:

SELECT DECODE (n,1, "one", 2, "two", "i cannot count that high") FROM some_table;

The last value is the default; if none is specified, it also defaults to NULL. However, unlike the standard's "simple case", Oracle's DECODE considers two NULLs to be equal with each other.

Exercise:

1. Execute the above Case expression example commands and learn to use CASE in SQL SERVER and Oracle.

Chapter - 18

View

In SQL, a view is a virtual table based on the result-set of an SQL statement. As you show required similar (same) query many times. So to avoid typing many time similar query you can create a view. A View is an Object of Current Database only. A view can have maximum 1024 Columns. You can't use a view if base table dropped or structure of base table got changed. In such case you need to drop the view and recreate it.

As you already show view creation during join exercise.

```
create view EmpDetails as
select Employees. Employee_Id, Employees. First_name,
Departments.DEPARTMENT_ID,Departments.MANAGER_ID
from Employees left outer join Departments
on Employees.DEPARTMENT_ID=Departments.department_id
```

So now instead of writing below query many times

```
select Employees.Employee_Id, Employees.First_name,
Departments.DEPARTMENT_ID,Departments.MANAGER_ID
from Employees left outer join Departments
on Employees.DEPARTMENT_ID=Departments.department_id
```

Output

Employee_Id	*First_name*	*Department_ID*	*Manager_ID*
100	Steven	90	100
101	Neena	90	100
102	Lex	90	100
103	Alexander	60	103
104	Bruce	60	103
107	Diana	60	103
124	Kevin	50	124
141	Trenna	50	124
142	Curtis	50	124
143	Randall	50	124
144	Peter	50	124
149	Eleni	80	149
174	Ellen	80	149
176	Jonathon	80	149
178	Kimberely	NULL	NULL
200	Jennifer	10	200
201	Mitchael	20	201
202	Pat	20	201
205	Shelley	110	205
206	William	110	205

You can use single line query as below to get similar result as above query result.

Select * from EmpDetails

OutPut

Employee_Id	*First_name*	*Department_ID*	*Manager_ID*
100	Steven	90	100
101	Neena	90	100
102	Lex	90	100
103	Alexander	60	103
104	Bruce	60	103
107	Diana	60	103
124	Kevin	50	124
141	Trenna	50	124
142	Curtis	50	124
143	Randall	50	124

(Contd...)

144	Peter	50	124
149	Eleni	80	149
174	Ellen	80	149
176	Jonathon	80	149
178	Kimberely	NULL	NULL
200	Jennifer	10	200
201	Mitchael	20	201
202	Pat	20	201
205	Shelley	110	205
206	William	110	205

Create view CaseWithHaving as

select EMPLOYEE_ID, FIRST_NAME, LAST_NAME, DEPARTMENT_ID, SUM (Salary) as Total_salary

from Employees

group by EMPLOYEE_ID, FIRST_NAME, LAST_NAME, DEPARTMENT_ID

Having max

CASE DEPARTMENT_ID WHEN 60 THEN Salary else Null End)>=6000 or

max (CASE WHEN DEPARTMENT_ID = 90 THEN Salary else Null End)>=17000

select * from CaseWithHaving

OutPut

Employee_ID	*First_Name*	*Last_Name*	*Department_ID*	*Total_Salary*
100	Steven	King	90	24000
101	Neena	Kochhar	90	17000
102	Lex	De Haan	90	17000
103	Alexander	Hunold	60	9000
104	Bruce	Emst	60	6000

Note: You can not use order by in create View Statement.

You show one benefit of using view. Now know more about View in brief.

Some Benefits of View

1. View takes very less space because it is a Virtual object in database.

2. By using view you can hide that complexity from its user.
3. View provides extra security to the base table and data.
4. In View you can club or join multiple tables' data in a single View.

18.1 View-Some Important point to keep in mind while creating a view.

1. You can't create any index on view.
2. In older version of some database you can't use subqueries in definition of view.
3. You can't use synonym instead of table name but you can use Alias of table name of the base table of view in definition.
4. You can create a sub view from a main view or supper view.
5. In New versions you can use subquery in view definition. Subquery can contain uo to 1000 expressions only.
6. If you use subquery and the subquery selects the ROWID, ROWNUM, or LEVEL pseudocolumns, then those columns must have aliases in the view subquery.

18.2 There are two types of View

18.2.1 Read only View : User can't update the data of the view is known as Read Only View. You can make a view Read only by giving Read only permission on that view. In SQL Lite View are only Read only. You can't update a view in SQL Lite. In SQL server if View contains data from more than one dependent table or using any Function then it will act like a Read only View. Else you can update it.

Example:

Create view updatableExample as

select Employee_ID, First_name from employees where Employee_ID=104

select * from updatableExample

Employee_ID	*First_name*
104	Bruce

update updatableExample set FIRST_NAME='BruceNew'

select * from updatableExample

Employee_ID	***First_name***
104	BruceNew

It will also update the base table.

select EMPLOYEE_ID, FIRST_NAME, LAST_NAME, DEPARTMENT_ID

from Employees where EMPLOYEE_ID=104

EMPLOYEE_ID	***FIRST_NAME***	***LAST_NAME***	***DEPARTMENT_ID***
104	BruceNew	Emst	60

Now if you want to update existing View CaseWithHaving

update CaseWithHaving set Total_salary=7000 where EMPLOYEE_ID=104

Then MS SQL Server will give an error like below:

'Update or insert of view or function 'CaseWithHaving' failed because it contains a derived or constant field'.

So it is Read Only View.

In Oracle you can also use 'With Read Only ' to make a view Read only.

Example:

Create view ReadOnlyViewExample

(EMPLOYEE_ID,FIRST_NAME,LAST_NAME,DEPARTMENT_ID) As select EMPLOYEE_ID, FIRST_NAME, LAST_NAME, DEPARTMENT_ID from Employees where EMPLOYEE_ID=104

with Read Only;

above view is depends on single base table, but you are using 'with Read Only. So It will be a read only View.

Note: In above example you are defining column name also before as select you can create a view without column definition also as you already show in other examples.

18.2.2 Updateable view: If the database system determines the reverse mapping from the view schema to the schema of the underlying base tables, then the view is updatable. INSERT, UPDATE, and DELETE operations can be performed on updateable views.

Example:

Create view updatableExample as

select Employee_ID, First_name from employees where Employee_ID=104

select * from updatableExample

Employee_ID	*First_Name*
104	Bruce

Here View updatableExample is an updatable View.

A view can be updatable if—

1. View created with only one base table.
2. View definition does not contains any aggregate function or set Operators or Group BY or having or Order by or Connect by or Subquery or Join with exceptions or check constraint.
3. Column you want to modify does not derived by using Group By, Having or Distinct clause.
4. If the join results in more than one table for which every primary key or unique key value in the base table is also unique in the join view, then Oracle Database deletes from the first table named in the FROM clause, whether or not the view was created WITH CHECK OPTION
5. For an INSERT statement, the view must not be created WITH CHECK OPTION, and all columns into which values are inserted must come from a one table for which every primary key or unique key value in the base table is also unique in the join view.

Note: MY SQL 4.0 Does not Support View. My SQL 5.0 and above supports View.

18.3 SQL Dropping a View

Dropping a view will remove view from that schema. To Drop a view you must be in same schema or else you need to refer that schema where view is created. And you must have relevant permission (privileges) on that view to Drop.

Example:

Drop view ReadOnlyView

18.4 Materialized View

Materialized views are local copies of remote tables. In today's distributed world, data resides on a central database server. The data is used by local users. In this kind of scenario, replicating data on local server can be helpful for gaining performance. Materialized views serve the same purpose. Materialized view contains data, same as if they were a table. These Materialized Views (MV) reside on local machines. Local users can query these MVs to get desired results. MVs can be complete replica of a table, or it can be a result of a query fired on multiple tables. Accuracy of a materialized view depends on the frequency of trigger mechanisms behind its updates.You will know more about Trigger in dedicated chapter for trigger in this book. IBM DB2 provides so-called MQT (materialized query tables) for the same purpose. MS SQL Server introduced in its 2000 version indexed views which only store a separate index from the table, but not the entire data. PostgreSQL implemented materialized views in its 9.3 release.

Materialized views improve query performance. When you create a materialized view, you create a set of query commands that aggregate or join data from multiple tables. Materialized views provide pre calculated data that can be reused or replicated to remote data marts. For example, data about company sales is widely sought throughout an organization.

When you create a materialized view, you can configure it to take advantage of the query rewrite and fast refresh features available in Oracle Database.

Fast Refresh for Materialized Views

You can configure a materialized view to refresh incrementally. When you update the base tables for a materialized view, the database stores updated record pointers in the materialized view log. Changes in the log tables are used to refresh the associated materialized views.

To ensure incremental refresh of materialized views, verify the following conditions:

The Refresh parameter must be set to Fast and the Base Tables parameter must list all base tables.

Each base table must have a PK constraint defined. Oracle Warehouse Builder generates a create statement based on the PK constraint and utilizes that log to refresh the dependent materialized views.

The materialized view must not contain references to non-repeating expressions such as SYSDATE, ROWNUM, and non-repeatable PL/SQL functions.

The materialized view must not contain references to RAW and LONG RAW data types.

There are additional restrictions for materialized views with statements for joins, aggregations, and unions. For information about additional restrictions.

Create a materialized view. - The word "snapshot" is synonymous with "materialized view".

Syntax: For Oracle only

Create materialized view **MYFIRST_MATERIALIZEDVIEW**

Refresh force

Startwith SysDate next SysDate + 7

As

Select * from Employee@REMOTE_CONNECT;

These are different parts of create statement, also these will be used to reference exactly one part at a time.

(1) The first part is the create statement itself with the MV name to be created. In this case MV name is "MYFIRST_MATERIALIZED-VIEW". Note that some parts are purposefully ignored here to avoid complexity. If no tablespace is provided then the MV is created in the current tablespace.

(2) The 'refresh' part has some options.

(a) Fast - Fast refreshes are only available if Oracle can match rows in the MV directly to rows in the base tables. They use tables called Materialized View Logs to send specific rows from the master table to the MV.

(b) Complete—Complete refreshes completely re-create the MV.

(c) Force - The force option for refreshes tells Oracle to use a fast refresh if it is available; otherwise, a complete refresh will be used.

(3) This part is the query. Note that the MV created in the above example is a Read-Only MV. You can create an updatable query with 'for update'

Syntax will be -

Create materialized view **MYFIRST_MATERIALIZEDVIEW**

Refresh force

Start with **SysDate next SysDate** + 7

For update as

Select* from **Employee@REMOTE_CONNECT;**

18.4.1 Types of Materialized View:

(1) Read-Only: This type of MVs cannot send data back to the server Master tables. These serves only one way communications. i.e. from server to the client.

(2) Updatable: This type of MVs can send the data, changed locally, back to the server.

Exercise:

What is the difference between tables/View and materialized Views?

Chapter - 19

Introduction of PL/SQL

PL/SQL is a programming language developed by Oracle Corporation in 1980s. it stands for Procedural language/Structured query language. So PL/SQL is a High level performance transaction-processing procedural language for SQL and the Oracle relational database.it provides a built-in interpreted and operating system independent programming environment. So it can directly called from the command line SQL*PLUS interface and also call can be called from external front end or backend language to database. PL/SQL Supports Object oriented programming language and developing web applications for running PL/SQL you need Oracle server installed on your machine for learning purpose you can install a free trial version of Express Edition from Oracle site.

19.1 Data Types: Every Variable and Constants should have a data type. Type determines storage type like format, constraints and range of data stored in that particular variable or constant.

19.2 Variables or Scalar Variable: Variables or Scalar Variable or program variable used to store the data for that program during execution of the code of program/query. You need to declare a variable before its use.

Declaration of variable:

Variable name datatype [Not Null] [:= Default value]

Variable name is mandatory to declare a variable. NOT NULL is a constraints here. So you can not store null value in this variable. It is not mandatory.

Test varchar2 (20);

Test varchar2 (20):= 'MyFirstVariable';

Test: = 'MySecondVariable';

19.3 Constants: Constant is optional. If you specify constant then you will not be able to change its value.

Constant name datatype [Not Null] [:= Default value]

Test Constant varchar2 (20):='MYVariablewithConstant';

The value of a Constant can not be changed.

19.4 Operators: In PL/SQL Many types of operators you can use. Below you will find tables of different types of operators. The Operations of an expression works in a particular order on their priority (precedence). See the default order of operations from list first to last (Top to Bottom) in below list.

Expressions and Comparisons	*Operation*
**	exponentiation
+, -	identity, negation
*, /	multiplication, division
+, -, ||	addition, subtraction, concatenation
=, <, >, <=, >=, <>, !=, ~=, ^=, IS NULL, LIKE, BETWEEN, IN	comparison
NOT	logical negation
AND	conjunction
OR	

See below table to know more about Comparison operators.

Operator	*Meaning*
=	equal to
<>, !=, ~=, ^=	not equal to
<	less than
>	greater than
<=	less than or equal to
>=	greater than or equal to

You will see use of operators in further chapters.

19.5 Conditions: Condition is uses to take alternative work done or to get conditional result set.

(A) IF Statement: works based on Boolean expressions.

```
IF condition then
    Statement
End IF;
```

Suppose you want to set bonus 20 per cent if sales data is more then 80:

```
IF Sales > 80 Then
    Bonus: =80
End IF
```

(b) If Then Else Statement: works based on Boolean expressions.

```
IF Condition then
    Statement
Else
    Default statement
End IF;
```

Suppose you want to set bonus 20 per cent if sales data is more then 80 and 13 if it is less than 80

```
IF Sales > 80 Then
    Bonus: =80
Else
    Bonus:=13
End IF
```

Below see conditional statement for multiple value check.

```
IF grade = 'A' THEN
    dbms_output.put_line('Excellent');
ELSIF grade = 'B' THEN
    dbms_output.put_line('Very Good');
ELSIF grade = 'C' THEN
    dbms_output.put_line('Good');
ELSIF grade = 'D' THEN
    dbms_output. put_line('Pass');
```

```
ELSE
    dbms_output.put_line('No such grade');
END IF;
```

(c) CASE Statement: the CASE statement uses a selector.

```
CASE grade
    WHEN 'A' THEN dbms_output.put_line('Excellent');
    WHEN 'B' THEN dbms_output.put_line('Very Good');
    WHEN 'C' THEN dbms_output.put_line('Good');
    WHEN 'D' THEN dbms_output.put_line('Pass');
    ELSE dbms_output.put_line('No such grade');
END CASE;
```

19.6 Loop Statement: A statement allows you to execute a sequence of statements multiple times known as LOOP statement.

LOOP statement Starts with LOOP keyword and ends with END LOOP keywords. To exit from a loop you need to use Exit / Exit when/ raise application error etc. keyword between LOOP and END LOOP. Also LOOP allows using FOR LOOP and WHILE LOOP. You will see later in this chapter.

Note: Before starting to use variable you need to Initialize/declare a variable. Use Exit/Exit when to exit from a loop if you will use exit without when then loop will execute only once.

19.6.1 Simple LOOP:

Syntax:

```
LOOP
    Statement;
EXIT;
END LOOP;
Or
LOOP
    Statement;
EXIT WHEN
    {Condition;}
END LOOP;
```

19.6.2 FOR LOOP: Allows you to get output value with lower bound and Upper bound

BEGIN

FOR i IN 1..10 LOOP - - I need to declare in declare section.i starts at 1, ends at 10

DBMS_OUTPUT.PUT_LINE(i); - - statements here execute 10 times

END LOOP;

END;

19.6.3 REVERSE LOOP: Allows you to get output value with Upper bound and Lower bound

BEGIN

FOR i IN REVERSE 10..1 LOOP - - i starts at 10, ends at 1

DBMS_OUTPUT.PUT_LINE (i); - - statements here execute 10 times

END LOOP;

END;

19.6.4 WHILE LOOP statement: It gives output statement while a condition is True.

WHILE *condition* LOOP

Statements

END LOOP;

You will see WHILE LOOP in more brief in below

Examples:

DECLARE
ToPrint BOOLEAN: = FALSE;
BEGIN
WHILE ToPrint LOOP
DBMS_OUTPUT.PUT_LINE ('this line will not print.');
ToPrint: = TRUE; — This assignment is not made.
END LOOP;

WHILE NOT ToPrint LOOP
DBMS_OUTPUT.PUT_LINE ('Hello, world!');

```
ToPrint: = TRUE;
END LOOP;
END;
/
```

Result:

Hello, world!

Exercise:

1. Print Hello World with
   Loop, While loop and For Loop
2. Write a PL/SQL program to print * in below given pattern

```
        *
     *  *  *
  *  *  *  *  *
```

   Do it with Loop, FOR Loop and while loop.
3. Write a PL/SQL program to print * in below given pattern

```
           *
      *    *    *
 *    *    *    *    *
      *    *    *
           *
```

With FOR Loop and Reverse for Loop

Chapter - 20

Stored Procedures

A procedure which stored in the Relational data base's data dictionary known as stored procedure. It can be called from any program with database connectivity or can be execute from database to perform desired task or get desired result.

You should use stored procedure to

Avoid network traffic, because stored procedure can run directly within the database engine on the production environment. It means stored procedures run on a specialized database server with direct access of data being processed or accessed.

Reduce Overhead, as it runs directly in the database, so it does not required compilation of queries again and again.

Encapsulation means it hides the complexity of query and codes from clients. At client place user can call it but can't see internal logic and can't make any changes in its logic.

Avoid unauthorized access, you can set permission and access rights for user for each stored procedure. So, unauthorized user can't access it.

Data level protection for relevant table/tables. User can pass parameter in prescribed format with precaution only. Else it will fail to insert/Update/ delete into table.

Example: For Oracle

Create or Replace procedure MyFirstStoredProcedure Is

Begin

```
    DBMS_OUTPUT.PUT_LINE ('Hello World.');
End;
/
```

OutPut

Hello World.

Example: For MS SQL Server

```
Create procedure MyFirstStoredProcedure AS
Begin
    Print ('Hello World.');
End;
Exec MyFirstStoredProcedure
```

OutPut

Hello World.

Note: AS- Specifies the actions the procedure is to take.

Example: For MySQL

```
Delimiter //
Create procedure MyFirstStoredProcedure AS
Begin
    Select 'Hello World!" ;
End; //
Call MyFirstStoredProcedure();
```

OutPut

Hello World!

Note: In My SQL you can change the delimiter for that Stored procedure and after that you can reset it as semicolon (;). Default delimiter is semicolon. Used to indicate the end of the stored procedure like you show resetting delimiter // for semicolon, and at end again setting it back to semicolon in above example.

20.1 Parameters Mode

There are three parameters modes for stored procedure IN, OUT, and INOUT. You will use these parameters in the stored procedure depending on the purpose of the parameter.

20.1.1 Parameter: IN – Parameter IN is the default parameter. Means, You no need to define it in Procedure definition. IN is optional, because if you will not defined and parameter type then stored procedure will consider as IN by default. When you use IN parameter in the stored parameter you must have to pass value of the parameter at the time of execution/call of the parameter. Oracle, DB2 and MySQL support this parameter. In SQL server By Default parameter is IN parameter.

Example: For Oracle

```
CREATE OR REPLACE PROCEDURE MyFirstSPwithIN
Parameter (param1 IN VARCHAR2)
IS
BEGIN
DBMS_OUTPUT.PUT_LINE ('Hello ' || param1);
END;
/
Exec MyFirstSPwithINParameter ('World);
```

OutPut

Hello World

Example: For MS SQL Server

```
Create PROCEDURE MyFirstSPwithINParameter
@param1 VARCHAR(20)
as
BEGIN
Print ('Hello ' + @param1);
END;
Exec MyFirstSPwithINParameter 'World'
```

OutPut

Hello World

Example 2: For MS SQL SERVER

Suppose you want to get employees data from employee table for specific employee_ID. And the employee_id user will enter at run time. Like when you search your data on bank's web site . you enters your login and it shows all data belong to you only. Or when you goes for shopping in any store and asks for product abc then and store keeper checks the product availability by searching the product detail. For such scenario user only enter login or product name or ID and gets all data.

```
Create PROCEDURE MyFirstSPwithINParameter
@param1 VARCHAR(20)
as
BEGIN
select EMPLOYEE_ID,FIRST_NAME,DEPARTMENT_ID from
Employees where EMPLOYEE_ID=@param1
END;
Exec MyFirstSPwithINParameter 101
```

EMPLOYEE_ID	*FIRST_NAME*	*DEPARTMENT_ID*
101	Neena	90

Alter existing Procedure:

Now if you want to alter above procedure to add one more column to get as output, then you need to alter the above stored procedure

```
Alter PROCEDURE MyFirstSPwithINParameter
@param1 VARCHAR(20)
as
BEGIN
select EMPLOYEE_ID,FIRST_NAME,Salary,DEPARTMENT_ID
from Employees where EMPLOYEE_ID=@param1
END;
Exec MyFirstSPwithINParameter 101
```

EMPLOYEE_ID	*FIRST_NAME*	*Salary*	*DEPARTMENT_ID*
101	Neena	17000	90

Example 3; For MS SQL SERVER (To insert values in Table locations)

```
select * from locations
```

Location_ID	*Street_Address*	*Postal_Code*	*City*	*State_Province*	*Country_ID*
1400	2014 Jabberwocky Rd	26192	Southlake	Texas	US
1500	2011 Interiors Bld	99236	South San Franciso	California	US
1700	2004 Charade Rd	98199	Seattle	Washington	US
1800	460 Bloor St. W.	ON M5S 1XB	Toronto	Ontario	CA
2500	Magdalen Centre, The Oxford Science Park	OX9 9ZB	Oxford	Oxford	UK

```
Create PROCEDURE Insert_Locations
(@Location_ID numeric(4,0),
@Street_address varchar(200),
@Postal_code varchar(50),
@City         varchar(50),
@State_province       varchar(50),
@Country_Id           varchar(50))
AS INSERT INTO Locations
     (LOCATION_ID
     ,STREET_ADDRESS
     ,POSTAL_CODE
     ,CITY
     ,STATE_PROVINCE
     ,COUNTRY_ID)
VALUES
     (@Location_ID,
     @Street_address,
     @Postal_code,
     @City,
     @State_province,
     @Country_Id)
GO
execute Insert_Locations 12,'202 streat no 4',300043, 'From SP',
'Wega', 'SP'
```

select * from locations

Location_ID	*Street_Address*	*Postal_Code*	*City*	*State_Province*	*Country_ID*
1400	2014 Jabberwocky Rd	26192	Southlake	Texas	US
1500	2011 Interiors Bld	99236	South San Francisco	California	US
1700	2004 Charade Rd	98199	Seattle	Washington	US
1800	460 Bloor St. W.	ON M5S 1XB	Toronto	Ontario	CA
2500	Magdalen Centre, The Oxford Science Park	OX9 9ZB	Oxford	Oxford	UK
12	202 streat no 4	300043	FromSP	Wega	SP

Example: For My SQL

```
CREATE OR REPLACE PROCEDURE MyFirstSPwithIN Parameter (param1 IN VARCHAR2)
IS
BEGIN
DBMS_OUTPUT.PUT_LINE ('Hello ' || param1);
END;
/
Exec MyFirstSPwithINParameter ('World);
```

OutPut

Hello World

Example 2 : With select statement

```
DELIMITER //
CREATE PROCEDURE MyFirstSPwithINParameter (IN param1 VARCHAR (255))
BEGIN
select EMPLOYEE_ID,FIRST_NAME,Salary,DEPARTMENT_ID from Employees where EMPLOYEE_ID=@param1
END //
DELIMITER;
CALL MyFirstSPwithINParameter (101)
```

OutPut

EMPLOYEE_ID	*FIRST_NAME*	*Salary*	*DEPARTMENT_ID*
101	Neena	17000	90

20.1.2 Parameter: OUT – When you use OUT parameter in the stored parameter you must get the value from the stored procedure at the time of execution/call of the parameter. Oracle, DB2 and MySQL support this parameter. In SQL server you can use Out or OUTPUT parameter. Out parameter is similar to return type in Functions. You will see more about Function in dedicated chapter for Functions.

Example: For Oracle

```
CREATE OR REPLACE PROCEDURE emp_name (id IN
    NUMBER, emp_name OUT NUMBER)
IS
BEGIN
SELECT first_name INTO emp_name
FROM employees WHERE employee_id = id;
END;
/
```

You can call stored procedure in PL/SQL block also.

```
DECLARE
EmpName varchar(20);
CURSOR id_cur SELECT employee_id FROM employees;
BEGIN
FOR emp_rec in id_cur
LOOP
emp_name(emp_rec.employee_id, empName);
dbms_output.putline('The employee ' || empName || ' has id ' ||
    emp-rec.employee_id);
END LOOP;
END;
/
```

Example: For Sql Server Out or Output

```
CREATE PROCEDURE spGetEmployeeCountByJobID
@JobID nvarchar(20),
```

```
@EmployeeCount int Output
AS
BEGIN
SELECT @EmployeeCount = COUNT(EMPLOYEE_ID)
FROM employees
WHERE JOB_ID = @JobID
END
```

You can Execute it with Declare

```
DECLARE @EmployeeTotal int
EXECUTE spGetEmployeeCountByJobID 'IT_PROG',
@EmployeeTotal output
PRINT @EmployeeTotal
```

Output

3

20.1.3 Parameter: IN OUT – When you use IN OUT parameter in the stored parameter you pass a value for the argument and get the value from the stored procedure at the time of execution/call of the parameter. Oracle, DB2 and My SQL support this parameter.

Note: The total data size of all input and all output parameters in a Stored PROCEDURE cannot exceed 64000 bytes.

Example: For Oracle (to swap value a to value b)

```
CREATE OR REPLACE PROCEDURE SWAPVALUE AS
A NUMBER :=1000;
B NUMBER :=5000;
PROCEDURE MYFIRSTSWAP(X IN OUT NUMBER,Y IN OUT
NUMBER) AS
C NUMBER;
BEGIN
C := X;
X := Y;
Y := C;
END MYFIRSTSWAP;
```

```
BEGIN
MYFIRSTSWAP (A,B);
DBMS_OUTPUT.PUT_LINE('A = ' || TO_CHAR(A));
DBMS_OUTPUT.PUT_LINE('B = ' || TO_CHAR(B));
END;
/
EXECUTE SWAP_TEST;
A = 5000
B = 1000
```

Example: with Employees and Departments table for Oracle

```
Declare
Mylast_name employees.last_name%TYPE;
- -% type will assign data type of last_name column data type to
- - Mylast_name.
MyDepartmentName departments.Department_name%Type
- -% type will assign data type of Department_name column data
- - type to MyDepartmentName.
Begin
Select last_name, department_name into Mylast_name, My
    Department Name
From employees.e, Departments d
Where e. department_id=d.department_id
And e.employee_id=101;
DBMS_OUT.PUT_LINE(Mylast_name || ' belongs to '|| My Depart-
ment Name ||' department.');
End;
/
```

Output

Kochhar belongs to Executive department

20.2 Drop Stored Procedure

Dropping a Stored procedure will remove that stored procedure from database.

Syntax: For Oracle /SQL Server

Drop Procedure Procedure name

Syntax: My SQL

Drop Procedure IF EXISTS Procedure name

The IF EXISTS clause is used to prevent an error in case the procedure does not exist.

Exercise

1. Write a stored procedure in Oracle to insert values in Departments table.
2. Write a stored procedure in Oracle to update values in Departments table.
3. Write a stored procedure in Oracle to update values in Location table.
4. Write a stored procedure in Oracle to swap values in Departments table.

Chapter - 21

Cursor

A Cursor is a pointer of the context area. Context area is a place of memory allocated by oracle, to contain necessary information to complete the process along with number of rows number of rows proceed by the statement. Cursor allows you to fetch and process all rows returned by the SQL select statement, one by one row. You can refer the named cursor in the program.

Example:

Declare

Cursor MyFirstCursor is

Select * from Employees where Employee_Id in (101,100,108)

21.1 Types of Cursors

There are two types of Cursor

21.1.1 IMPLICIT CURSOR: Implicit Cursor is by default cursor. Whenever you don't define a cursor for SQL DML statement Implicit cursor works for that to receive the data that is to select, insert, delete or update. Like each insert statement need a place to receive the data that is to be inserted in the data base table, Implicit cursor makes it available for that. Implicit cursor can't tell you the number of rows will get affect by an update or delete.The most recently open statement's cursor know as 'SQL %' implicit cursor.

Example:

```
Begin
    Update table EMP set ename ='Imp_CUR_UPDATE'
    Where ename like 'A%';
    DBMS_OUTPUT.PUT_LINE (SQL% ROWCOUNT);
End;
```

21.1.2 EXPLICIT CURSOR: Explicit cursor is those which defined by user explicitly in PL/SQL block. You have all control over explicit Cursor. You need to declare it first in declaration section and then you can use it in that PL/SQL Program.

Explicit cursor consist of the following steps:

1. DECLARING- Explicit cursor need to declare in declaration section to initialize in it memory.
2. OPENING –need to open before using it to allocate memory.
3. FETCHING-After opening you can use that cursor to fetch data from it.
4. CLOSING-After use you need to close the cursor to release the memory allocation.

Example:

```
Declare
Cursor MyFirstCursor is
Select * from Employees where Employee_Id in (101,100,108)
```

21.2 Attributes of cursor

There are four attributes of Cursor.

%NOTFOUND - is a Boolean attribute that returns TRUE if FETCH does not return a row, and FALSE if it does.

%FOUND - is a Boolean attribute that re-turns TRUE if FETCH returns a row, and FALSE if it does not.

%ROWCOUNT – Returns number of records fetched from a cursor at that point in time.

%ISOPEN - is a Boolean attribute that re-turns TRUE if cursor is open, FALSE if it is not.

21.3 Cursor Declaration, Opening, Fetching and closing

```
declare
    ename varchar(20);
    Cursor MyCur_ename is select First_name from Employees
    where EMPLOYEE_ID = 101;
begin
    Open MyCur_ename;
    Fetch MyCur_ename into ename;
    dbms_output.put_line('Employee Name is'|| ename);
    Close Cur_ename;
end;
```

Output

Employee Name is Neena

Exercise

1. Write a PL/SQL program with cursor to select * record from employees table and print with department name.

Chapter - 22

Function

A Function in data base also known as user defined function or stored function. Function is a set of PL/SQL statement which can be called by its name. It is similar like store procedure except it must return a value. Function can be called from SQL and PL/SQL. You can't use User defined functions in situations that require an unchanging definition. Thus, you cannot use user-defined functions -In a CHECK constraint clause of a CREATE TABLE or ALTER TABLE statement and In a DEFAULT clause of a CREATE TABLE or ALTER TABLE statement. When you call a function from within a query or DML statement, the function cannot have OUT or IN OUT parameters.

22.1. Function creation

```
CREATE FUNCTION get_sal(empid IN NUMBER)
RETURN NUMBER
IS sal NUMBER(11,2);
BEGIN
SELECT salary
INTO sal
FROM employees
WHERE employee_id = empid;
RETURN(sal);
END;
/
```

```
Select get_sal(101) from dual;
```

Example: MS SQL SERVER

```
Alter FUNCTION MyFirstFuncforemp
(
@input VARCHAR(250)
)
RETURNS table
AS Return
(
Select EMPLOYEE_ID, FIRST_NAME, DEPARTMENT_ID from
    Employees where FIRST_NAME=@input
)
```

Note: In above Example you noticed Alter instead of Create. After Creation you will find that for any change in created function you will use Alter to update existent function.

22.2 Calling function

Example: For Oracle

```
Select get_sal (101) from dual;
```

Example: For MS SQL Server

```
select * from MyFirstFuncforemp ('Steven')
```

Output

EMPLOYEE_ID	*FIRST_NAME*	*DEPARTMENT_ID*
100	Steven	90

23.3 Dropping Function

```
Drop Function MyFirstFuncforemp
```

Exercise

1. Create a function to get bonus for each employee, which is
   If salary <6000 then 20
   Else 25

Chapter - 23

Trigger

Database allows you to create and store a procedure to implicitly execute when insert, update or Delete statement is issued against the related table, that stored procedure known as Trigger. Stored procedure and trigger are similar but there are difference like: stored procedure you need to execute explicitly. Trigger executes implicitly on insert, update or delete on relevant table.You can create trigger in MS SQL Server and Sybase also. In SQL server and Sybase triggers are after trigger. Means trigger fires after Insert, update or delete. And if not satisfied the condition of trigger then do rollback on table statement. In Oracle you have on, before and after all types of triggers for update, insert and delete. Also you have row level and statement level triggers. Oracle stores the pcode (pseudo-code) after coalition of trigger just like stored procedure. You can keep trigger in either Enabled or disabled mode.

Example: To Enable a trigger
Alter Trigger MyFirstTrigger Enable;
Example: To disable a trigger
Alter Trigger MyFirstTrigger Disable;
Example: To disable all trigger created on a table
Alter Trigger Employees Disable all triggers;
Example: To Enable all trigger created on a table
Alter Trigger Employees Enable all triggers;
Example: create a table dept (deptno, total_sal) to store total salary for each department from employees table. Then run below code.

```
CREATE TRIGGER total_salary
AFTER DELETE OR INSERT OR UPDATE OF Deaprtment_ID,
    Salary ON employees
FOR EACH ROW BEGIN
IF DELETING OR (UPDATING AND :old.Deaprtment_ID != :
    new.Deaprtment_ID)
THEN UPDATE dept
SET total_sal = total_sal - : old.sal
WHERE deptno = : old.deptno;
END IF;
IF INSERTING OR (UPDATING AND :old.deptno != :new.deptno)
THEN UPDATE dept
SET total_sal = total_sal + :new.sal
WHERE deptno = : new.deptno;
END IF;
IF (UPDATING AND :old.deptno = :new.deptno AND :old.sal !=
    :new.sal )
THEN UPDATE dept
SET total_sal = total_sal - :old.sal + :new.sal
WHERE deptno = :new.deptno;
END IF;
END;
```

Now whenever user will insert/update/delete any row from employees table this trigger will fire and update dept table accordingly.

23.1 Types of Trigger- in different database there are different types of triggers

Oracle: In oracle

1. Statement level Trigger: when schema level like table modified and when user logon or logoff events occur. Oracle 10g and above only supports this type of trigger. Schema-level triggers refer and fire on different event like.

After creation- Fires after Creation of schema object like Table
Before Alter- Fires before altering the schema object like Table
After Alter- Fires after altering the schema object like Table

Before Drop- Fires before dropping the schema object like Table

After Drop- Fires after dropping the schema object like Table

2. Row level Trigger-Fires before or after *any column value of a row* changes

3. Column Level Trigger Fires before or after the *specified column* changes

4. For Each Row Type – Fires once for each row of the result set affected by an insert/update/delete

5. For Each statement Type -Fire only once for the entire result set, but fires each time the statement is executed

Example: MS SQL Server

Microsoft SQL Server supports triggers either after or instead of insert, update or delete operation. They can be set on tables. view can be referenced only by an INSTEAD OF trigger.

23.2 Triggering a Trigger

```
Create or replace trigger MyFirstTrigger
    After Delete on Employees
    For each row
Begin
    If : old.employee_id =101 then
    Raise _aaplication_error ('you can't delete this row');
    End if;
End;
/
Delete from employees where employee.id=101;
Output -You can't delete this row
```

Exercise

1. Create a trigger to ask question before deleting any row from employees table.

Chapter - 24

Collections

An Orders Group of same types of elements called as collection. Lists and Array are example of collection. In collection each element must have a unique subscript that determines its positions. collection must have one dimension. You can also create collection with multiple dimension by making collection as an element of collection.

24.1 Types of Collections

1. Nested Table – No upper limit or dynamically increasable upper limit).
2. Index by Table also known as associative array. In other programming language it is also known as hash table.
3. Varrays also known as variable size array.

24.1.1 Nested Table – In general an array have fixed Upper limit with consecutive subscript. In nested table you can create an array with no explicit Upper limit. You can increase its upper limit and its size dynamically. And you can have nested table with non-consecutive subscript. Means in nested table you can delete elements. To delete element you can use built in procedure DELETE. You can use built in function next to iterate any series of subscript. You can declare it inside or outside of PL/SQL block with Create Type. In case of referencing non-existent element it raises system defined error SUBSSCRIPT_BEYOND_COUNT. you must have to initialize and extend it before assigned an element. There are some limitation of using element type in Nested Table. Like you can't use below listed element type in Nested Table:

BINARY_INTEGER, PLS_INTEGER, STRING, REF CURSOR, BOOLEAN, LONG, LONG ROW etc.

Example: General array for 10 elements (number)

1	2	3	4	5	6	7	8	9	10
x1	x2	x3	x4	x5	x6	x7	x8	x9	x10

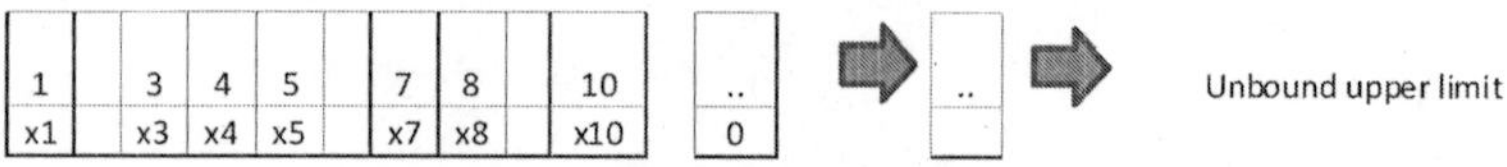

You can use nested table when you don't have upper limit of index values or your index values are not consecutive or you need to delete or update some on the value.

Example: For Oracle

```
CREATE TYPE Locations AS TABLE OF VARCHAR2(64);
CREATE TABLE department (
    name VARCHAR2(20),
    director VARCHAR2(20),
    office VARCHAR2(20),
    courses CourseList);
/
NESTED TABLE courses STORE AS courses_tab;
/
```

Example 2: Nested table for oracle

```
CREATE TYPE Dept AS TABLE OF VARCHAR2(10) — you
    - - create a type
/
CREATE TYPE emp1 AS OBJECT
( empid_num INTEGER(4),
fname VARCHAR2(25),
lname VARCHAR2(35),
deptid CHAR(2),
deptdetails dept)
/- - you declared nested table as attribute of dept type
/
```

You can also create a type of table's column. When you create a type Of column data then that type will work like associated table'Column type.

Example:

Declare Type EmployeeList is Type of employees.employee_ID%Type

You can also create a type of table's column with NOT NULL

Example:

Declare Type EmployeeList is Type of employees.employee_ID%Type NOT NULL

You can also create a type of another existing type

Example:

Declare

Type EmployeeListNew is Type of EmployeeList;

You can also create a type of Cursor type:

Example:

Declare

Type EmployeeList is Type of employees.employee_ID%Type

Cursor MyFirstCursor is Select * from Departments

- - You will learn more about Cursor in dedicated chapter of Cursor - - in this book.

Type DEPTTYPE is Type of MyFirstCursor%ROWTYPE

In above example DEPTTYPE will work like MyFirstCursor Rowtype

You can use %ROWTYPE to define a type of rowtype of a cursor or table.

In Nested table you can pass multiple element, because there are no upper limit .

Example: for passing multiple elements

```
DECLARE
TYPE EmployeeList IS TABLE OF VARCHAR2 (16);
MyEmployeeEmployeeList;
BEGIN
my_MyEmployee:=MyEmployee ('NEWEMPLOYEE', 'NEW-
    EMPLOYEE2', 'NEWEMPLOYEE2');
END;
```

Example: programming to reference a Nested table element with loop

```
DECLARE
TYPE EmployeeList IS TABLE OF VARCHAR2 (16);
MyEmployeeEmployeeList:=
MyEmployee ('NEWEMPLOYEE', 'NEWEMPLOYEE2', 'NEW-
EMPLOYEE2');
BEGIN
    FOR i IN MyEmployee.FIRST..MyEmployee.LAST
    LOOP
        IF MyEmployee (i) = 'NEWEMPLOYEE2' THEN
        NULL;
    END IF;
        END LOOP;
END;
```

24.1.2 Variables-Size Array or VArray–Varrays are array of fixed number of elements, used sequential number as subscript and always have space allocated for each of the elements. You can increase the number of elements at run time. It can be automatically NULL. You can declare it inside or outside of PL/SQL block with Create Type. You must have to initialize it before assigning an element. You can also store it in database table. In case of referencing nonexistent element it raises system defined error SUBSSCRIPT_BEYOND_COUNT.

Example:

1	2	3	4	5	6				
x1	x2	x3	x4	x5	x6				

Upper limit=10

Varray minimum lower limit is 1 and upper limit is extendable, but you must have to define its upper limit at definition.

Example: For Oracle

```
CREATE TYPE Dept AS VARRAY(100) OF VARCHAR2(20) - -
you create a type
/
CREATE tableemp1
    (empid_num INTEGER(4),
        fname VARCHAR2(20),
        lname VARCHAR2(20),
        deptid CHAR(2),
        empdetails dept
);
/
```

You can declare a variable of the type of collection

Example:

```
DECLARE
    TYPE nested_typecollection IS TABLE OF VARCHAR2 (100);
    TYPE varray_typecollection IS VARRAY (100) OF INTEGER;
v1 nested_ typecollection;
v2 varray_ typecollection;
```

Example 2: With % TYPE – it gives you flexibility of changing variables data type by changing the collection's element definition.

```
DECLARE
    TYPE FirstName IS VARRAY(50) OF emp;
F1 FirstName;
F2 F1 %TYPE;
```

Example: With %TYPE and % ROWTYPE

```
Declare
Type EmployeeList is Type of employees.employee_ID % Type
Cursor MyFirstCursor is Select * from Departments
Type DEPTTYPE is Varray(25) of MyFirstCursor% ROWTYPE
```

Example: Varray of Record Type-You can also use RECORD TYPE to define a VARRAY element type.

```
Declare
    Type EmployeeList IS record
    (First_Name varchar(25),
    Last_name varchar(25));
    Type DEPTTYPE is Varray (25) of EmployeeList;
```

Example: using varray in SQL Query

```
Create Type DeptList as varray(25) of departments;
Declare
    My Dept DeptList;
Begin
    Select Department_Name into MyDept from departments where
    department_ID=60;
End;
```

Example: with Bulk and SQL for inserting data into Table of type varray

```
Create type A1 is varray(20) of integer;
/
Create table B1 (Col1A1);— Col1is a column in table B1 of type
    A1
Insert into B1values (A1 (1,3,5));
    Insert into B1values (A1 (1000, 3000, 5000));
    Insert into B1 values (A1 (123, 456, 789));
    Insert into B1 values (A1 (147, 258, 369));
    Insert into B1 values (A1 (321, 654, 987));
Declare
Type A2 is table of A1;
Var1 A2;
Begin
    Select Col1 BULK COLLECT INTO Var1 from B1;
dbms_output.put_line (Var1.count);
End;
/
```

OutPut

5

- - total 5 rows inserted into table B1

24.1.3 Index By tables/ Associative Array–An Associative array or Index by Table is a set of Positive or negative key values each should be unique and locate to a corresponding value in the array. Key can be integer or string. You can not store it in database table. It has no explicit upper limit. You can sparse it with non-sequential values. You can declare it inside PL/SQL blocks only also you can assign directly without initialization. It can store data by using primary key value as INDEX where key values are not sequential. In case of referencing non-existent element it raise system defined error NO_DATA_FOUND. You can use below listed element type BINARY_INTEGER, PLS_INTEGER, STRING, REF CURSOR, BOOLEAN, LONG etc.

Example:

TYPE *typename* IS TABLE OF *elementtype* [NOT NULL]
INDEX BY [BINARY_INTEGER | PLS_INTEGER | VARCHAR2 (*sizelimit*)];
INDEX BY *keytype*;

Note: In Associative Array keytype can be any of the data type except Char, Character, ROW, LONG ROW and ROWID.

Example: declaring Collection Types

```
DECLARE
TYPE nestedtype IS TABLE OF VARCHAR2 (200);
TYPE varraytype IS VARRAY (100) OF INTEGER;
TYPE associativearraytype IS TABLE OF NUMBER
    INDEXED BY BINARY_INTEGER;
Var1 nestedtype;
Var2 varraytype;
Var3 associativearraytype;
```

24.2 Collection Methods- Is a built-in function or procedure that operates on collections and you can call it using dot (.) notation. There are 10 types of collection methods.

24.2.1 FIRST and LAST–It returns first(smallest) and last (largest) index number of a collection. You can use it in loop to start with first and end with last record/index.

Example:

FOR i IN Dept.FIRST..Dept.LAST LOOP

PRIOR and NEXT –PRIOR returns preceding index number and NEXT returns succeeding index number.in case no preceding number of index then PRIOR returns NULL and in case no succeeding index number then NEXT returns NULL.

i:=dept.NEXT(i);

i:=dept.PRIOR(i);— will return NULL

24.2.2 EXISTS –It return true if given number of element exist in collection. Else it will return false. You can use EXISTS (n) with number or variable to check either element or value does existing or not. If you are using an element which does not exist then PL/SQL raises Error SUBSCRIPTION_OUTSIDE_LIMIT in Nested Table or Varray and NO_DATA_FOUND in associative array. To avoid such error you should use EXISTS to check existence of element.

Example:

IF dept.EXISTS (i) THEN dept (i):= new_dept;

24.2.3 COUNT –It returns number of element of a collection.

Example:

```
Select Col1 BULK COLLECT INTO Var1 from B1;
     dbms_output.put_line (Var1.count);
```

24.2.4 LIMIT –It Returns upper limit of index by table. And returns NULL in Nested table or Varray which has no upper limit.

Example:

IF MyFirstType.LIMIT = 25 THEN...

24.2.5 EXTEND –It increases the size of a nested table or varray. You cant use it in associative Array.

Example:

A1.EXTEND - - it will append one NULL element to A1 varray.

A1.EXTEND (2) - - it will append 2 NULL elements to A1 varray.

A1.EXTEND (2, 1) - - it will append 2 copy of element 1

24.2.6 TRIM –you can use it to remove number of elements from collection.

Example:

A1.TRIM- - - it will remove 1 element from A1
A1.TRIM (2) - - it will remove 2 elements from A1

Note: if you will use value of n>A1.count then it will raise error SUBSCRIPT_BEYOND_COUNT.

24.2.7 DELETE –you can use it to remove elements from collection.

Example:

A1.DELETE - - it will delete all elements from A1
A1.DELETE (2) - - it will delete 2 elements from A1
A1.DELETE (1000) - - it will delete all elements from A1 with key value 1000.

Exercise

1. Create an associative array to insert 10 new rows in employees table.
2. Create an associative array to delete 2 rows with key value 100 and 101 if exist.

Chapter - 25

Exceptions

Exceptions are used to handle run time error in PL/SQL program. You can see errors at the time of compilation also those are dedicated PL/SQL engine error to report error message to user. You can't handle compile time error through PL/SQL program. You have to correct the cause of error in your program and then can compile again. You can declare exception in declarative section of the PL/SQL block and can handle in exception section. There are two types of Exceptions User Defined and Predefined.

25.1 Syntax of Exception handing

```
Declare
Expname     EXCEPTION;     - - declared exception with name Expname
...
...
BEGIN
...
RAISE Expname;
...            - - any program code here will not be executed.
EXCEPTION
When Expname Then            - - exception will be handle here
....
- - Any program code here will be execute.
END;
```

25.2 Raising Exceptions

Data base raises Exception automatically when internal database error found, but you can raise exception explicitly with RAISE.

Example:

```
BEGIN
    ...
    RAISE Expname; - - Raising Exception here.
    ...        - - any program code here will not be executed.
EXCEPTION
    When Expname Then - - exception wiil be handle here
    ....
    - - Any program code here will be executed.
END;
```

25.3 User Defined Exception

In PL/SQL you can define your own Exception according to your requirement in the program. You can raise user defined exception explicitly, using either a RAISE statement or the procedure DBMS_ STANDARD.RAISE_APPLICATION_ERROR.

Example:

```
DECLARE
  emp_id employees.employee_id % type: = &e_id;
  e_name employees.First_Name % type;
    Exception_invalid_empid EXCEPTION; - - user defined
    exception
  BEGIN
    IF emp_id <= 0 THEN
       RAISE Exception_invalid_empid;
    ELSE
  SELECT First_name INTO e_name
    FROM employees
    WHERE employee_id = emp_id;
    DBMS_OUTPUT.PUT_LINE ('First name of the Employee
    is: '|| e_name);
  END IF;
```

```
EXCEPTION
WHEN Exception_invalid_empid THEN
    dbms_output.put_line ('explicitly Id Should not be negative.');
WHEN No_Data_Found THEN - - predefined exception of database
    dbms_output.put_line ('Employee not Found');
WHEN others THEN
    dbms_output.put_line ('Error!');
END;
/
```

25.4 Pre-Defined Exceptions

PL/SQL provides predefined exception which executes on any violation of programming rule.

Like in above example you can see a predefined exception NO_DATA_FOUND. It will raise when you will provide value of e_id which is not available in table employee.

You have many more predefined exception in PL/SQL.

Pre-Defined Exceptions	*Description*
DUP_VAL_ON_INDEX	raises when duplicate values are to be stored in a column with unique index.
INVALID_CURSOR	raises when opening or closing an unopened/undefined cursor.
INVALID_NUMBER	raises when the conversion of a character string into a number fails because the string does not represent a valid number.
TOO_MANY_ROWS	raises when s SELECT INTO statement returns more than one row.
VALUE_ERROR	raises when an arithmetic, conversion, truncation, or size-constraint error occurs.
ZERO_DIVIDE	raises when an attempt is made to divide a number by zero.

Exercise

1. Write a program to handle Too_Many_Rows pre-defined exception along with unwanted salary like >=50000 for Department id 90.

Chapter - 26

Packages

PL SQL packages are schema object, used to groups logically related PL/SQL Subprograms, types, variables etc. It has two parts Specification (Public) and Body(Private). Specification part is mandatory part. There are some advantages of using package:

26.1 Advantages of Package

1. Information Hiding- In Package specification you can specify subprograms, cursor, variable, type. And in body you can implement all as per your requirement. So implementation part user can't see. So you protect integrity of the package by using this.
2. Reuse of same specification- in Package specification you can do specify subprograms, cursor, variable, type. And in body you can implement all as per your requirement. Another user can also use same specification with different implementation. Or you can also use same specification with different program.
3. Performance- in Package specification you can specify subprograms, cursor, variable, type. And in body you can implement all as per your requirement. You can also use same specification with different program. Reusability of same specification does not need to compile the specification again and again. Once compiled, it stores in memory. So you can only call it with no disk input output (I/O) to increased performance.

4. Modularity- package having separate specification and body as per your requirement. so it is easy to understand and, the interface between package are simple and clearly defined.

26.2 Package specification is the interface part of a package allows you to declare types, cursor, subprograms and variables for use in your programs. Declaration under specification parts are public. And can be call or use from outside of the package.

Example:

```
CREATE PACKAGE MyFirstPackage AS
    PROCEDURE Sal(empid employees.employee_id%type);
END MyFirstPackageSpec;
/
Output
Package created.
```

26.3 Package body Body allows you to do implementation and private declarations. Any subprograms or type or variable etc. not specified in the package specification and available in the package body are private object. You can't call or use from outside of the body.

Example:

```
CREATE OR REPLACE PACKAGE BODY MyFirstPackage AS
    PROCEDURE Sal (empid employees.employee_id%type);
IS
GetSal employees.Salary%type
  BEGIN
    SELECT salary INTO GetSal
    FROM Employees
    WHERE Employees_ID= empid;
    dbms_output.put_line('Salary: '|| GetSal);
  END Sal;
END MyFirstPackage;
/
```

26.4 Using Package elements – you can use package Element with (.) dot notation.

Example:

```
DECLARE
id Employees.Employee_id%type := &emp_id;
BEGIN
MyFirstPackage.Sal (id);
END;
/
```

If you will enter 101 as the value of emp_id

You will get output as :

Salary: 17000

PL/SQL procedure successfully completed.

Exercise

1. Create a package with cursor to fetch all row from employees table
2. Use same package spec and create a body to fetch date from employees table for employee_id > 107.

Chapter - 27

DBMS-Output

DBMS _OUTPUT is a built in package use to display output message from PL/SQL blocks, Subprograms, triggers and packages.

Example:

```
IF grade = 'A' THEN
    dbms_output.put_line('Excellent');
ELSIF grade = 'B' THEN
    dbms_output.put_line('Very Good');
ELSIF grade = 'C' THEN
    dbms_output.put_line('Good');
ELSIF grade = 'D' THEN
    dbms_output. put_line('Pass');
ELSE
    dbms_output.put_line('No such grade');
END IF;
```

27.1 DBMS_OUTPUT Subprograms –it has below listed subprograms.

DBMS_OUTPUT's SubPrograms	***Description***
DBMS_OUTPUT.DISABLE;	Used to disable the package to support output message feature of the package.
DBMS_OUTPUT.ENABLE;	Used to disable the package to output message. Maximum buffer size is 20000 and minimum size is 2000.

	It will raise Exception ORU-10027-Buffer overflow in case cross the maximum buffer size.
DBMS_OUTPUT.GET_LINE	Retrieves a single line of buffered information. Maximum line size is 32767. It will raise Exception ORU-10028- .Line length overflow in case cross the maximum line size.
DBMS_OUTPUT.GET_LINES	Retrieves an array of lines from the buffer.
DBMS_OUTPUT.NEW_LINE;	Terminates a line created with DBMS_OUTPUT.PUT
DBMS_OUTPUT.PUT	Places a line in the buffer
DBMS_OUTPUT.PUT_LINE	Places a partial line in the buffer

Example:

```
DECLARE
Lines dbms_output.char_arr;
Num_lines number;
BEGIN
dbms_output.enable; — enable the package to print message.
dbms_output.put_line('Hello Friends');
dbms_output.put_line('Have a great future with SQL & PL/SQL.');
num_lines := 2;
dbms_output.get_lines(lines, num_lines);
FOR i IN 1..num_lines LOOP
    dbms_output.put_line(lines(i));
END LOOP;
END;
/
```

OutPut
Hello Friends
Have a great future with SQL & PL/SQL.

Exercise

1. Use all subprograms of DBMS_OUTPUT and notice the difference and uses.

Chapter 28

Practice set for Oracle Certification

Exhibit of Employee table.

Employee_id	*First_Name*	*Last_Name*	*E-mail*	*Hire_Date*	*Job_ID*	*Salary*	*Manager_ID*	*Department_ID*
100	Steven	King	SKING	6/17/1987	AD_PRES	24000	NULL	90
101	Neena	Kochhar	NKOCHHAR	9/21/1989	AD_VP	17000	100	90
102	Lex	De Haan	LDEHAAN	1/13/1993	AD_VP	17000	100	90
103	Alexander	Hunold	AHUNOLD	1/3/1990	IT_PROG	9000	102	60
104	Bruce	Emst	BERNST	5/21/1991	IT_PROG	6000	103	60
107	Diana	Lorentz	DLORENTZ	2/7/1999	IT_PROG	4200	103	60
124	Kevin	Mourgos	KMOURGOS	11/16/1999	ST_MAN	5800	100	50
141	Trenna	Rajas	TRAJAS	10/17/1995	ST_CLERK	3500	124	50
142	Curtis	Davies	CDAVIES	1/29/1997	ST_CLERK	3100	124	50
143	Randall	Matos	RMATOS	3/15/1998	ST_CLERK	2600	124	50
144	Peter	Vargas	PVARGAS	7/9/1998	ST_CLERK	2500	124	50
149	Eleni	Zlotkey	EZLOTKEY	1/29/2000	SA_MAN	10500	100	80
174	Ellen	Abel	EABEL	5/11/1996	SA_REP,	1100	149	80
176	Jonathon	Taylor	JTAYLOR	3/24/1998	SA_REP	8600	149	80
178	Kimberely	Grant	KGRANT	5/24/1999	SA_REP	7000	149	NULL
200	Jennifer	Whalen	JWHALEN	9/17/1987	AD_ASST	4400	101	10
201	Mitchael	Hartstein	MHARTSTE	2/17/1996	MK_MAN	13000	100	20
202	Pat	Fay	PFAY	8/17/1997	MK_REP	6000	201	20
205	Shelley	Higgins	SHIGGINS	6/7/1994	AC_MGR	12000	101	110
206	William	Gietz	WGEITZ	6/7/1994	AC_ACCOUNT	8300	205	110

Exhibit of Departments table.

Department_ID	*Department_Name*	*Manager_ID*	*Location_ID*
10	Administration	200	1700
20	Marketing	201	1800
50	Shipping	124	1500
60	IT	103	1400
80	Sales	149	2500
90	Executive	100	1700
110	Accounting	205	1700
190	Contracting	NULL	1700

Exhibit of Locations table.

Location_id	*Street_address*	*Postal_code*	*City*	*State_ province*	*Coun-try_id*
1400	2014 Jabberwocky Rd	26192	Southlake	Texas	US
1500	2011 Interiors Bld	99236	South San Franciso	California	US
1700	2004 Charade Rd	98199	Seattle	Washington	US
1800	460 Bloor St. W.	ON M5S 1XB	Toronto	Ontario	CA
2500	Magdalen Centre, The Oxford Science Park	OX9 9ZB	Oxford	Oxford	UK

Exhibit of Order_Iterms table.

Order_id	*Line_item_id*	*Product_id*	*Unit_price*	*Quantity*
2355	1	2276	1000	31
2356	2	2274	158.5	23
2356	5	2323	15	65
2356	6	2312	495	21
2356	8	2311	987	35
2356	1	2265	365	14
2357	9	2276	23	35

1. You need to load information about new customers from the NEW_CUST table into the tables CUST and CUST_SPECIAL. If a new customer has a credit limit greater than 10,000, then the details have to be inserted into CUST_SPECIAL. All new customer details have to be inserted into the CUST table. Which technique should be used to load the data most efficiently?

A. External table
B. The MERGE command
C. The multi table INSERT command
D. INSERT using WITH CHECK OPTION

2. Which three tasks can be performed using regular expression support in Oracle Database 10g? (Choose three.)

A. It can be used to concatenate two strings.
B. It can be used to find out the total length of the string.
C. It can be used for string manipulation and searching operations.
D. It can be used to format the output for a column or expression having string data.
E. It can be used to find and replace operations for a column or expression having string data.

3. Evaluate the CREATE TABLE statement:

CREATE TABLE products (product_id NUMBER(6) CONSTRAINT prod_id_pk PRIMARY KEY, product_name VARCHAR2(15));

Which statement is true regarding the PROD_ID_PK constraint?

A. It would be created only if a unique index is manually created first.
B. It would be created and would use an automatically created unique index.
C. It would be created and would use an automatically created no unique index.
D. It would be created and remains in a disabled state because no index is specified in the Command.

4. Which two statements are true? (Choose two.)

A. The USER_SYNONYMS view can provide information about private synonyms.
B. The user SYSTEM owns all the base tables and user-accessible views of the data dictionary.
C. All the dynamic performance views prefixed with V$ are accessible to all the database users.
D. The USER_OBJECTS view can provide information about the tables and views created by the user only.

E. DICTIONARY is a view that contains the names of all the data dictionary views that the user can access.

5. View the Exhibit and examine the description of the EMPLOYEES table.

Your company decided to give a monthly bonus of $50 to all the employees who have completed five years in the company. The following statement is written to display the LAST_NAME, DEPARTMENT_ID, and the total annual salary:

SELECT last_name, department_id, salary+50*12 "Annual Compensation" FROM employees.

WHERE MONTHS_BETWEEN(SYSDATE, hire_date)/12 >= 5;

When you execute the statement, the "Annual Compensation" is not computed correctly. What changes would you make to the query to calculate the annual compensation correctly?

A. Change the SELECT clause to SELECT last_name, department_id, salary*12+50 "Annual Compensation".
B. Change the SELECT clause to SELECT last_name, department_id, salary+(50*12) "Annual Compensation".
C. Change the SELECT clause to SELECT last_name, department_id, (salary+50)*12 "Annual Compensation".
D. Change the SELECT clause to SELECT last_name, department_id, (salary*12)+50 "Annual Compensation".

6. Evaluate the following CREATE SEQUENCE statement:

CREATE SEQUENCE seq1

START WITH 100

INCREMENT BY 10

MAXVALUE 200

CYCLE

NOCACHE;

The sequence SEQ1 has generated numbers up to the maximum limit of 200. You issue the

Following SQL statement:

SELECT seq1.nextval FROM dual;

What is displayed by the SELECT statement?

A. 1
B. 10
C. 100
D. an error

7. View the Exhibit and examine the description of the EMPLOYEES table. You want to display the EMPLOYEE_ID, FIRST_NAME, and DEPARTMENT_ID for all the employees who work in the same department and have the same manager as that of the employee having EMPLOYEE_ID 104. To accomplish the task, you execute the following SQL statement:

```
SELECT employee_id, first_name, department_id
FROM employees
WHERE (manager_id, department_id) =(SELECT department_id, manager_id
FROM employees
WHERE employee_id = 104)
AND employee_id <> 104;
```

When you execute the statement it does not produce the desired output. What is the reason for this?

A. The WHERE clause condition in the main query is using the = comparison operator, instead of EXISTS.
B. The WHERE clause condition in the main query is using the = comparison operator, instead of the IN operator.
C. The WHERE clause condition in the main query is using the = comparison operator, instead of the = ANY operator.
D. The columns in the WHERE clause condition of the main query and the columns selected in the subquery should be in the same order.

8. View the Exhibit and examine the description of the Employees table.

You want to add a constraint on the FIRST_NAME column of the Employees table so that the value inserted in the column does not have numbers.

Which SQL statement would you use to accomplish the task?

A. ALTER TABLE EMPLOYEES ADD CONSTRAINT f_name CHECK(REGEXP_LIKE(first_name,'^A-Z')) NOVALIDATE;
B. ALTER TABLE EMPLOYEES ADD CONSTRAINT f_name CHECK(REGEXP_LIKE(first_name,'^[0-9]')) NOVALIDATE;
C. ALTER TABLE EMPLOYEES ADD CONSTRAINT f_name CHECK(REGEXP_LIKE(first_name,'[[:alpha:]]')) NOVALI DATE;
D. ALTER TABLE EMPLOYEES ADD CONSTRAINT f_name CHECK (REGEXP_LIKE (first_name,'[[:digit:]]'))NOVALIDATE;

9. Which three tasks can be performed using regular expression support in

Oracle Database 10g? (Choose three.)

A. It can be used to concatenate two strings.
B. It can be used to find out the total length of the string.
C. It can be used for string manipulation and searching operations.
D. It can be used to format the output for a column or expression having string data.
E. It can be used to find and replace operations for a column or expression having string data.

10. View the Exhibit and examine the structure of the Employee table which is not partitioned and not an index-organized table.

Evaluate the following SQL statement:

ALTER TABLE Employees

DROP COLUMN first_name;

Which two statements are true regarding the above command? (Choose two.)

A. The FIRST_NAME column would be dropped provided it does not contain any data.
B. The FIRST_NAME column would be dropped provided at least one or more columns remain in the table.
C. The FIRST_NAME column can be rolled back provided the SET UNUSED option is added to the above SQL statement.

D. The FIRST_NAME column can be dropped even if it is part of a composite PRIMARY KEY provided the CASCADE option is used.

11. Which two statements are true? (Choose two.)

A. The USER_SYNONYMS view can provide information about private synonyms.

B. The user SYSTEM owns all the base tables and user-accessible views of the data dictionary.

C. All the dynamic performance views prefixed with V$ are accessible to all the database users.

D. The USER_OBJECTS view can provide information about the tables and views created by the user only.

E. DICTIONARY is a view that contains the names of all the data dictionary views that the user can access.

12. View the Exhibit and examine the description of the EMPLOYEES table.

You want to display the EMPLOYEE_ID, FIRST_NAME, and DEPARTMENT_ID for all the employees who work in the same department and have the same manager as that of the employee having EMPLOYEE_ID 104. To accomplish the task, you execute the following SQL statement:

```
SELECT employee_id, first_name, department_id
FROM employees
WHERE (manager_id, department_id) =(SELECT department_id,
    manager_id
FROM employees
WHERE employee_id = 104)
AND employee_id <> 104;
```

When you execute the statement it does not produce the desired output. What is the reason for this?

A. The WHERE clause condition in the main query is using the = comparison operator, instead of EXISTS.

B. The WHERE clause condition in the main query is using the = comparison operator, instead of the IN operator.

C. The WHERE clause condition in the main query is using the = comparison operator, instead of the = ANY operator.

D. The columns in the WHERE clause condition of the main query and the columns selected in the subquery should be in the same order.

13. View the Exhibit and examine the structure of the EMPLOYEES table.

You want to retrieve hierarchical data of the employees using the top-down hierarchy. Which SQL clause would let you choose the direction to walk through the hierarchy tree?

A. WHERE
B. HAVING
C. GROUP BY
D. START WITH
E. CONNECT BY PRIOR

14. Which two statements are true regarding the execution of the correlated subqueries? (Choose two.)

A. The nested query executes after the outer query returns the row.
B. The nested query executes first and then the outer query executes.
C. The outer query executes only once for the result returned by the inner query.
D. Each row returned by the outer query is evaluated for the results returned by the inner query.

15. OE and SCOTT are the users in the database. The ORDERS table is owned by OE. Evaluate the statements issued by the DBA in the following sequence:

```
CREATE ROLE r1;
GRANT SELECT, INSERT ON oe.orders TO r1;
GRANT r1 TO scott;
GRANT SELECT ON oe.orders TO scott;
REVOKE SELECT ON oe.orders FROM scott;
```

What would be the outcome after executing the statements?

A. SCOTT would be able to query the OE.ORDERS table.
B. SCOTT would not be able to query the OE.ORDERS table.

C. The REVOKE statement would remove the SELECT privilege from SCOTT as well as from the roleR1.

D. The REVOKE statement would give an error because the SELECT privilege has been granted to the roleR1.

16. Evaluate the following SQL statement:

ALTER TABLE hr.emp

SET UNUSED (mgr_id);

Which statement is true regarding the effect of the above SQL statement?

A. Any synonym existing on the EMP table would have to be re-created.

B. Any constraints defined on the MGR_ID column would be removed by the above command.

C. Any views created on the EMP table that include the MGR_ID column would have to be dropped and re-created.

D. Any index created on the MGR_ID column would continue to exist until the DROP UNUSED COLUMNS command is executed.

17. EMPDET is an external table containing the columns EMPNO and ENAME. Which command would work in relation to the EMPDET table?

A. UPDATE empdet SET ename = 'Amit' WHERE empno = 1234;

B. DELETE FROM empdet WHERE ename LIKE 'J%';

C. CREATE VIEW empvu AS SELECT * FROM empdept;

D. CREATE INDEX empdet_idx ON empdet(empno);

18. In which scenario would you use the ROLLUP operator for expression or Columns within a GROUP BY clause?

A. to find the groups forming the subtotal in a row

B. to create group-wise grand totals for the groups specified within a GROUP BY clause

C. to create a grouping for expressions or columns specified within a GROUP BY clause in one direction, from right to left for calculating the subtotals

D. to create a grouping for expressions or columns specified within a GROUP BY clause in all possible directions, which is cross-tabular report for calculating the subtotals.

19. View the Exhibit and examine the details of the EMPLOYEES table.

Evaluate the following SQL statement:

SELECT phone_number,

REGEXP_REPLACE(phone_number,'([[:digit:]]{3})\.([[:digit:]]{3})\.([[:digit:]]{4})', '(\1) \2-\3')

"PHONE NUMBER"

FROM employees;

The query was written to format the PHONE_NUMBER for the employees. Which option would be the correct format in the output?

A. xxx-xxx-xxxx

B. (xxx) xxxxxxx

C. (xxx) xxx-xxxx

D. xxx-(xxx)-xxxx

20. Which statement correctly grants a system privilege?

A. GRANT EXECUTE ON proc1TO PUBLIC;

B. GRANT CREATE VIEW ON table1 TO user1;

C. GRANT CREATE TABLE TO user1, user2;

D. GRANT CREATE SESSION TO ALL;

21. Which statement is true regarding external tables?

A. The default REJECT LIMIT for external tables is UNLIMITED.

B. The data and metadata for an external table are stored outside the database.

C. ORACLE_LOADER and ORACLE_DATAPUMP have exactly the same functionality when used with an external table.

D. The CREATE TABLE AS SELECT statement can be used to unload data into regular table in the database from an external table.

22. Which two statements are true regarding the EXISTS operator used in the correlated subqueries? (Choose two.)

A. The outer query stops evaluating the result set of the inner query when the first value is found.
B. It is used to test whether the values retrieved by the inner query exist in the result of the outer query.
C. It is used to test whether the values retrieved by the outer query exist in the result set of the inner query.
D. The outer query continues evaluating the result set of the inner query until all the values in the result set are processed.

23. non-correlated subquery can be defined as ____.

A. a set of sequential queries, all of which must always return a single value
B. a set of sequential queries, all of which must return values from the same table
C. a SELECT statement that can be embedded in a clause of another SELECT statement only
D. a set of one or more sequential queries in which generally the result of the inner query is used as the search value in the outer query

24. You need to create a table for a banking application with the following considerations:

(1) You want a column in the table to store the duration of the credit period.
(2) The data in the column should be stored in a format such that it can be easily added and subtracted with
(3) date type data without using the conversion functions.
(4) The maximum period of the credit provision in the application is 30 days.
(5) The interest has to be calculated for the number of days an individual has taken a credit for.

Which data type would you use for such a column in the table?

A. INTERVAL YEAR TO MONTH
B. INTERVAL DAY TO SECOND
C. TIMESTAMP WITH TIME ZONE
D. TIMESTAMP WITH LOCAL TIME ZONE

25. Which statements are true regarding the hierarchical query in Oracle

Database 10g? (Choose all that apply.)

A. It is possible to retrieve data only in top-down hierarchy.
B. It is possible to retrieve data in top-down or bottom-up hierarchy.
C. It is possible to remove an entire branch from the output of the hierarchical query.
D. You cannot specify conditions when you retrieve data by using a hierarchical query.

26. Which two statements are true regarding views? (Choose two.)

A. A simple view in which column aliases have been used cannot be updated.
B. A subquery used in a complex view definition cannot contain group functions or joins.
C. Rows cannot be deleted through a view if the view definition contains the DISTINCT keyword.
D. Rows added through a view are deleted from the table automatically when the view is dropped.
E. The OR REPLACE option is used to change the definition of an existing view without dropping and re-creating it.
F. The WITH CHECK OPTION constraint can be used in a view definition to restrict the columns displayed through the view.

27. Evaluate the following SQL statements in the given order:

```
DROP TABLE dept;

CREATE TABLE dept

(deptno NUMBER(3) PRIMARY KEY,

deptname VARCHAR2(10));

DROP TABLE dept;

FLASHBACK TABLE dept TO BEFORE DROP;
```

Which statement is true regarding the above FLASHBACK operation?

A. It recovers only the first DEPT table.
B. It recovers only the second DEPT table.

C. It does not recover any of the tables because FLASHBACK is not possible in this case.
D. It recovers both the tables but the names would be changed to the ones assigned in the RECYCLEBIN.

28. Evaluate the following statements:

CREATE TABLE digits

(id NUMBER(2),

description VARCHAR2(15));

INSERT INTO digits VALUES (1,'ONE');

UPDATE digits SET description ='TWO' WHERE id=1;

INSERT INTO digits VALUES (2,'TWO');

COMMIT;

DELETE FROM digits;

SELECT description FROM digits

VERSIONS BETWEEN TIMESTAMP MINVALUE AND MAXVALUE;

What would be the outcome of the above query?

A. It would not display any values.
B. It would display the value TWO once.
C. It would display the value TWO twice.
D. It would display the values ONE, TWO, and TWO.

29. Which statements are correct regarding indexes? (Choose all that apply.)

A. When a table is dropped, the corresponding indexes are automatically dropped.
B. For each DML operation performed, the corresponding indexes are automatically updated.
C. Indexes should be created on columns that are frequently referenced as part of an expression.
D. A non-deferrable PRIMARY KEY or UNIQUE KEY constraint in a table automatically creates a unique index.

30. SCOTT is a user in the database.

Evaluate the commands issued by the DBA:

1. CREATE ROLE mgr;
2. GRANT CREATE TABLE, SELECT ON oe.orders TO mgr;
3. GRANT mgr, create table TO SCOTT;

Which statement is true regarding the execution of the above commands?

A. Statement 1 would not execute because the WITH GRANT option is missing.

B. Statement 1 would not execute because the IDENTIFIED BY <password> clause is missing.

C. Statement 3 would not execute because role and system privileges cannot be granted together in a single GRANT statement.

D. Statement 2 would not execute because system privileges and object privileges cannot be granted together in a single GRANT command.

31. Which statement best describes the GROUPING function?

A. It is used to set the order for the groups to be used for calculating the grand totals and subtotals.

B. It is used to form various groups to calculate total and subtotals created using ROLLUP and CUBE operators.

C. It is used to identify if the NULL value in an expression is a stored NULL value or created by ROLLUP or CUBE.

D. It is used to specify the concatenated group expressions to be used for calculating the grand totals and subtotals.

32. Which two statements are true regarding operators used with subqueries?

(Choose two)

A. The NOT IN operator is equivalent to IS NULL.

B. The <ANY operator means less than the maximum.

C. =ANY and =ALL operators have the same functionality.

D. The IN operator cannot be used in single-row subqueries.

E. The NOT operator can be used with IN, ANY and ALL operators.

33. Given below are the SQL statements executed in a user session:

```
CREATE TABLE product
(pcode NUMBER(2),
pname VARCHAR2(10));
INSERT INTO product VALUES(1, 'pen');
INSERT INTO product VALUES (2,'pencil');
SAVEPOINT a;
UPDATE product SET pcode = 10 WHERE pcode = 1;
SAVEPOINT b;
DELETE FROM product WHERE pcode = 2;
COMMIT;
DELETE FROM product WHERE pcode=10;
ROLLBACK TO SAVEPOINT a;
```

Which statement describes the consequences?

A. SQL statement would be rolled back.

B. Both the DELETE statements would be rolled back.

C. Only the second DELETE statement would be rolled back.

D. Both the DELETE statements and the UPDATE statement would be rolled back.

34. Evaluate the following CREATE TABLE command:

```
CREATE TABLE order_item
(order_id NUMBER(3),
item_id NUMBER(2),
qty NUMBER(4),
CONSTRAINT ord_itm_id_pk
PRIMARY KEY (order_id,item_id)
USING INDEX
(CREATE INDEX ord_itm_idx
ON order_item(order_id,item_id)));
```

Which statement is true regarding the above SQL statement?

A. It would execute successfully and only ORD_ITM_IDX index would be created.

B. It would give an error because the USING INDEX clause cannot be used on a composite primary key.
C. It would execute successfully and two indexes ORD_ITM_IDX and ORD_ITM_ID_PK would be created.
D. It would give an error because the USING INDEX clause is not permitted in the CREATE TABLE command.

35. View the Exhibit and examine the description of EMPLOYEES and

DEPARTMENTS tables. You want to display the EMPLOYEE_ID, LAST_NAME, and SALARY for the employees who get the maximum salary in their respective departments. The following SQL statement was written:

```
WITH
SELECT employee_id, last_name, salary
FROM employees
WHERE (department_id, salary) = ANY (SELECT *
FROM dept_max)
dept_max as ( SELECT d.department_id, max(salary)
FROM departments d JOIN employees j
ON (d.department_id = j.department_id)
GROUP BY d.department_id);
```

Which statement is true regarding the execution and the output of this statement?

A. The statement would execute and give the desired results.
B. The statement would not execute because the = ANY comparison operator is used instead of =.
C. The statement would not execute because the main query block uses the query name before it is even created.
D. The statement would not execute because the comma is missing between the main query block and the query name.

36. View the Exhibit and examine the data in the DEPARTMENTS tables.

Evaluate the following SQL statement:

SELECT department_id "DEPT_ID", department_name , 'b' FROM departments.

WHERE department_id=90

UNION

SELECT department_id, department_name DEPT_NAME, 'a'

FROM departments WHERE department_id=10

Which two ORDER BY clauses can be used to sort the output of the above statement? (Choose two.)

A. ORDER BY 3;
B. ORDER BY 'b';
C. ORDER BY DEPT_ID;
D. ORDER BY DEPT_NAME;

37. View the Exhibit and examine the description of the EMPLOYEES table.

You want to know the EMPLOYEE_ID and FIRST_NAME of all the records in the EMPLOYEES table wherein the JOB_ID column has ST_CLERK or ST_MAN values, the DEPARTMENT_ID column has value 30, and the SALARY column has a value greater than 3,000. Which SQL statement would get you the desired result?

A. SELECT employee_id, first_name FROM employees
WHERE job_id like 'MAN%' OR job_id like 'CLERK%'
AND department_id = 30 AND salary > 3000;

B. SELECT employee_id, first_name FROM employees
WHERE job_id like '%MAN' OR job_id like '%CLERK'
AND (department_id = 30 OR salary > 3000);

C. SELECT employee_id, first_name FROM employees
WHERE (job_id like '%MAN' AND job_id like '%CLERK')
AND department_id = 30 OR salary > 3000;

D. SELECT employee_id, first_name FROM employees
WHERE (job_id like '%MAN' OR job_id like '%CLERK')
AND department_id = 30 AND salary > 3000;

38. Which two statements are true about sequences created in a single instance

database? (Choose two.)

A. The numbers generated by a sequence can be used only for one table.

B. DELETE <sequencename> would remove a sequence from the database.
C. CURRVAL is used to refer to the last sequence number that has been generated.
D. When the MAXVALUE limit for a sequence is reached, you can increase the MAXVALUE limit by using the ALTER SEQUENCE statement.
E. When a database instance shuts down abnormally, the sequence numbers that have been cached but not used would be available once again when the database instance is restarted.

39. View the Exhibit and examine the structure of the EMPLOYEES and

DEPARTMENTS tables. Which SET operator would you use in the blank space in the following SQL statement to list the departments where all the employees have managers?

```
SELECT department_id
FROM departments
SELECT department_id
FROM employees
WHERE manager_id IS NULL;
```

A. UNION
B. MINUS
C. INTERSECT
D. UNION ALL

40. Which mandatory clause has to be added to the following statement to successfully create an external table called EMPDET?

```
CREATE TABLE empdet
(empno CHAR(2), ename CHAR(5), deptno NUMBER(4))
ORGANIZATION EXTERNAL (LOCATION ('emp.dat'));
```

A. TYPE
B. REJECT LIMIT
C. DEFAULT DIRECTORY
D. ACCESS PARAMETERS

41. Evaluate the following statement:

CREATE TABLE bonuses (employee_id NUMBER, bonus NUMBER DEFAULT 100);

The details of all employees who have made sales need to be inserted into the BONUSES table. You can obtain the list of employees who have made sales based on the SALES_REP_ID column of the ORDERS table. The human resources manager now decides that employees with a salary of $8,000 or less should receive a bonus. Those who have made sales get a bonus of 1 per cent of their salary and also a salary increase of 1 per cent. The salary of each employee can be obtained from the EMPLOYEES table.

Which option should be used to perform this task most efficiently?

A. MERGE
B. Unconditional INSERT
C. Conditional ALL INSERT
D. Conditional FIRST INSERT

42. Which statement is true regarding the ROLLUP operator specified in the

GROUP BY clause of a SQL statement?

A. It produces only the subtotals for the groups specified in the GROUP BY clause.
B. It produces only the grand totals for the groups specified in the GROUP BY clause.
C. It produces higher-level subtotals, moving from right to left through the list of grouping columns specified in the GROUP BY clause.
D. It produces higher-level subtotals, moving in all the directions through the list of grouping columns specified in the GROUP BY clause.

43. View the Exhibit and examine DEPARTMENTS and the LOCATIONS tables. Evaluate the following SQL statement:

SELECT location_id, city FROM locations l WHERE NOT EXISTS (SELECT location_id

FROM departments WHERE location_id <> l.location_id);

This statement was written to display LOCATION_ID and CITY where there are no departments located. Which statement is true regarding the execution and output of the command?

A. The statement would execute and would return the desired results.

B. The statement would not execute because the = comparison operator is missing in the WHERE clause of the outer query.

C. The statement would execute but it will return zero rows because the WHERE clause in the inner query should have the = operator instead of <>.

D. The statement would not execute because the WHERE clause in the outer query is missing the column name for comparison with the inner query result.

44. Evaluate the following SQL statements that are issued in the given order:

```
CREATE TABLE emp
(emp_no NUMBER(2) CONSTRAINT emp_emp_no_pk PRIMARY KEY,
ename VARCHAR2(15),
salary NUMBER(8,2),
mgr_no NUMBER(2) CONSTRAINT emp_mgr_fk REFERENCES
    emp);
ALTER TABLE emp
DISABLE CONSTRAINT emp_emp_no_pk CASCADE;
ALTER TABLE emp
ENABLE CONSTRAINT emp_emp_no_pk;
```

What would be the status of the foreign key EMP_MGR_FK?

A. It would be automatically enabled and deferred.

B. It would be automatically enabled and immediate.

C. It would remain disabled and has to be enabled manually using the ALTER TABLE command.

D. It would remain disabled and can be enabled only by dropping the foreign key constraint and re-creating it.

45. View the Exhibit and examine the structure of the LOCATIONS and

DEPARTMENTS tables.Which SET operator should be used in the blank space in the following SQL statement to display the cities that have departments located in them?

```
SELECT location_id, city
FROM locations

____
SELECT location_id, city
FROM locations JOIN departments
USING(location_id);
```

A. UNION

B. MINUS

C. INTERSECT

D. UNION ALL

46. Which CREATE TABLE statement is valid?

A. CREATE TABLE ord_details
(ord_no NUMBER(2) PRIMARY KEY,
item_no NUMBER(3) PRIMARY KEY,
ord_date date NOT NULL);

B. CREATE TABLE ord_details
(ord_no NUMBER(2) UNIQUE, NOT NULL,
item_no NUMBER(3),
ord_date date DEFAULT SYSDATE NOT NULL);

C. CREATE TABLE ord_details
(ord_no NUMBER(2) ,
item_no NUMBER(3),
ord_date date DEFAULT NOT NULL,
CONSTRAINT ord_uq UNIQUE (ord_no),
CONSTRAINT ord_pk PRIMARY KEY (ord_no));

D. CREATE TABLE ord_details
(ord_no NUMBER(2),
item_no NUMBER(3),
ord_date date DEFAULT SYSDATE NOT NULL,
CONSTRAINT ord_pk PRIMARY KEY (ord_no, item_no));

47. Which statement is true regarding Flashback Version Query?

A. It returns versions of rows only within a transaction.
B. It can be used in subqueries contained only in a SELECT statement.
C. It will return an error if the undo retention time is less than the lower bound time or SCN specified.
D. It retrieves all versions including the deleted as well as subsequently reinserted versions of the rows.

48. Which two statements are true regarding multiple-row subqueries? (Choose two.)

A. They can contain group functions.
B. They always contain a subquery within a subquery.
C. They use the < ALL operator to imply less than the maximum.
D. They can be used to retrieve multiple rows from a single table only.
E. They should not be used with the NOT IN operator in the main query if NULL is likely to be a part of the result of the subquery.

49. The following are the steps for a correlated subquery, listed in random order:

(1) The WHERE clause of the outer query is evaluated.
(2) The candidate row is fetched from the table specified in the outer query.
(3) The procedure is repeated for the subsequent rows of the table, till all the rows are processed.
(4) Rows are returned by the inner query, after being evaluated with the value from the candidate row in the outer query.

Identify the option that contains the steps in the correct sequence in which the Oracle server evaluates a correlated subquery.

A. 4, 2, 1, 3
B. 4, 1, 2, 3
C. 2, 4, 1, 3
D. 2, 1, 4, 3

50. View the Exhibit and examine the structure of the EMPLOYEES table. Evaluate the following SQL statement:

SELECT employee_id, last_name, job_id, manager_id

FROM employees

START WITH employee_id = 101

CONNECT BY PRIOR employee_id=manager_id;

Which statement is true regarding the output for this command?

A. It would return a hierarchical output starting with the employee whose EMPLOYEE_ID is 101, followed by his or her peers.
B. It would return a hierarchical output starting with the employee whose EMPLOYEE_ID is 101, followed by the employee to whom he or she reports.
C. It would return a hierarchical output starting with the employee whose EMPLOYEE_ID is 101, followed by employees below him or her in the hierarchy.
D. It would return a hierarchical output starting with the employee whose EMPLOYEE_ID is101, followed by employees up to one level below him or her in the hierarchy.

51. Which two statements are true about the GROUPING function? (Choose two.)

A. It is used to find the groups forming the subtotal in a row.
B. It is used to identify the NULL value in the aggregate functions.
C. It is used to form the group sets involved in generating the totals and subtotals.
D. It can only be used with ROLLUP and CUBE operators specified in the GROUP BY clause.

52. Given below is a list of datetime data types and examples of values stored in them in a random order: Datatype Example

(1) INTERVAL YEAR TO MONTH a) '2003-04-15 8:00:00 -8:00'
(2) TIMESTAMP WITH LOCAL TIME ZONE b) '+06 03:30:16.000000'
(3) TIMESTAMP WITH TIME ZONE c) '17-JUN-03 12.00.00.000000 AM'
(4) INTERVAL DAY TO SECOND d) '+02-00'

Identify the option that correctly matches the data types with the values.

A. 1-d, 2-c, 3-a, 4-b
B. 1-b, 2-a, 3-c, 4-d
C. 1-b, 2-a, 3-d, 4-c
D. 1-d, 2-c, 3-b, 4-a

53. You need to load information about new customers from the NEW_CUST table into the tables CUST and CUST_SPECIAL. If a new customer has a credit limit greater than 10,000, then the details have to be inserted into CUST_SPECIAL. All new customer details have to be inserted into the CUST table. Which technique should be used to load the data most efficiently?

A. external table
B. the MERGE command
C. the multitable INSERT command
D. INSERT using WITH CHECK OPTION

54. View the Exhibit and examine the details of the ORDER_ITEMS table. Evaluate the following SQL statements:

Statement 1:
SELECT MAX(unit_price*quantity) "Maximum Order"
FROM order_items;

Statement 2:
SELECT MAX(unit_price*quantity) "Maximum Order"
FROM order_items
GROUP BY order_id;

Which statements are true regarding the output of these SQL statements? (Choose all that apply.)

A. Statement 1 would return only one row of output.
B. Both the statements would give the same output.
C. Statement 2 would return multiple rows of output.
D. Statement 1 would not return any row because the GROUP BY clause is missing.
E. Both statements would ignore NULL values for the UNIT_PRICE and QUANTITY columns.

55. View the Exhibit and examine the ORDER_ITEMS table.

You need to display the ORDER_ID of the order that has the highest total value among all the orders in the ORDER_ITEMS table.

Which query would produce the desired output?

A. SELECT order_id FROM order_items
WHERE(unit_price*quantity) = MAX(unit_price*quantity)
GROUP BY order_id;

B. SELECT order_id FROM order_items
WHERE(unit_price*quantity) = (SELECT MAX (unit_price* quantity) FROM order_items)

GROUP BY order_id;

C. SELECT order_id FROM order_items
WHERE (unit_price*quantity) = (SELECT MAX (unit_price* quantity) FROM order_items

GROUP BY order_id);

D. SELECT order_id FROM order_items GROUP BY order_id
HAVING SUM (unit_price* quantity) =(SELECT MAX (SUM(unit_price* quantity))

FROM order_items GROUP BY order_id);

Answer

1. C	20. C	39. B
2. C, D, E	21. D	40. C
3. B	22. A,C	41. A
4. A, E	23. D	42. C
5. C	24. B	43. C
6. A	25. B, C	44. C
7. D	26. C,E	45. C
8. C	27. B	46. D
9. C, D, E	28. C	47. D
10. B, D	29. A,B,D	48. A,E
11. A,E	30. D	49. C
12. D	31. C	50. C
13. E	32. B,E	51. A,D
14. A,D	33. A	52. A
15. A	34. A	53. C
16. B	35. C	54. A,C,E
17. C	36. A,C	55. D
18. C	37. D	
19. C	38. C,D	

Chapter - 29

Some Important Questions and answers For SQL and PL/SQL

1. What is Normalization?

Database normalization is a data design and organization process applied to data structures based on rules that help building relational databases. In relational database design, the process of organizing data to minimize redundancy is called normalization. Normalization usually involves dividing a database into two or more tables and defining relationships between the tables The objective is to isolate data so that additions, deletions, and modifications of a field can be made in just one table and then propagated through the rest of the database via the defined relationships. It reduces the need of restructuring the relations, in case new types of data- introduced .

2. What is De-normalization?

De-normalization is the process of attempting to optimize the performance of a database by adding redundant data. It is sometimes necessary because current DBMSs implement the relational model poorly. A true relational DBMS would allow for a fully normalized database at the logical level, while providing physical storage of data that is tuned for high performance. De-normalization is a technique to move from higher to lower normal forms of database modeling in order to speed up database access.

3. What are the Different Normalization Forms?

1NF: Eliminate Repeating groups and Make a separate table for each set of related attributes, and give each table a primary key. Each field contains at most one value from its attribute domain.

2NF: Eliminate Redundant Data If an attribute depends on only part of a multi-valued key, then remove it to a separate table.

3NF: Eliminate Columns Not Dependent On Key If attributes do not contribute to a description of the key, then remove them to a separate table. All attributes must be directly dependent on the primary key.

BCNF: Boyce-Codd Normal Form If there are non-trivial dependencies between candidate key attributes, then separate them out into distinct tables.

4. What's the Difference between a Primary Key and a Unique Key?

Both primary key and unique key enforce uniqueness of the column on which they are defined. But by default, the primary key creates a clustered index on the column, whereas unique key creates a non-clustered index by default. Another major difference is that primary key doesn't allow NULLs, but unique key allows one NULL only.

5. What is Difference between DELETE and TRUNCATE Commands?

Delete command removes the rows from a table on the basis of the condition that we provide with a WHERE clause. Truncate will actually remove all the rows from a table, and there will be no data in the table after we run the truncate command.

TRUNCATE

TRUNCATE is faster and uses fewer system and transaction log resources than DELETE.

TRUNCATE removes the data by de allocating the data pages used to store the table's data, and only the page de allocations are recorded in the transaction log.

TRUNCATE removes all the rows from a table, but the table structure, its columns, constraints, indexes and so on remains.

You cannot use TRUNCATE TABLE on a table referenced by a FOREIGN KEY constraint.

Using T-SQL – TRUNCATE cannot be rolled back unless it is used in TRANSACTION. OR TRUNCATE can be rolled back when used with BEGIN … END TRANSACTION using T-SQL.

TRUNCATE is a DDL Command.

TRUNCATE resets the identity of the table.

DELETE

DELETE removes rows one at a time and records an entry in the transaction log for each deleted row.

DELETE does not reset Identity property of the table.

DELETE can be used with or without a WHERE clause

DELETE activates Triggers if defined on table.

DELETE can be rolled back.

DELETE is DML Command.

DELETE does not reset the identity of the table.

6. What is subquery?

A query within a query known as subquery. A subquery is executed by enclosing in a set of parentheses. Subqueries are generally used to return a single row value although they may be used to compare values against multiple rows with the IN or NOT IN keyword.

7. What are Different Types of Join?

Cross Join

A cross join that does not have a WHERE clause produces the Cartesian product of the tables involved in the join.

Inner Join

A join that displays only the rows that have a match in both joined tables is known as inner Join. This is the default type of join in the Query.

Outer Join

A join that includes rows even if they do not have related rows in the joined table is an Outer Join. You can create three different outer join:

Left Outer Join: Left Outer Join fetch all the rows from the Left table and matched rows From right table.

Right Outer Join: Right Outer Join fetch all the rows from the Right table and matched rows From Left table.

Full Outer Join: In Full Outer Join, all the rows from all joined tables are included, whether they are matched or not.

Self Join: This is a particular case when one table joins to itself with one or two aliases to avoid confusion. The common example is when company has a hierarchal reporting structure whereby one member of staff reports to another.

8. What are Primary Keys and Foreign Keys?

Primary keys are the unique identifiers for each row. They must contain unique values and cannot be null. A table can have only one primary key. In MS SQL server A primary key cannot exceed 16 columns and a total key length of 900 bytes.

foreign key is a field in one child table that uniquely identifies a row of another table parent table (having primary key).

9. What is CHECK Constraint?

A CHECK constraint is used to limit the values that can be placed in a column. The check constraints are used to enforce domain integrity.

10. What is NOT NULL Constraint?

A NOT NULL constraint enforces that the column will not accept null values.

11. What is the difference between UNION and UNION ALL?

UNION command is used to select related information from two tables, much like the JOIN command. However, when using the UNION command all selected columns need to be of the same data type. With UNION, only distinct values are selected (removes duplicate record).

UNION ALL command is equal to the UNION command, except that UNION ALL selects all values (includes duplicate records).

12. What is Difference between Commit and Rollback when Used in Transactions?

Commit stores the transaction.

ROLLBACK restore the state of the database to the last commit point.

13. How to Implement One-to-One, One-to-Many and Many-to-Many Relationships while Designing Tables?

One-to-One relationship can be implemented as a single table and rarely as two tables with primary and foreign key relationships. One-to-Many relationships are implemented by splitting the data into two tables with primary key and foreign key relationships.

Many-to-Many relationships are implemented using a junction table with the keys from both the tables forming the composite primary key of the junction table.

14. What is the difference between INNER JOIN and JOIN?

Both are equal to each other. There is absolutely no difference between them. Both are equal in performance as well as implementation. JOIN is actually shorter version of *INNER JOIN.*

15. HOW to swap the values of two columns in SQL Server

Suppose you have a Customer table in the database with the following data and you want to interchange the values of columns Name and Address then how do you do?

SELECT* FROM CUSTOMER

	Cust ID	*Name*	*Address*	*Contact No*
1	2	Rahul	Gurgaon	8797897979
2	3	Hans	Noida	9444444444
3	4	Jeetu	Delhi	9560344074
4	7	Tushar	Delhi	9878908978
5	9	Deepak	Noida	9878909878
6	10	Ram	Noida	9778987890
7	11	Saksham	Noida	8988787878

UPDATE Customer SET Name=Address, Address=Name

SELECT * FROM CUSTOMER

Cust ID	*Address*	*Name*	*Contact No*
2	Gurgaon	Rahul	8797897979
3	Noida	Hans	9444444444
4	Delhi	Jeetu	9560344074
7	Delhi	Tushar	9878908978
9	Noida	Deepak	9878909878
10	Noida	Ram	9778987890
11	Noida	Saksham	8988787878

16. Describe the differences between MySQL and Microsoft SQL Server

Following are some specific technical differences in MySQL and SQL Server when it comes down to the ANSI SQL standard:

My SQL does not support Triggers, User Defined Functions, Cursor, Stored Procedures, FULL JOIN capabilities. SQL Server does.

MySQL has limited Import/Export capabilities; SQL Server has full support for Import/Export.

MySQL has limited Transaction Support while SQL Server offers full Transaction Support.

17. What are the Rules for Naming Objects in IBM DB2 UDB

Following are the rules for naming objects in a DB2 module:

Object names and column names must be unique.

The maximum length for the object name is 128 characters.

The maximum length for each column name is 30 characters.

The following characters are illegal in names: ‘, *, +, |, [,], :, ;, “, ‘, &, <, >, ?, /, and Space

Names cannot begin with a space, a digit, or with any of the following characters: _, ‘, &, *, +, |, [,], :, ;, “, ‘, <, >, ?, and /.

Note: Enclosed illegal characters are only enabled in names when you import objects. You cannot use illegal characters within Oracle Warehouse Builder.

18. What are the Rules for Naming Objects in Microsoft SQL SERVER?

Following are the rules for naming objects in Microsoft SQL Server:

Object names and column names must be unique.

The maximum length for the object name is 128 characters.

The following characters are illegal in names: ~, ‘, !, %, ^, &, ;, *, (,), {, }, [,], |, \, :, “, /, ?, >, and <.

Names cannot contain spaces, periods, or mathematical symbols.

Names cannot begin with a space or with any of the following characters: ~, ‘, !, %, ^, &, *,(,) {, }, [,], |, \, :, ;, “, ‘, /, ?, <, >, and $.

Column names cannot begin with mathematical symbols or periods.

19. What is the difference between Tables/Views and Materialized Views ?

There must be some difference between Views and MVs. Views do not contain any data, but MVs do contain data. This difference can be easily pointed out from the definition of MVs itself. But then, what is the difference between Tables and MVs? The difference is that, MVs can refresh data from the Master tables after a specified time interval. I used a term Master tables. What are these Master tables? Master tables are the base for MV. As specified above MV can be an exact replica or result of a query. These tables on which query are fired on the server side are Master tables.

20. Oracle version 9.2.0.4.0 what does each number refers to?

Oracle version number refers

9-Major database release number

2-Database Maintenance release number

0-Application server release number

4-Component Specific release number

0-Platform specific release number

21. How do you find current date and time in oracle?

SYSDATE function is used in oracle to find current date and time of operating system on which the database is running return type of function is DATE.

Syntax: SELECT TO_CHAR (SYSDATE, 'MM-DD-YYYY HH24:MI:SS') "Current_Date" FROM DUAL.

22. Write the syntax to find current date and time in format "YYYY-MM-DD".

SELECT TO_CHAR (SYSDATE, 'YYYY-MM-DD HH24:MI:SS') "Current_Date" FROM DUAL;

or

SELECT to_char(to_date('11-01-2012, 'DD-MM-YYYY') , 'DD-MM-YYYY') FROM dual;

23. What is Save Points in Oracle database?

SAVE POINTS are used to divide a transaction into smaller parts. It enables rolling back part of a transaction. Maximum of five save points are allowed. Whenever we encounter error we can rollback from the point where we set our SAVEPOINT. This is useful for multistage transaction and conditional transaction where commit and rollback depend on certain condition.

24. How will you convert string to a date in oracle database?

To_date function is used to convert string to a date function.

Syntax: to_date (string, format)

Example: to_date ('2012/06/12', 'yyyy/mm/dd') It will return June 12, 2012

25. What is Snap shot in Oracle database?

Snapshots are read-only copies of a master table located on a remote node which is periodically refreshed to reflect changes made to the master table.

26. Define a temp table

A temp table is a temporary storage structure. you can use a temp table to store data temporarily so you can manipulate and change it before it reaches its destination format.

27. What is the difference between a HAVING CLAUSE and a WHERE CLAUSE?

HAVING can be used only with the SELECT statement. HAVING

is typically used in a GROUP BY clause. When GROUP BY is not used, HAVING behaves like a WHERE clause. Having Clause is basically used only with the GROUP BY function in a query whereas WHERE Clause is applied to each row before they are part of the GROUP BY function in a query.

28. How to implement one-to-one, one-to-many and many-to-many relationships while designing tables?

One-to-One relationship can be implemented as a single table and rarely as two tables with primary and foreign key relationships. One-to-Many relationships are implemented by splitting the data into two tables with primary key and foreign key relationships. Many-to-Many relationships are implemented using a junction table with the keys from both the tables forming the composite primary key of the junction table.

29. How does one eliminate duplicates rows from a table?

Choose one of the following queries to identify or remove duplicate rows from a table leaving only unique

Records in the table:

Method 1:

```
SQL> DELETE FROM table_name A WHERE ROWID > (
SELECT min (rowid) FROM table_name B
WHERE A.key_values = B.key_values);
```

Method 2:

```
create table table_name2 as select distinct * from table_name1;
drop table_name1;
rename table_name2 to table_name1;
- - Remember to recreate all indexes, constraints, triggers, etc.
on table...
```

Method 3:

```
delete from my_table t1
where exists (select 'x' from my_table t2
where t2.key_value1 = t1.key_value1
and t2.key_value2 = t1.key_value2
and t2.rowid > t1.rowid);
```

30. How does one count different data values in a column?

```
select my_table_column, count(*)
from my_table
group by my_table_column;
```

A more sophisticated example...

```
select dept, sum( decode(sex,'M',1,0)) MALE,
sum ( decode(sex,'F',1,0)) FEMALE,
count (decode(sex,'M',1,'F',0)) TOTAL
from my_emp_table
group by dept;
```

31. How does one select EVERY Nth row from a table?

Method 1: Using a subquery

```
SELECT *
FROM emp
WHERE (ROWID,0) IN (SELECT ROWID, MOD(ROWNUM,4)
FROM emp);
```

Method 2: Use dynamic views

```
SELECT *
FROM ( SELECT rownum rn, empno, ename
FROM emp)
temp
WHERE MOD(temp.ROWNUM,4) = 0;
```

32. What's the difference between a primary key and a unique key?

Both primary key and unique key enforces uniqueness of the column on which they are defined. But by default primary key creates a clustered index on the column, where are unique creates a non-clustered index by default. Another major difference is that, primary key doesn't allow NULLs, but unique key allows one NULL only.

33. Can a table have more than one foreign key defined?

Yes. table can have any number of foreign keys defined. It can have only one primary key defined.

34.What is Decode function

Decode facilitates conditional inquires by doing the work of a case or if then else statement.

35. Advantages of Views

- Views restrict access to the data because the view can display selective columns from the table.
- Views can be used to make simple queries to retrieve the results of complicated queries. For Example, views can be used to query information from multiple tables without the user knowing
- Views provide data independence for ad hoc users and application programs. One view can be used to retrieve data from several tables.
- Views provide groups of user's access to data according to their particular criteria.

Provide an additional level of table security, by restricting access to a predetermined set of rows and columns of a table.

- Hide data complexity.
- Simplify commands for the user.
- Present the data in a different perspective from that of the base table.
- View Stores complex queries.

36. Does View contain Data?

Views do not contain or store data.

37. Can a View based on another View?

Yes.

38. Difference between SUBSTR and INSTR?

INSTR (String1, String2 (n,(m)),

INSTR returns the position of the nth occurrence of the string 2 in string1. The search begins from nth position of string1.

SUBSTR (String1 n, m)

SUBSTR returns a character string of size m in string1, starting from nth position of string1.

39. Explain UNION, MINUS, UNION ALL, INTERSECT?

INTERSECT returns all distinct rows selected by both queries.

MINUS - returns all distinct rows selected by the first query but not by the second.

UNION - returns all distinct rows selected by either query

UNION ALL - returns all rows selected by either query, including all duplicates.

40. What is the fastest way of accessing a row in a table?

Using ROWID.

41. What is ROWID ?

ROWID is a pseudo column attached to each row of a table. It is 18 character long, blockno, rownumber are the components of ROWID.

42. How many LONG columns are allowed in a table? Is it possible to use LONG columns in WHERE clause or ORDER BY?

Only one LONG columns is allowed in a table. It is not possible to use LONG column in WHERE or ORDER BY clause.

43. Which is faster - IN or EXISTS?

EXISTS is faster than IN because EXISTS returns a Boolean value whereas IN returns a value.

44. What does COMMIT do?

Saving all changes made by DML statements

45. Which operator do you use to return all of the rows from one query except rows are returned in a second query?

You use the MINUS operator.

46. Which Operator you will uses to return duplicate rows which are found in a second query?

The UNION operator returns all rows from both queries minus duplicates. The UNION ALL operator returns all rows from both queries including duplicates. The INTERSECT operator returns only those rows that exist in both queries.

47. Differences between Oracle and My SQL Schema objects

Schema Objects in Oracle and MySQL

Oracle	MySQL
AFTER trigger	trigger
BEFORE trigger	trigger
Check constraint	Check constraint
Column default	Column default
Database	Database
Foreign key	Foreign key
Index	Index
Package	N/A
PL/SQL function	Routine
PL/SQL procedure	Routine
Primary key	Primary key
Role	Role
Schema	Schema
Sequence	AUTO_INCREMENT for a column
Snapshot	N/A
Synonym	N/A
Table	Table
Tablespace	N/A
Temporary table	Temporary table
Trigger for each row	Trigger for each row
Unique key	Unique key
User	User
View	View

48. Write a SQL query to find the products which have continuous increase in sales every year?

Select p.product_name, s.year, s.quantity,

Lead (s.quantity, 1, 0) over (partition by p.product_id)

Order by s.year desc) quan_prev_year

From productsp, sales

Where p.product_id= s.product_id

49. Write a query to find the number of products sold in each year/

Select year, count (1) num_products

From sales group by year;

50. Write a query to generate sequence number from 1 to the specified number N?

Select LEVEL from dual connect by level <=&N;

51. Write a query to display each letter of word "SMILE" in a separate row?

Select substr ('SMILE', LEVEL, 1) A from dual

Connect by level <= length ('SMILE');

52. Write a query to convert the string 'SMILE' to Ascii values? The output look like as 83,77,73,76,69. Where 83 is the Ascii of S and so on.

Select substr (dump ('SMILE'), 15) from dual;

Or

Select WM_CONCAT (A) from (Select ASCII (SUBSTR ('SMILE', LEVEL, 1)) A

From Dual connect by Level <=length ('SMILE'));

53. To fetch ALTERNATE records from a table. (EVEN NUMBERED)

select * from emp where rowid in (select decode (mod (rownum, 2), 0, rowid, null) from emp);

54. To select ALTERNATE records from a table. (ODD NUMBERED)

select * from emp where rowid in (select decode (mod (rownum,2), 0, null, rowid) from emp);

55. Find the 3rd MAX salary in the EMP table.

Select distinct sal from EMP e1 where 3 = (select count (distinct sal) from emp e2 where e1.sal <= e2.sal);

56. Find the 3rd MIN salary in the EMP table.

Select distinct sal from EMP e1 where 3 = (select count (distinct sal) from EMP e2where e1.sal >= e2.sal);

57. Select FIRST n records from a table.

Select * from EMP where rownum <= &n;

58. Select LAST n records from a table

select * from emp minus select * from emp where rownum <= (select count(*) - &n from emp);

59. List dept no., Dept name for all the departments in which there are no employees in the department.

select * from dept where deptno not in (select deptno from emp);

or

select * from dept a where not exists (select * from emp b where a.deptno = b.deptno);

or

select empno,ename,b.deptno,dname from emp a, dept b where a.deptno(+) = b.deptno and empno is null;

60. How to get 3 Max salaries?

Select distinct sal from emp a where 3 >= (select count (distinct sal) from emp b where a.sal <= b.sal) order by a.sal desc;

61. How to get 3 Min salaries?

Select distinct sal from EMP a where 3 >= (select count (distinct sal) from emp b where a.sal >= b.sal);

62. How to get nth max salaries?

Select distinct hiredate from EMP a where &n = (select count (distinct sal) from EMP b where a.sal >= b.sal);

63. Select DISTINCT RECORDS from EMP table.

Select * from EMP a where rowid = (select max (rowid) from EMP b where a.empno=b.empno);

64. How to delete duplicate rows in a table?

Delete from EMP a where rowid! = (select max (rowid) from EMP b where a.empno=b.empno);

65. Count of number of employees in department wise.

Select count (EMPNO), b.deptno, dname from emp a, dept b where a.deptno (+)=b.deptno group by b.deptno,dname;

In Oracle you can use (+) instead of outer join name. Its side will denote the name and functionality of join. If you put this in left side it will give output of left outer join. And if you put it in right side you will get result of Right outer join.

66. Suppose there is annual salary information provided by EMP table. How to fetch monthly salary of each and every employee?

Select ename, sal/12 as monthlysal from EMP;

67. Select all record from EMP table where deptno =10 or 30.

Select * from EMP where deptno=30 or deptno=10;

68. Select all record from EMP table where deptno=30 and sal>1500.

Select * from EMP where deptno=30 and sal>1500;

69. Select all record from emp where job not in SALESMAN or CLERK.

Select * from EMP where job not in ('SALESMAN','CLERK');

70. Select all record from EMP where ename in 'BLAKE', 'SCOTT', 'KING' and 'FORD'.

Select * from EMP where ename in ('BLAKE', 'SCOTT', 'KING', 'FORD');

71. Select all records where ename starts with 'S' and its length is 6 char.

Select * from EMP where ename like'S_____';

72. Select all records where ename may be any no of character but it should end with 'R'.

Select * from EMP where ename like'%R';

73. Count MGR and their salary in EMP table.

Select count (MGR), count (sal) from EMP;

74. In EMP table add comm+sal as total sal.

Select ename,(sal+nvl(comm,0)) as totalsal from emp;

75. Select any salary <3000 from EMP table.

Select * from EMP where sal>any (select sal from EMP where sal<3000);

76. Select all salary <3000 from EMP table.

Select * from EMP where sal>all (select sal from EMP where sal<3000);

77. Select the entire employee group by deptno and sal in descending order.

Select ename, deptno, sal from emp order by deptno,sal desc;

78. How can I create an empty table emp1 with same structure as emp?

Create table emp1 as select * from EMP where 1=2;

79. How to retrieve record where sal between 1000 to 2000?

Select* from EMP where sal>=1000 and sal<2000

80. Select all records where dept no of both EMP and dept table matches.

Select * from EMP where exists (select * from dept where emp. deptno=dept.deptno)

81. If there are two tables emp1 and emp2, and both have common record. How can I fetch all the records but common records only once?

(Select * from EMP) Union (Select * from emp1)

82. How to fetch only common records from two tables emp and emp1?

(Select * from EMP) Intersect (Select * from emp1)

83. How can I retrive all records of emp1 those should not present in emp2?

(Select * from EMP) Minus (Select * from emp1)

84. Count the totalsal deptno wise where more than 2 employees exist.

SELECT deptno, sum (sal) as totalsal

FROM EMP

GROUP BY deptno

HAVING COUNT (empno) > 2

85. How do i eliminate the duplicate ename rows from emp table?

Delete ename from EMP a where rowid< (select min (rowid) from emp b

Where a.ename=b.ename;

86. If commission is null then text 'NA' should displays, instead of blank space.write a query.

Select nvl (to_char (commission),'NA') from EMP;

87. Find out nth highest salary from EMP table;

Select distinct (a.sal) from emp a where &N=(select count (distinct (b.sal)) from emp b where a.sal=b.sal);

88. Display Odd/ Even number of records

Odd number of records:

select * from emp where (rowid,1) in (select rowid, mod(rownum,2) from emp);

1

3

5

Even number of records:

select * from emp where (rowid,0) in (select rowid, mod(rownum,2) from emp)

1

2

6

89. How to generate row number in SQL without Rownum

Select name, sal, (select count(*) from employee i where o.name >= i.name) row_num

From employee o order by row_num

90. What is PL SQL ?

PL/SQL is a procedural programming language

91. What you know about % TYPE and % ROWTYPE?

% TYPE is used to define a variable of column type of a table.

% ROWTYPE is used to define a variable of ROW type of a table's column.

92. What is cursor?

A Cursor is a named pointer a private SQL, are that stored information about the processing of a select.

Steps to use cursor .

Define a cursor

Open cursor

Fetch record from explicit cursor or do programming (loop or DML) with output of cursor

Close cursor.

93. What are the differences between stored procedure and function?

1. You can call function in sql statement. you can not call Stored procedure in SQL statement.

2. Function must return 1 value. Procedure may or may not return value.
3. Function return 1 value only procedure can return maximum 1024 values.
4. You can use DDL in stored procedure using execute immediate statement but in function you can't use DDL.

94. Explain all virtual tables available at the time of database trigger execution.

In Trigger Table columns are referred as THEN.column_name and NOW.column_name.

For INSERT related triggers, NOW.column_name values are available only.

For DELETE related triggers, THEN.column_name values are available only.

For UPDATE related triggers, both Table columns are available.

95. Define types of Cursors.

There are two types of cursor Implicit Cursor and explicit cursor. A cursor is implicit by default. user cannot control or process the information in this cursor. If a query returns multiple rows of data, the program defines an explicit cursor. This allows you to process each row sequentially as the cursor returns it.

96. What are SQLCODE and SQLERRM?

SQLCODE returns the value of the number of error for the last encountered error and SQLERRM returns the message for the last error.

97. Explain cursor attributes of PL/SQL.

% ISOPEN: Is used to checks if the cursor is open or not

% ROWCOUNT: returns number of rows that are updated, deleted or fetched.

% FOUND: Is used to checks if the cursor has fetched any row. It is true if rows are fetched.

% NOT FOUND: Is used to checks if the cursor has fetched any row. It is true if rows are not fetched.

98. What is Raise_application_error?

Raise_application_error is a procedure of the package DBMS_STANDARD that allow issuing a user_defined error messages from the database trigger or stored sub-program.

99. What is Trigger?

Trigger is a PL/SQL stored procedure fires automatically on defined event like insert, update or delete on table etc.

100. How to find Employee name, employee manager from employee table. Employees table which contains rows for normal employees as well as managers. So, to find out the managers of all the employees, you need a self join.

```
CREATE TABLE emp
(
empid int,
mgrid int,
empname char(10)
)
INSERT emp SELECT 1,2,'Vyas'
INSERT emp SELECT 2,3,'Mohan'
INSERT emp SELECT 3,NULL,'Shobha'
INSERT emp SELECT 4,2,'Shridhar'
INSERT emp SELECT 5,2,'Sourabh'
SELECT t1.empname [Employee], t2.empname [Manager]
FROM emp t1, emp t2
WHERE t1.mgrid = t2.empid
```

Employee	*Manager*
Vyas	Mohan
Mohan	Shobha
Shridhar	Mohan
Sourabh	Mohan

```
SELECT t1.empname [Employee], isnull (t2.empname, 'No
    manager') [Manager]
FROM emp t1
LEFT OUTER JOIN
emp t2 ON t1.mgrid = t2.empid
```

Employee	***Manager***
Vyas	Mohan
Mohan	Shobha
Shobha	No manager
Shridhar	Mohan
Sourabh	Mohan

Chapter - 30

Glossary

ADDM

Automatic Database Diagnostic Monitor. An Oracle Database infrastructure that enables a database to diagnose its own performance and determine how identified problems could be resolved.

B-tree index

An index organized like an upside-down tree known as B-tree Index. A B-tree index has two types of blocks: branch blocks for searching and leaf blocks that store values. The leaf blocks contain every indexed data value and a corresponding rowid used to locate the actual row. The "B" stands for "balanced" because all leaf blocks automatically stay at the same depth.

Background Process

A process that consolidates functions that would otherwise be handled by multiple Oracle programs running for each client process. The background processes a synchronously perform I/O and monitor other Oracle processes.

Bind Variable

A place holder in a SQL statement that must be replaced with a valid value or value address for the statement to execute successfully. By using bind variables, you can write a SQL statement that accepts inputs or parameters at run time. The following example shows a query that uses v_empid as a bind variable:

SELECT * FROM employees WHERE employee_id = :v_empid;

Bitmap index

A database index in which the database stores a bitmap for each index key instead of a list of rowids.

Bitmap merge

An operation that merges bitmaps retrieved from bitmap index scans. For example, if the gender and DOB columns have bitmap indexes, then the database may use a bitmap merge if the query predicate is WHERE gender='F' AND DOB > 1966.

Client process

A process that executes the application or Oracle tool code. When users run client applications such as SQL*Plus, the operating system creates client processes to run the applications.

Column

Vertical space in a table that represents a domain of data. A table definition includes a table name and set of columns. Each column has a name and data type.

Commit

Action that ends a database transaction and makes permanent all changes performed in the transaction.

Concurrency

Simultaneous access of the same data by many users. A multiuser database management system must provide adequate concurrency controls so that data cannot be updated or changed improperly, compromising data integrity.

Condition

The combination of one or more expressions and logical operators in a SQL statement that returns a value of TRUE, FALSE, or UNKNOWN. For example, the condition 1=1 always evaluates to TRUE.

Connection

Communication pathway between a client process and an Oracle database instance.

Cube

An organization of measures with identical dimensions and other shared characteristics. The edges of the cube contain the dimension members, whereas the body of the cube contains the data values.

Cursor

A cursor is a control structure used for sequential processing of data for fetch the data from database table through Query. You need to follow steps to use cursor

1. Declare a cursor that defines a result set.
2. Open the cursor to establish the result set.
3. Fetch the data into local variables from the cursor, one row at a time.
4. Close the cursor after completion of record fetch and process.

Database

Data base is a organized collection of data treated as a unit. The purpose of a database is to store and retrieve related information. Every database instance accesses only one database in its lifetime.

Database user

An account through which you can log in to an Oracle database.

Data consistency

A consistent view of the data by each user in a multiuser database.

Data dictionary

A read-only collection of database tables and views containing reference information about the database, its structures, and its users.

Data integrity

Business rules that dictate the standards for acceptable data. These rules are applied to a database by using integrity constraints and triggers to prevent invalid data entry.

Data type

In Database, a fixed set of properties associated with a column value or constant. Examples include VARCHAR2 and NUMBER. Oracle Database treats values of different data types differently.

data warehouse

A relational database designed for query and analysis rather than for OLTP.

DDL

Data definition language. Includes statements such as CREATE TABLE or ALTER INDEX that define or change a data structure.

Deadlock

A situation in which two or more users are waiting for data locked by each other. Such deadlocks are rare in Oracle Database and Ms SQL server.

Dedicated server

A database configuration in which a server process handles requests for a single client process.

DML

Data manipulation language. Includes statements such as SELECT, INSERT, UPDATE, and DELETE.

Execution plan

The combination of steps used by the database to execute a SQL statement. Each step either retrieves rows of data physically from the database or prepares them for the user issuing the statement. You can override execution plans by using hints.

Expression

A combination of one or more values, operators, and SQL functions that evaluates to a value. For example, the expression 2×2 evaluates to 4. In general, expressions assume the data type of their components.

Extent

Multiple contiguous data blocks allocated for storing a specific type of information. A segment is made up of one or more extents.

External table

A read-only table whose metadata is stored in the database but whose data in stored in files outside the database. The database uses the metadata describing external tables to expose their data as if they were relational tables.

Fact

Data that represents a business measure, such as sales or cost data.

Foreign key

An integrity constraint that requires each value in a column or set of columns to match a value in the unique or primary key for a related table. Integrity constraints for foreign keys define actions dictating database behavior if referenced data is altered.

Function

A schema object, similar to a procedure that always returns a single value.

Grid computing

A computing architecture that coordinates large numbers of servers and storage to act as a single large computer.

Implicit query

A component of a DML statement that retrieves data without a subquery. An UPDATE, DELETE, or MERGE statement that does not explicitly include a SELECT statement uses an implicit query to retrieve the rows to be modified.

Index

Optional schema object associated with a non-clustered table, table partition, or table cluster. In some cases indexes speed data access.

Index clustering factor

A measure of the row order in relation to an indexed value such as last name. The more order that exists in row storage for this value, the lower the clustering factor.

Index-organized table

A table whose storage organization is a variant of a primary B-tree index. Unlike a heap-organized table, data is stored in primary key order known as Index-organized table.

Index segment

A segment that stores data for a non-partitioned index or index partition.

Initialization parameter

A configuration parameter such as DB_NAME or SGA_TARGET that affects the operation of a database instance. Settings for initialization parameters are stored in a text-based initialization parameter file or binary server parameter file.

Initialization parameter file

A text file that contains initialization parameter settings for a database instance.

Instance

The combination of the system global area (SGA) and background processes. An instance is associated with one and only one database. In an Oracle Real Application Clusters configuration, multiple instances access a single database simultaneously.

Join

A statement that retrieves data from multiple tables specified in the FROM clause. Join types include inner joins, outer joins, self join and Cartesian joins.

Join condition

A condition that compares two columns, each from a different table or same table with two different name, in a join. The database combines pairs of rows, each containing one row from each table, for which the join condition evaluates to TRUE.

Key

Column or set of columns included in the definition of certain types of integrity constraints.

LOB

Large object. An Oracle data type designed to hold large amounts of data.

Lock

A database mechanism that prevents destructive interaction between transactions accessing a shared resource such as a table, row, or system object not visible to users. The main categories of locks are DML locks, DDL locks, and latches and internal locks.

Log sequence number

A number that uniquely identifies a set of redo records in a redo log file. When the database fills one online redo log file and switches to a different one, the database automatically assigns the new file a log sequence number.

Lookup table

A table containing a code column and an associated value column. For example, a job code corresponds to a job name. In contrast to a master table in a pair of master-detail tables, a lookup table is not the means to obtain a detailed result set, such as a list of employees. Rather, a user queries a table such as employees for an employee list and then joins the result set to the lookup table.

Materialized view

A schema object that stores the result of a query. Oracle materialized views can be read-only or updatable.

Null

Absence of a value in a column of a row. Nulls indicate missing, unknown, or inapplicable data.

Object type

A schema object that abstracts a real-world entity such as a purchase order. Attributes model the structure of the entity, whereas methods implement operations an application can perform on the entity.

operator

1. In memory management, operators control the flow of data. Examples include sort, hash join, and bitmap merge operators.
2. In SQL, an operator manipulates data items called operands or arguments and returns a result. The SQL operators are

represented by special characters or by keywords. For example, the multiplication operator is represented by an asterisk (*).

PL/SQL

Procedural Language/SQL. The Oracle Database procedural language extension to SQL. PL/SQL enables you to mix SQL statements with programmatic constructs such as procedures, functions, and packages.

Precompiler

A programming tool that enables you to embed SQL statements in a high-level source program written in a language such as C, C++, or COBOL.

Predicate

The WHERE condition in a SQL statement.

Primary key

The column or set of columns that uniquely identifies a row in a table. Only one primary key can be defined for each table.

Primary key constraint

An integrity constraint that disallows duplicate values and nulls in a column or set of columns.

Privilege

The right to run a particular type of SQL statement, or the right to access an object that belongs to another user, run a PL/SQL package, and so on. The types of privileges are defined by Oracle Database.

Procedure

A schema object that consists of a set of SQL statements and other PL/SQL constructs, grouped together, stored in the database, and run as a unit to solve a specific problem or perform a set of related tasks.

Query

An operation that retrieves data from tables or views. For example, SELECT * FROM employees is a query.

Query plan

The execution plan used to execute a query.

read-only database

A database that is available for queries only and cannot be modified.

Referential integrity

A rule defined on a key in one table that guarantees that the values in that key match the values in a key in a related table (the referenced value).

Role

A set of privileges that can be granted to database users or to other roles.

Row

A set of column information corresponding to a single record in a table. The database stores rows in data blocks.

Rowid

A globally unique address for a row in a database.

Savepoint

A named SCN in a transaction to which the transaction can be rolled back.

Schema

A named collection of database objects, including logical structures such as tables and indexes. A schema has the name of the database user who owns it.

Schema object

A logical structure of data stored in a schema. Examples of schema objects are tables, indexes, sequences, and database links.

Selectivity

In a query, the measure of how many rows from a row set pass a predicate test, for example, WHERE last_name = 'Smith'. A selectivity of 0.0 means no rows, whereas a value of 1.0 means all rows. A predicate becomes more selective as the value approaches 0.0 and less selective (or more unselective) as the value approaches 1.0.

Sequence

A schema object that generates a serial list of unique numbers for table columns.

Server

In a client/server architecture, the computer that runs Oracle software and handles the functions required for concurrent, shared data access. The server receives and processes the SQL and PL/SQL statements that originate from client applications.

SQL

Structured Query Language. A non-procedural language to access a relational database. Users describe in SQL what they want done, and the SQL language compiler automatically generates a procedure to navigate the database and perform the task. Oracle SQL includes many extensions to the ANSI/ISO standard SQL language.

SQL*Plus

Oracle tool used to run SQL statements against Oracle Database.

Standby database

An independent copy of a production database that you can use for disaster protection in a high availability environment.

Statement-level rollback

A database operation in which the effects of an unsuccessful SQL statement are rolled back because the statement caused an error during execution.

Stored procedure

A named PL/SQL block or Java program that Oracle Database stores in the database. Applications can call stored procedures by name.

Subquery

A query nested within another SQL statement. Unlike implicit queries, subqueries use a SELECT statement to retrieve data.

Synonym

An alias for a schema object. You can use synonyms to provide data independence and location transparency.

Table

Basic unit of data storage in Oracle Database. Data in tables are stored in rows and columns.

Table cluster

A schema object that contains data from one or more tables, all of which have one or more columns in common. In table clusters, the database stores together all the rows from all tables that share the same cluster key.

Table compression

The compression of data segments to reduce disk space in a heap-organized table or table partition.

Tablespace

A database storage unit that groups related logical structures together. The database data files are stored in tablespaces.

Temp file

A file that belongs to a temporary tablespace. The temp files in temporary tablespaces cannot contain permanent database objects.

Temporary table

A table that holds an intermediate result set for the duration of a transaction or a session. Only the current session can see the data in temporary tables.

Transaction

Logical unit of work that contains one or more SQL statements. All statements in a transaction commit or roll back together. The use of transactions is one of the most important ways that a database management system differs from a file system.

Transaction ID

An identifier is unique to a transaction and represents the undo segment number, slot, and sequence number.

Transaction recovery

A phase of instance recovery in which uncommitted transactions are rolled back.

Transaction table

The data structure within an undo segment that holds the transaction identifiers of the transactions using the undo segment.

Trigger

A PL/SQL or Java procedure that fires when a table or view is modified or when specific user or database actions occur. Procedures are explicitly run, whereas triggers are implicitly run.

Undo data

Records of the actions of transactions, primarily before they are committed. The database can use undo data to logically reverse the effect of SQL statements. Undo data is stored in undo segments.

User name

The name by which a user is known to Oracle Database and to other users. Every user name is associated with a password, and both must be entered to connect to Oracle Database.

View

A custom-tailored presentation of the data in one or more tables. The views do not actually contain or store data, but derive it from the tables on which they are based.

Virtual column

A column that is not stored on disk. The database derives the values in virtual columns on demand by computing a set of expressions or functions.